Clinical Practice Guideline
Number 5

Depression in Primary Care:
Volume 2.
Treatment of Major Depression

Depression Guideline Panel

U.S. Department of Health and Human Services
Public Health Service
Agency for Health Care Policy and Research
Rockville, Maryland

AHCPR Publication No. 93–0551
April 1993

Guideline Development and Use

Guidelines are systematically developed statements to assist practitioner and patient decisions about appropriate health care for specific clinical conditions. This guideline was developed by a private sector panel convened by the Agency for Health Care Policy and Research (AHCPR). The panel employed an explicit, science-based methodology and expert clinical judgment to develop specific statements on patient assessment and management for the clinical condition selected.

Extensive literature searches were conducted and critical reviews and syntheses were used to evaluate empirical evidence and significant outcomes. Peer review and field review were undertaken to evaluate the validity, reliability, and utility of the guideline in clinical practice. The panel's recommendations are primarily based on the published scientific literature. When the scientific literature was incomplete or inconsistent in a particular area, the recommendations reflect the professional judgment of panel members and consultants.

The guideline reflects the state of knowledge, current at the time of publication, on effective and appropriate care. Given the inevitable changes in the state of scientific information and technology, periodic review, updating, and revision will be done.

We believe that the AHCPR-assisted clinical practice guidelines will make positive contributions to the quality of care in the United States. We encourage practitioners and patients to use the information provided in this *Clinical Practice Guideline*. The recommendations may not be appropriate for use in all circumstances. Decisions to adopt any particular recommendation must be made by the practitioner in light of available resources and circumstances presented by individual patients.

J. Jarrett Clinton, MD
Administrator
Agency for Health Care Policy and Research

Foreword

This *Clinical Practice Guideline* (*Depression in Primary Care: Volume 1. Detection and Diagnosis*; and *Volume 2. Treatment of Major Depression*) was developed with support from the Agency for Health Care Policy and Research (AHCPR) by the Depression Guideline Panel to assist primary care providers (e.g., general practitioners, family practitioners, internists, nurse practitioners, registered nurses, mental health nurse specialists, physician assistants, and others) in the diagnosis of depressive conditions and the treatment of major depressive disorder. The panel hopes that the general principles embodied in these guidelines will also provide a framework for other medical and nonmedical practitioners who assume responsibilities for the recognition and care of depressed persons.

Depression was selected as a topic for guideline development because:

- Depressive disorders are commonly encountered in primary care, as well as in other treatment settings.
- Most depressed patients seek care from primary care practitioners.
- A range of effective treatments are available and commonly provided for these conditions.
- There is a large body of scientific evidence on which to base these guidelines.
- Practice surveys indicate that improvements are needed in primary care practitioners' ability to recognize and treat depressive disorders.
- Depressive disorders result in significant morbidity and mortality.
- Depressive disorders have a high prevalence in the general population.

These guidelines are not aimed at rendering selected procedures reimbursable or not reimbursable; that decision logically falls to third-party payors. Nor do they specify which professionals should conduct which procedures, an issue addressed by licensing/privileging bodies. Should the recommended steps in the diagnosis or treatment of depression fall outside the expertise of the practitioner, he or she should seek a consultation with, or a referral to, someone knowledgeable in these matters.

The Depression Guideline Panel is composed of experts from diverse disciplines, as well as a consumer representative. The guidelines are based on systematic literature reviews commissioned by the panel and conducted by experts in numerous areas relevant to depression, with special attention to the clinical issues most pertinent to the diagnosis and treatment of depression in primary care. Guideline development also included input from a broad range of professional and consumer organizations and individuals. The guidelines have undergone peer review and field review with intended users in clinical sites to evaluate the document both conceptually and operationally. For practitioners, patients, and their families, we hope these guidelines provide a richer understanding of depression. For researchers, we hope we have identified key areas of uncertainty for further investigation.

Research develops knowledge. The synthesis and specification of current knowledge do not mitigate (in fact increase) the need for careful translation and application of this knowledge. Practitioners translate and apply that knowledge. However, in many cases they have to act without sufficient scientifically based data.

The panel's inferences as to what is optimal patient care are not expected to apply to all patients or situations. Knowledge developed through research can only provide a starting point for approaching a particular patient. Algorithms are not applicable in every case, and often provide only coarse road maps for managing patients. Adaptation of guidelines to particular patients requires practitioners to have skill, training, knowledge, and experience, and patients and families to have patience, understanding, trust, and knowledge.

This is the first edition of the *Clinical Practice Guideline*. We plan to revise the guidelines based on new knowledge, empirical evaluation of their impact on patient outcome, and critiques from users. The panel welcomes comments and suggestions for use in the next edition. Please send written comments to Director, Office of the Forum for Quality and Effectiveness in Health Care, AHCPR, Executive Office Center, Suite 401, 2101 East Jefferson Street, Rockville, MD 20852.

Depression Guideline Panel

Abstract

Despite the high prevalence of depressive symptoms and major depressive episodes in patients of all ages, depression is underdiagnosed and undertreated, especially by primary care and other nonpsychiatric practitioners, who are, paradoxically, the providers most likely to see these patients initially. Depression may co-occur with nonpsychiatric medical disorders or with other psychiatric disorders; it may also be brought on by the use of certain medications. Major risk factors for depression include a personal or family history of depressive disorder, prior suicide attempts, female gender, lack of social supports, stressful life events, and current substance abuse. The social stigma surrounding depression is substantial and often prevents the optimal use of current knowledge and treatments. The cost of the illness in pain, suffering, disability, and death is high.

Once identified, depression can almost always be treated successfully, either with medication, psychotherapy, or a combination of both. Not all patients respond to the same treatment. A patient who fails to respond to the first treatment attempted is highly likely to respond to a different treatment.

Once major depressive disorder is diagnosed, interventions that predictably decrease symptoms and morbidity earlier than would occur naturally in the course of the illness are logically tried first. The key initial objectives of treatment, in order of priority, are (1) to reduce and ultimately to remove all signs and symptoms of the depressive syndrome, (2) to restore occupational and psychosocial function to that of the asymptomatic state, and (3) to reduce the likelihood of relapse and recurrence. Given the strong evidence that treatments are effective, third-party coverage for the diagnosis and treatment of depression should be equal to that available for other medical disorders.

Depression Guideline Panel. *Depression in Primary Care: Volume 2. Treatment of Major Depression. Clinical Practice Guideline, Number 5.* Rockville, MD. U.S. Department of Health and Human Services, Public Health Service, Agency for Health Care Policy and Research. AHCPR Publication No. 93–0551. April 1993.

Dedication

Depression in Primary Care is dedicated to the memory of Gerald L. Klerman, MD, who passed away while serving as one of our scientific reviewers. Dr. Klerman, in his lifetime of research, teaching, and clinical work, and in his years of government service as the administrator of the Alcohol, Drug Abuse, and Mental Health Administration, Public Health Service, Washington, DC (1977–80), worked diligently to develop scientifically based information to help clinicians better serve their patients. We remain indebted to him for his contribution to our panel and to the field of psychiatry in general.

Panel Members

A. John Rush, MD, *Chair*
Betty Jo Hay Distinguished Chair in Mental Health
Professor and Vice Chairman for Research, Department of Psychiatry
University of Texas Southwestern Medical Center
Dallas, Texas
Specialty: Psychiatry

William E. Golden, MD
Director, General Internal Medicine
Associate Professor, Department of Medicine
University of Arkansas for Medical Sciences
Little Rock, Arkansas
Specialty: General Internal Medicine

Gladys Walton Hall, PhD, MSW
Associate Professor, School of Social Work
Howard University
Washington, District of Columbia
Specialty: Social Work

Col. Moses Herrera, MD
Chief, Primary Care Clinic
Robins Air Force Base Hospital
Robins Air Force Base, Georgia
Specialty: Family Medicine

Artie Houston
Consumer Representative
Fort Worth, Texas

Roger G. Kathol, MD
Professor of Psychiatry and Internal Medicine
University of Iowa Hospitals and Clinics
Iowa City, Iowa
Specialty: Psychiatry and Internal Medicine

Wayne Katon, MD
Professor of Psychiatry
Chief of Consultation-Liaison Psychiatry
University of Washington Medical School
Seattle, Washington
Specialty: Psychiatry

Catherine L. Matchett, MD
Matchett Medical Center, President
Grapevine, Texas
Specialty: Family Medicine

Frederick Petty, PhD, MD
Associate Professor, Department of Psychiatry
Veterans Administration Medical Center
University of Texas Southwestern Medical Center
Dallas, Texas
Specialty: Psychiatry

Herbert C. Schulberg, PhD
Professor of Psychiatry, Psychology and Medicine
University of Pittsburgh School of Medicine
Pittsburgh, Pennsylvania
Specialty: Psychology and Community Mental Health

G. Richard Smith, Jr., MD
Professor and Director
Centers for Mental Healthcare Research
VA HSR&D Field Program for Mental Health
University of Arkansas for Medical Sciences
Little Rock, Arkansas
Specialty: Psychiatry and Health Services Research

Gail Wiscarz Stuart, PhD, RN, CS
Associate Professor and Chief, Division of Psychiatric Nursing
Department of Psychiatry and Behavioral Sciences
Professor, College of Nursing
Medical University of South Carolina
Charleston, South Carolina
Specialty: Psychiatric Nursing

Acknowledgments

These guidelines were developed with the help of many dedicated contributors. The reviewing consultants for treatment issues searched and compiled a vast literature. The scientific reviewers critiqued the reviews and several drafts of the guideline document. A variety of professional organizations, patient groups, and individuals provided peer review and pilot-tested the guidelines. Finally, critical administrative, scientific, technical, and secretarial support made the entire effort feasible. A full listing of all those involved in this effort appears in the lists of contributors at the end of this document.

Special recognition goes to David Schriger, MD, MPH, UCLA School of Medicine, Los Angeles, California, panel methodologist, who critiqued all reviews and drafts of the guidelines and helped to conceptualize the overall approach, specify clinical issues, and organize the relevant data. Extraordinary credit also goes to Madhukar Trivedi, MD, Instructor, Department of Psychiatry, University of Texas Southwestern Medical Center, Dallas, Texas, scientific assistant to the chair, who helped to conceptualize the overall approach, conduct all meta-analyses, and review most studies of medication efficacy. Without him, this project would not have been possible.

Contents

Tables

Figures

Executive Summary

Up to one in eight individuals may require treatment for depression during their lifetimes. The direct costs of treatment for major depressive disorder combined with the indirect costs from lost productivity are significant, accounting for approximately $16 billion per year in 1980 dollars.

Despite the high prevalence of depressive symptoms and major depressive episodes in patients of all ages, depression is underdiagnosed and undertreated by primary care and other nonpsychiatric practitioners, who are, paradoxically, the providers most likely to see these patients initially. Depression may co-occur with other nonpsychiatric, general medical disorders or with other psychiatric disorders; it may also be brought on by the use of certain medications. Major risk factors for depression include a personal or family history of depressive disorder, prior suicide attempts, female gender, lack of social supports, stressful life events, and current substance abuse. The social stigma surrounding depression is substantial and often prevents the optimal use of current knowledge and treatments. The cost of the illness in pain, suffering, disability, and death is high.

Once identified, depression can almost always be treated successfully with medication, psychotherapy, or a combination of both. Not all patients respond to the same therapy, but a patient who fails to respond to the first treatment attempted is highly likely to respond to a different treatment. The threshold for accepting a scientific report regarding treatment efficacy was the randomized controlled clinical trial, as this methodology is the most stringent test of treatment efficacy. Therefore, where studies are cited and data are available, conclusions are virtually certain.

Once major depressive disorder is diagnosed, interventions that predictably decrease symptoms and morbidity earlier than would occur naturally in the course of the illness are logically tried first. The key initial objectives of treatment, in order of priority, are (1) to reduce and ultimately to remove all signs and symptoms of the depressive syndrome, (2) to restore occupational and psychosocial function to that of the asymptomatic state, and (3) to reduce the likelihood of relapse and recurrence.

All treatments are administered in the context of clinical management, which is defined as education of and discussion with patients and, when appropriate, their families about the nature of depression, its course, and the relative costs and benefits of treatment options. Clinical management is to be distinguished from formal supportive therapy; the latter focuses on the management and resolution of current difficulties and life decisions using the patient's strengths and available resources. Supportive therapy is often combined with medication and clinical management in more severe, complex, or chronic cases. However, good clinical management is important with all depressed patients, whose pessimism, low motivation and energy, and sense of social isolation or guilt may lead them to give up, not to adhere to treatment, or even to drop out of treatment.

Effective treatment rests on accurate diagnosis. The practitioner must first distinguish clinical depression, which is sufficiently severe and disabling to require intervention, from sadness or distress that is a normal part of the human experience. A formal mood syndrome should be treated. Treatments with established efficacy are preferred initially over less well tested or untested interventions.

In selecting an appropriate treatment, the clinician weighs the certainty of treatment response against the likelihood and severity of potential adverse treatment effects. The optimal treatment is highly acceptable to patients, predictably effective, and associated with minimal adverse effects. It results in complete removal of symptoms and restoration of psychosocial and occupational functioning. Treatment proceeds in three phases: acute treatment, continuation treatment, and maintenance treatment.

Acute treatment aims to remove all signs and symptoms of the current episode of depression and to restore psychosocial and occupational functioning (a remission). A remission (absence of symptoms) may occur either spontaneously or with treatment. If the patient improves significantly, but does not fully remit with treatment, a response is declared. If the symptoms return and are severe enough to meet syndromal criteria within 6 months following remission, a relapse (return of symptoms of the current episode) is declared.

Continuation treatment is intended to prevent this relapse. Once the patient has been asymptomatic for at least 4 to 9 months following an episode, recovery from the episode is declared. At recovery, continuation treatment may be stopped. For those with recurrent depressions, however, a new episode (recurrence) may occur months or years later. Maintenance treatment is aimed at preventing a new episode of depression and may be prescribed for 1 year to a lifetime, depending on the likelihood of recurrences.

Formal treatments for major depressive disorder fall into five broad domains: medication, psychotherapy, the combination of medication and psychotherapy, electroconvulsive therapy (ECT), and light therapy. Each domain has benefits and risks, which must be weighed carefully in selecting a treatment option for a given patient. Once selected, the initial treatment should be applied for a sufficient length of time to permit a reasonable assessment of the patient's response (or lack of response). If the treatment is going to be effective, a 4- to 6-week trial of medication or a 6- to 8-week trial of psychotherapy usually results in at least a partial symptomatic response; a 10- to 12-week trial usually results in a symptomatic remission, though full recovery of psychosocial function appears to take longer. The selection of the first and subsequent treatments should, whenever possible, be a collaborative decision between practitioner and patient. Such shared decision making is likely to increase patient adherence and, therefore, treatment effectiveness.

If the patient shows a partial response to treatment by 4 to 6 weeks, the same treatment should be continued for 4 or 6 more weeks. If the patient does not respond at all by 6 weeks or responds only partially by 10 to 12 weeks, other treatment options should be considered. If the initial treatment is the administration of an antidepressant medication, available evidence suggests that both partial responders and nonresponders will benefit from either switching to a different medication class or adding a second medication to the first. If psychotherapy alone is the initial treatment and it produces no response at all by 6 weeks or only a partial response by 12 weeks, clinical experience and logic suggest a trial of medication, given the strong evidence for the specific efficacy of medication. If the initial acute treatment is combined treatment and it produces no response by 6 weeks, switching to another medication is a strong consideration. For some patients, especially those who have had previous medication trials, medication augmentation rather than switching may be preferred.

Medications have been shown to be effective in all forms of major depressive disorder. Given the evidence to date, it is appropriate to treat patients with moderate to severe major depressive disorder with medication whether or not formal psychotherapy is also used. Medication is administered in dosages shown to alleviate symptoms. No one antidepressant medication is clearly more effective than another, and no single medication results in remission for all patients. The specific medication choice is based on side-effect profiles, patient's history of prior response, family history of response, and type of depression. Some patients respond well to one antidepressant medication, while others respond to a different medication. If the patient has previously responded well to and has had minimal side effects with a particular drug, that agent is preferred. Similarly, if the patient has previously failed to respond to an adequate trial of or could not tolerate the side effects of a particular compound, that agent should generally be avoided.

In general, of the tricyclics, the secondary amines (e.g., desipramine, nortriptyline) have equal efficacy, but fewer side effects, than do the parent tertiary amines (e.g., imipramine, amitriptyline). The newer antidepressants (e.g., bupropion, fluoxetine, paroxetine, sertraline, trazodone) are associated with fewer long-term side effects, such as weight gain, than are the older tricyclic medications. Patients whose disorder has atypical features appear to fare better on monoamine oxidase inhibitors (MAOIs) or selective serotonin reuptake inhibitors (SSRIs) than on tricyclic antidepressants (TCAs).

A history of failure to respond to a truly adequate trial of a drug in one class strongly suggests that it would be appropriate to try a medication from a different class rather than another drug from the same class. If the patient has not responded at all or has only a modest symptomatic response to medication by 6 weeks, the practitioner is advised to reevaluate the accuracy of diagnosis and the adequacy of treatment. Options for further treatment include continuing the current medication at a corrected dosage, discontinuing the first medication and beginning a second, augmenting the first medication with a second, adding psychotherapy to the initial medication, or obtaining a consultation/referral.

Patients with milder forms of major depressive disorder may be unwilling to tolerate medication side effects, and those with certain coexisting medical conditions may be physically unable to tolerate these drugs. Psychotherapy alone to reduce the symptoms of major depressive disorder may be considered a first-line treatment if (1) the depression is mild to moderate, nonpsychotic, not chronic, and not highly recurrent and (2) the patient desires psychotherapy as the first-line therapy. Preferred psychotherapy approaches are those shown to benefit patients in research trials, such as interpersonal psychotherapy, cognitive therapy, behavioral therapy, and marital therapy. The therapies that target depressive symptoms (i.e., cognitive or behavioral therapies) or specific interpersonal or current psychosocial problems related to the depression (i.e., interpersonal psychotherapy) are more similar than different in efficacy.

The efficacy of long-term psychotherapies for the acute phase treatment of major depressive disorder is not known; therefore, these therapies are not recommended for first-line treatment. The psychotherapy should generally be time-limited, focused on current problems, and aimed at symptom resolution rather than personality change. The therapist should be experienced and trained in the use of the therapy with patients who have major depressive disorder. Regular visits once or twice a week are typical.

If the patient being treated with psychotherapy fails to show any improvement in depressive symptoms by 6 weeks or only partial response by 12 weeks, a reevaluation and potential switch to, or addition of, medication are indicated. Medication is almost always recommended for those who do not respond to therapy at all. Given the evidence for the efficacy of medication and the lack of information regarding the efficacy of formal psychotherapy alone, the panel does not advise practitioners to treat severe and/or psychotic major depressive disorders with psychotherapy alone.

Combined treatment with both medication and psychotherapy may have an advantage for patients who have responded partially to either treatment alone or who have a history of chronic episodes or poor interepisode recovery, a history of chronic psychosocial problems (both in and out of episodes of major depression), and/or a history of treatment adherence difficulties. However, combined treatment may provide no unique advantage for patients with uncomplicated, nonchronic major depressive disorder. The possibility that these patients need adjunctive psychotherapy may be better gauged once the depressive syndrome has largely resolved with medication, since medication that induces a symptomatic remission also, as a consequence, improves psychosocial difficulties in many patients. The condition of patients given the combination of medication and psychotherapy who have not responded at all by week 6 or only partially by week 12 should be reevaluated to ensure that an alternative cause of symptoms has not been overlooked.

Electroconvulsive therapy is not recommended as first-line therapy for uncomplicated, nonpsychotic cases of major depressive disorder in primary care, as effective treatments that are less invasive and less expensive are available. It is a first-line option for patients suffering from severe or psychotic forms of major depressive disorder, whose symptoms are intense, prolonged, and associated with neurovegetative symptoms and/or marked functional impairment, especially if these patients have failed to respond fully to several adequate trials of medication. Electroconvulsive therapy may also be considered for patients who do not respond to other therapies, those at imminent risk of suicide or complications, and those with medical conditions precluding the use of medications. Very few patients will be sufficiently ill to require ECT. However, when ECT is indicated, it must be provided by a specialist.

Light therapy—a relatively new treatment option—is a consideration only for well-documented mild to moderately severe seasonal, nonpsychotic, winter depressive episodes in patients with recurrent major depressive or bipolar II disorders. Training in the administration and potential risks of light therapy is requisite to its use. Medication may also be effective for seasonal depression.

If a patient has a major depressive episode thought to be biologically caused by a nonpsychiatric, general medical disorder, the practitioner is advised to (1) treat optimally the associated general medical condition, (2) reevaluate the patient's condition, and (3) treat the major depression as an independent disorder if it is still present. In some cases, treatment of the major depression must proceed simultaneously with efforts to optimize treatment of the general medical condition. When major depressive disorder occurs with another psychiatric disorder, the practitioner has three options: (1) to treat the major depressive disorder as the primary target and reevaluate the patient's condition once he or she has responded to determine whether additional treatment is needed for the associated condition (for example, major depressive disorder with personality disorder or generalized anxiety disorder), (2) to treat the associated condition as the initial treatment focus (for example, major depression co-occurring with anorexia nervosa, bulimia nervosa, obsessive-compulsive disorder, or substance abuse), or (3) to attempt to decipher which condition is "primary" and select it as the initial treatment target (for example, major depressive disorder with panic disorder). The option selected will depend on the nature and severity of the co-occurring disorder.

Patients who respond to acute phase medication are generally continued on the drug at the same dosage for 4 to 9 months after they have returned to the clinically well state (continuation treatment). Unless maintenance treatment is planned, antidepressant medication is discontinued at 4 to 9 months or tapered over several weeks (depending on the type of medication). Patients are followed during the next several months to ensure that a new depressive episode does not occur. If a recurrence does begin, the patient is likely to respond to the same medication at the same dosage that was effective previously, which should then be continued for 4 to 9 months.

Although antidepressant medications are generally safe, even with long-term use, they should be discontinued if they are not required. All patients who have had a single episode of major depressive disorder are advised to discontinue medication after 4 to 9 months of continuation treatment, since only 50 percent will have another episode of major depressive disorder. Even then, the next episode may be years hence. If the full depressive episode recurs during or shortly after the discontinuation of medication, the depressive episode has not "run its course," and the full therapeutic dosage is generally reinstated.

The decision to implement continuation phase psychotherapy depends on the patient's residual symptoms, psychosocial problems, history of psychological functioning between episodes, and the practitioner's and patient's judgment about the need for such treatment. Continuation psychotherapy can be added to continuation medication following acute phase response to either medication alone or combined treatment.

Patients who relapse once continuation medication is ended may require long-term maintenance medication to prevent a new episode of depression. Patients who have had three or more episodes of major depression have a 90 percent chance of having another and are, therefore, potential candidates for long-term maintenance antidepressant medication. The maintenance medication given is generally the same type and dosage found effective in acute phase treatment. Maintenance psychotherapy does not appear to be effective in preventing a recurrence, although it may delay the onset of the next episode in those with highly recurrent major depressive disorder.

Mental health care professionals must be readily available (same day or next day) to provide a consultation (second opinion) or to receive a referral from busy primary care providers. The consultation is most useful when the mental health care professional outlines specific options or steps for the primary care provider and provides patients with the same information. Mental health care professionals should be open to subsequent patient visits, if needed.

Overview

The clinical practice guideline statements contained in *Depression in Primary Care* were developed to assist both patients and primary care practitioners in the diagnosis of depressive conditions and the treatment of major depressive disorder. This guideline is an abbreviated version of a far larger *Depression Guideline Report* and is divided into two volumes: this one, Volume 2: *Treatment of Major Depression*, and its companion volume, Volume 1: *Detection and Diagnosis*. The *Depression Guideline Report* contains more than 3,500 relevant references.

Treatment of Major Depression systematically reviews the indications, contraindications, benefits, and harms of the four major treatments for major depressive disorder: medication, psychotherapy, combined medication and psychotherapy, and electroconvulsive therapy (ECT). It also makes brief reference to other less frequently used treatments and the special circumstances in which they may be appropriate. The guideline considers the three phases of treatment for major depressive disorder—acute, continuation, and maintenance—and the indications for each.

Major depressive disorder consists of one or more episodes of major depression with or without full recovery between episodes. The clinically depressed patient must suffer either a sustained sad mood or a significant loss of interest/pleasure plus associated criterion symptoms for a period of 2 weeks or more. Nearly all patients with major depressive disorder also report significant life stresses. Up to one in eight individuals may require treatment for depression during their lifetimes; up to 70 percent of psychiatric hospitalizations are associated with mood disorders. According to data obtained from a 1980 population base, the total number of cases of major depressive disorder among those 18 or older in a 6-month period would be 4.8 million; in addition, over 60 percent of suicides can be attributed to major depressive disorder.

Based on 1980 data, mood disorders account for more than 565,000 hospital admissions, 7.4 million hospital days, and 13 million physician visits annually. The total cost of mood disorders to society, including the indirect costs that result from lost productivity, is estimated to be $16 billion annually. In addition to economic costs, depression can carry great personal costs because of the social stigma associated with the diagnosis and treatment of a "mental" illness. This stigma likely plays a large role in patients' reluctance to seek, accept, and adhere to treatment. Yet, when identified, depression can almost always be treated successfully, either with medication, psychotherapy, or a combination of the two. The potential savings to be derived from the appropriate treatment of people who suffer from depression are socially and economically significant.

The high prevalence of depression and the success of available treatments prompted these guidelines. The Depression Guideline Panel that prepared them is composed of experts from various mental health and primary care disciplines and a consumer representative, selected for their range and diversity of expertise. The guidelines are based on systematic literature reviews commissioned by the panel and conducted by experts in numerous areas relevant to depression, with special attention to the clinical issues most pertinent to the diagnosis and treatment of depression in primary care. Guideline development also included input from a broad range of professional and consumer organizations and individuals. The guidelines have undergone peer review and field review with intended users in clinical sites to evaluate the document both conceptually and operationally.

In making its recommendations for interventions, the panel chose to focus on randomized controlled clinical trials as the highest level of credible evidence for treatment efficacy. Thus, where data are available, conclusions are virtually certain. Where evidence is either lacking or incomplete, this is noted; in these instances, either no guideline has been derived or options are provided, based on logical inference, available data, and panel consensus.

Because of space and time constraints, this guideline does not address the treatment of children and adolescents, bipolar disorder, or depressive symptoms insufficient to meet the criteria for major depressive disorder. Development of guidelines in these areas would be fruitful areas for followup activities.

1 Guideline Development and Methodology

Rationale for Guideline Development—The Cost of Depression

Up to one in eight individuals may require treatment for depression during their lifetimes; up to 70 percent of psychiatric hospitalizations are associated with mood disorders (Secunda, Katz, Friedman, et al., 1973). The direct costs of treatment for major depressive disorder, combined with the indirect costs from lost productivity, are significant. According to one study based on a 1980 population base, the total number of cases of major depressive disorder among those aged 18 or older in a 6-month period would be 4.8 million; in addition, 60 percent of suicides could be attributed to major depressive disorder (Stoudemire, Frank, Hedemark, et al., 1986). This translates to more than 16,000 suicides or 7 deaths per 100,000 annually. In 1980, mood disorders accounted for more than 565,000 hospital admissions, 7.4 million hospital days, and 13 million physician visits annually. Office-based psychiatrists' and psychologists' costs were $453 million, pharmaceutical costs were $138 million, the cost of home and institutional care was $141 million, and total direct costs were more than $2.1 billion. Indirect morbidity costs were estimated to be $10 billion; total mortality costs due to lost productivity, $4 billion. The total cost of mood disorders to society was roughly $16 billion.

Patients with major depressive disorder experience substantial pain; suffering; and psychological, social, and occupational disability during the depression (Johnson, Weissman, and Klerman, 1992; von Korff, Ormel, Katon, et al., 1992; Wells, Golding, and Burnam, 1988a,b). If depressive conditions accompany selected nonpsychiatric medical conditions (e.g., coronary artery disease, diabetes), the outcome of these concurrent general medical disorders is likely to be worse than if depression were not present (Carney, Rich, Freedland, et al., 1988; Carney, Rich, teVelde, et al., 1987a,b; Keitner, Ryan, Miller, et al., 1991; Lustman, Amado, and Wetzel, 1983; Lustman, Griffith, and Clouse, 1988; Lustman, Griffith, Clouse, et al., 1986).

In addition to economic costs, depression can carry great personal costs because of the social stigma associated with the diagnosis and treatment of a "mental" illness. This stigma likely plays a large role in patients' reluctance to seek, accept, adhere to, and continue treatment. Evidence compatible with the notion of stigma includes the following:

- Those with mental illnesses are often required to report them when applying for driver's licenses, security clearances, jobs, and other routine purposes, while those with other medical conditions are not. (The recent Americans with Disabilities Act has rectified this problem somewhat.)

- Third parties reimburse providers for treatment of mental illnesses at reduced rates and with marked capitations on total costs, although there are very few such restrictions on treatment for general medical disorders.
- A recent preliminary survey of physicians revealed that many cases of depression may not be coded in medical records, partly because of a desire to protect patients from stigmatization (Rost and Smith, 1992).
- Only about 20 percent or fewer patients with depression are treated in the mental health sector (Hough, Landsverk, Karno, et al., 1987; Shapiro, Skinner, Kessler, et al., 1984).
- Only 12 percent of people are willing to take medication for clinical depression, while more than 70 percent would take medication for a headache (Roper Reports, 1986).

As a result of stigma, depressed patients often incorrectly believe that they have caused their own illness or are solely responsible for its cure. They fear (sometimes correctly) subsequent discrimination in hiring, promotion, and other occupational opportunities. It is logical to infer that until depression is dealt with on an equal footing with nonpsychiatric medical disorders (attitudinally, economically, socially, occupationally, and politically), it will be underreported and national health statistics will likely remain misleading.

Given this stigmatization, it is vital to educate patients (and their families, if appropriate) about the nature, prognosis, and treatment of depression to increase adherence to treatment, relieve unnecessary guilt, and raise hope. Patients need to know the full range of suitable treatment options before agreeing to participate in treatment.

This *Clinical Practice Guideline* was developed with support from the Agency for Health Care Policy and Research (AHCPR) by the Depression Guideline Panel to assist both patients and primary care providers (e.g., general practitioners, family practitioners, internists, nurse practitioners, registered nurses, physician assistants, and others) in the treatment of major depressive disorder. The general principles embodied in these guidelines should also provide a framework for others who treat depressed persons. A detailed description of the development of these guidelines is found in *Depression in Primary Care: Volume 1. Detection and Diagnosis* (AHCPR Publication No. 93–0550, 1993) and in Chapter 1 of the *Depression Guideline Report* (Depression Guideline Panel, forthcoming).

These guidelines are not intended to render selected procedures reimbursable or not reimbursable. That decision logically falls to third-party payors. Likewise, the guidelines do not specify which professionals should conduct which procedures, an issue addressed by licensing/privileging bodies. Should the recommended steps in the treatment of depression fall outside the expertise of the practitioner or be impractical, given constraints of time or availability of appropriate resources, the practitioner should consult with, or refer the patient to, someone knowledgeable in these matters.

Methodological Background

This *Clinical Practice Guideline* is an abbreviated version of a far larger document, the *Depression Guideline Report*, to which the reader may refer for further detail. These treatment guidelines focus on outpatients with major depressive disorder, particularly those seen in primary care settings. They do not address the treatment of children or adolescents, bipolar disorder, or depressive symptoms insufficient to meet the criteria for major depressive disorder. The panel members believe that the steps and procedures proposed here form a reasonable general treatment plan in many cases; they have attempted to be as explicit as possible in making recommendations, such as how often to see a patient, when to increase a medication dosage, and when to change to a different treatment. However, the treatment of an individual patient requires adaptation of both the general (strategic) and specific (tactical) recommendations to suit the patient's particular situation.

The guidelines are based on systematic reviews of the available scientific literature. The reviews commissioned involved a comprehensive examination of literature published through December 1990. However, articles published after this date were included when they provided information that would otherwise have been unavailable. The panel chose to focus on randomized controlled trials as the highest level of credible evidence for treatment efficacy for two major reasons. First, many non–mental health care practitioners and many in the general public are not fully aware of the striking evidence for the efficacy of various treatments. Second, the statements derived from such evidence can be made with substantial certainty. Where evidence is either lacking or incomplete, this is noted; in these cases, either no guideline has been derived or options are provided, based on logical inference, available data, and panel consensus. When the evidence is reasonably clear though modest in amount, these findings are noted, and a tentative recommendation is offered. Thus, the guidelines that follow are coded according to the strength of the available evidence as interpreted by the panel:

A Good research-based evidence, with some panel opinion, to support the guideline statement.

B Fair research-based evidence, with substantial panel opinion, to support the guideline statement.

C Guideline statement based primarily on panel opinion, with minimal research-based evidence, but significant clinical experience.

The full guideline development process is illustrated in Figure 1.

Figure 1. Guideline development process

Topic chosen by AHCPR

↓

Panel chair chosen by AHCPR

↓

Panel members recommended by the chair and AHCPR

↓

Panel members approved/appointed by AHCPR

↓

Panel convened and focus for literature reviews refined

↓

21 diagnostic and 18 treatment topics selected for review

↓

Literature reviewers for specific topics selected by panel

↓

NLM literature searches conducted using key words selected for each topic by panel/reviewers with MEDLINE and Psychiatric Abstracts for each topic

↓

Abstracts received by literature reviewers

↓

Abstracts reviewed for inclusion/exclusion criteria by literature reviewers

↓

Full copy of each article selected read by literature reviewers

↓

Literature review and evidence tables created by literature reviewers

↓

Review read/critiqued by panel chair, methodologist, and a minimum of 3 panel members

↓

Reviews revised where indicated

↓

Relevant parts of each review abstracted by panel for *Depression Guideline Report*

↓

Depression Guideline Report drafted by panel

↓

All reviews independently reviewed by all panel members and 14 scientific reviewers

↓

Depression Guideline Report revised

↓

Depression Guideline Report synopsized to *Clinical Practice Guideline*, *A Patient's Guide*, and *Quick Reference Guide for Clinicians*

↓

Peer review requested from 73 organizations and 14 new scientific reviewers, pilot review of *A Patient's Guide, Quick Reference Guide for Clinicians*, and *Clinical Practice Guideline* in nine sites

↓

Critiques from peer/pilot review considered by panel

↓

All versions of guidelines reviewed by panel

↓

Final copy of all versions of guidelines submitted to AHCPR

In applying these guidelines, several caveats are in order. First, the reader should not confuse the absence of studies with the absence of efficacy. In certain situations, there is little direct evidence for the efficacy of various treatments, based on randomized controlled trials (for example, with patients who have major depressive disorder and concurrent general medical conditions). Furthermore, several commonly used treatments, such as supportive psychotherapy, have not been subjected to randomized controlled trials. In the absence of evidence, no scientifically based statement about the efficacy of a treatment can be made. However, case reports, case series, clinical experience, and logical inference form a basis for selecting treatments for particular patients.

Second, the primary care practitioner is cautioned not to persist with extensive, multiple medication trials or with prolonged psychotherapy to which the patient is not responding because the longer the patient's depressive episode lasts, the more difficult it may be to treat (Bielski and Friedel, 1976; Rush, Hollon, Beck, et al., 1978). For example, patients who have not remitted with one or two well-conducted antidepressant medication trials (with or without psychotherapy) or, for less severe cases, a trial of psychotherapy not exceeding 12 weeks are likely candidates for consultation or referral.

Third, a consultation or referral to a specialist is always an option throughout the patient's management. It may be called for immediately, for example, if the patient is suicidal, or later. Consultation or referral to a specialist is particularly appropriate in the following instances:

- The practitioner is not skilled in making the diagnosis.
- The diagnosis is unclear.
- The practitioner is not skilled in providing the recommended treatment.
- Treatment does not result in successful outcome.
- These recommendations cannot be adapted or followed for practical, clinical reasons.

Specific Methodological Strategies

This summary of the methods used by the panel to evaluate treatments considered in this document provides the reader with a better understanding of the scientific basis and limitations of these guidelines, as well as an appreciation of the current state of the depression literature and the methodological and research issues that need further investigation. (See Depression Guideline Panel, forthcoming, for more detail.)

The Depression Guideline Panel's charge was to determine the efficacy of various treatments for major depressive disorder in patients likely to be seen by primary care providers. The ideal evidence on which to base conclusions would be randomized controlled trials of the various therapies conducted in primary care settings with outpatients who have major depressive disorder. A perusal of the literature reveals few such studies.

The panel, therefore, constructed an indirect model, incorporating information from non–primary care settings, and extrapolated this information to the setting of interest. The general strategy was to identify all relevant literature, summarize the results in evidence tables, combine results across each study using meta-analysis, and compare the efficacy of alternative therapies.

Review of the Literature

The literature was reviewed systematically by establishing a priori criteria for relevant studies, specifying key words (see Depression Guideline Panel, forthcoming), reviewing abstracts selected by computer searches, compiling and reviewing the full articles, compiling evidence tables summarizing these articles, and conducting meta-analyses where possible.

Selection of Evidence. The panel considered only published, peer-reviewed randomized controlled trials as appropriate evidence to support these guidelines for the treatment of major depressive disorder. This decision was based on the notion that absolute confirmation of the efficacy of a treatment was a prerequisite for any consideration of effectiveness.[1] The randomized controlled trial is the clearest scientific method for judging comparative efficacy. The panel made this decision with knowledge of the limitations of randomized controlled trials, particularly considerations of generalizability with respect to patient selection and treatment quality.

Analysis of Treatment Effect. The success of a treatment studied in a randomized controlled trial can be reported in a number of ways. Some may ask, "How many patients randomized to the treatment got better?" This question is answered by an intent-to-treat analysis, which uses the number of patients who got better (regardless of whether they remained in the study) as the numerator and the number randomized to the treatment as the denominator. Others may wonder, "Of those who received at least the minimal amount of treatment thought to be effective, how many got better?" This question is answered by an adequate treatment analysis, which considers only those patients who received a predetermined minimum amount of treatment (typically 3 to 4 weeks for medication and 4 to 6 weeks for psychotherapy in major depressive disorder) as the denominator and counts as the numerator those who responded. Finally, a completer analysis includes only those who received the full treatment package in both the numerator and the denominator.

[1]"Efficacy" refers to the performance of the treatment under controlled, research-defined conditions. "Effectiveness" refers to the actual outcomes obtained in routine practice.

These distinctions are critical. For example, 100 patients may be randomized to the treatment; 80 may continue the treatment for 3 weeks (the minimum amount of time necessary to achieve a response), and 40 may continue the treatment until its termination. Imagine that a full course of treatment is 95 percent efficacious, that an adequate course of treatment is 75 percent efficacious, and that none of the patients who drop out get better. In this example, the intent-to-treat response rate is (.95) (40/100) or 38 percent, the adequate treatment response rate is (.75) (40) + (.95) (40/80) or 78 percent, and the completer response rate is (.95) (40/40) or 95 percent. Thus, depending on which parameter is chosen, an investigator can claim a success rate anywhere between 38 and 95 percent.

A modified intent-to-treat analysis was used in the treatment section of these guidelines. The denominator for this analysis was the number of patients randomized to the treatment. In most studies, the numerator was the number of patients who stayed in treatment and got better. This modification was made because few studies presented sufficient data to permit calculation of true intent-to-treat numbers, while many provided enough information to permit calculation of the modified percentage. If some patients who left a study got better anyway (which is quite probable), these modified percentages may be lower than those derived from a true intent-to-treat analysis. It is unlikely, however, that this bias would be substantially different among treatments; thus, the between-treatment comparisons should remain valid.

Outcome Measures. As it is the patients who experience the pain and suffering associated with depression, the best way to measure a treatment's effectiveness is to determine whether the patients are feeling and functioning better. Most randomized trials of therapies for major depressive disorder use standardized measures of depressive symptoms completed by the clinician (e.g., the Hamilton Rating Scale for Depression [HAM-D; Hamilton, 1960, 1968], the Clinical Global Impression [CGI; Guy, 1976]) or by the patient (e.g., the Beck Depression Inventory [BDI; Beck, Ward, Mendelson, et al., 1961]) to determine treatment effectiveness. Less often, measures of marital, social, or occupational functioning are used to supplement depression symptom ratings. Ideally, future studies will use a battery of outcome measures that, together, create a complete vision of the patient's level of well-being and functioning.

For medication studies, the panel chose to use the percentage of patients with a 50 percent reduction in HAM-D score or a CGI response of 1 or 2 (markedly or very much improved) as the primary outcome measure, because these were the most commonly reported categorical outcome measures, thereby rendering the greatest number of studies eligible for inclusion in the meta-analysis.

For psychotherapy studies, the BDI was by far the most commonly used measure. Analysis showed a correlation coefficient of .84 between the BDI and the HAM-D, demonstrating that the two are well correlated with each other. A meta-analysis of the difference in percent response as determined by HAM-D and BDI in the 18 limbs of the six studies that reported both of these parameters resulted in a distribution with a mean of 2.6 percent, suggesting that the BDI may report a 2.6 percent greater response than does the HAM-D when applied to similar patients. However, there is a 19.6 percent chance that the HAM-D will show a higher response rate than does the BDI; therefore, until further evidence is accrued, it is best to think of the two measures as generally equivalent. Such an assumption does not appear to put psychotherapy at a disadvantage when it is compared to medication trials that used the HAM-D.

Scoring of Outcomes. Treatment outcome in a randomized trial is commonly reported in one of two ways. In categorical scoring, a set of rules is used to place all patients into two or more categories (e.g., "better" versus "not better"), and the percentage of patients in each category is reported. In continuous scoring, a standardized measure of depressive symptoms is administered before and after treatment, and the change in group mean score is reported. Categorical scoring addresses the question that interests most patients: How likely am I to get better if I take this treatment? The results of continuous scoring are of interest to researchers: What is the average amount of improvement a patient can expect by taking this treatment?

The two methods are not mutually exclusive, and it would be best if both were reported in all trials. In this analysis, the panel used categorical data, because they are of greatest interest to patients. Sufficient data were available to provide a reasonable number of studies for meta-analysis.

Preparation of Evidence Tables. To evaluate the literature systematically, each article that met inclusion criteria was read and scored by the author of the review and then abstracted to the appropriate evidence table. (See Depression Guideline Panel, forthcoming, for the evidence tables.) For medication studies, three summaries were prepared for each treatment. The first reports the percentage of patients who recovered and contains an entry for every eligible trial that included the treatment as one of its arms. The second reports the difference in response rate between the treatment of interest and placebo. This summary includes an entry for each study that has both an arm containing the treatment of interest and a placebo limb. The third compares the response rate of the treatment of interest to all other established treatments. This listing includes an entry for each study with a limb containing the treatment of interest and a limb containing another established treatment. Thus, a single study may be listed in one, two, or three summaries for a given treatment and may appear in evidence tables for more than one treatment.

A similar approach was used for psychotherapy studies, with tables outlining the percentage of patients who responded to the treatment of interest, the results of treatment compared to the results of another fully representative psychotherapy package or medication, and the effectiveness of therapy versus placebo and versus wait-list.

Meta-Analysis

Methodology and Limitations. The panel used meta-analysis following the confidence profile method (CPM) to calculate summary statistics that describe the likely effects of each treatment considered. (Details can be found in Eddy, Hasselblad, and Schacter, 1990.) Using a hierarchical Bayesian random-effects model, the panel calculated the probability distribution describing the results that would be expected if a hypothetical additional study, similar to the ones included in the analysis, were performed. By taking into account the heterogeneity of study results, this type of analysis depicts the range of results that practitioners can expect should they use the treatment in their own practice settings.

Each meta-analysis produces a probability distribution depicting the likelihood that the parameter of interest falls within any particular range of values. For example, the meta-analysis result depicted in Figure 2 indicates the difference in success rate for two alternative therapies. The curve represents the percent difference in success rate between the therapies. It can be said that the mean difference between them is 5 percent (.05), with a standard deviation of 6.6, that 95 percent of the area under the curve (the Bayesian equivalent of a 95 percent confidence interval) lies between -8 and 17.7 percent, or that there is a 22.5 percent chance that the actual

Figure 2. Example of a meta-analysis result (mean 5 percent, standard deviation 6.6)

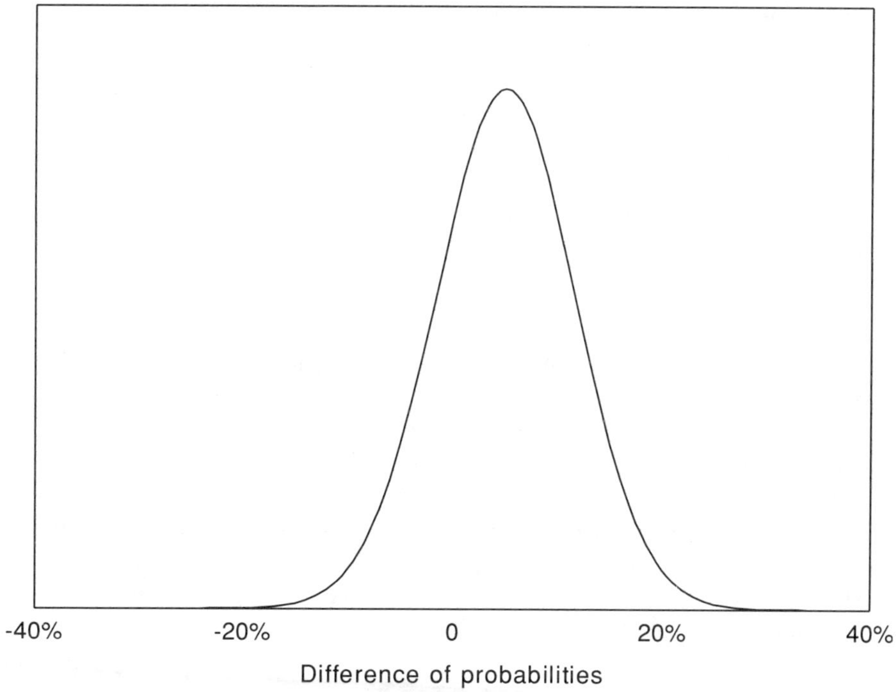

difference is less than zero. Since Figure 2 is a probability distribution, it is easy to determine the probability that the true difference in the effect of the treatment is greater than, less than, or equal to any selected value. The standard deviation suggests the shape of the distribution; distributions with small standard deviations relative to their mean are tall and narrow, indicating a high degree of certainty regarding the result.

Several factors can compromise the internal validity of the meta-analyses. First, while the random effects model accounts for among-study variations and, therefore, for random bias, it cannot account for any systematic biases that occurred in all of the studies. Second, to be included in the meta-analysis, studies had to include sufficient data to permit calculation of the percent response for each treatment, based on a modified intent-to-treat analysis that used either the HAM-D or the CGI (medication trials) or the BDI (psychotherapy trials). If studies without sufficient data to permit inclusion were fundamentally different from those that were included, summary statistics may be biased. Similarly, a variety of publication biases (particularly the tendency to publish only those studies with positive findings) may result in biased summary statistics.

On the other hand, the hierarchical random effects model is robust. Sensitivity analyses reveal that it would take a huge number of very large studies to change the results in any important way.

Threats to the external validity of the meta-analysis relate primarily to the generalizability of the study populations. While most studies entered a well characterized group of patients with major depressive disorder, others included small, but unspecified, numbers of patients with bipolar disorder or other psychiatric co-morbidities. It is, therefore, difficult to state with certainty the patient populations that the meta-analyses describe. Evidence suggests that patients with different types of depression have different prognoses and react differently to treatment. For example, the placebo response rate for nonpsychotic major depressive disorder is on the order of 25 percent, while the placebo response rate for psychotic depressions is only about 10 percent (Schatzberg and Rothschild, in press). In the absence of knowledge about the exact case mix included in the meta-analysis, caution is necessary to avoid overstating the degree of certainty that is assigned to the results.

Limitations in Comparisons Across Trials. After the meta-analyses have been performed, there is a great temptation to make direct comparisons between summary statistics for medication and psychotherapy trials. Such comparisons should be approached with caution because of the following limitations;

- Patients who agree to participate in studies that provide both medication and psychotherapy treatment cells may differ from patients who participate in medication trials with two active medication cells or in psychotherapy trials that do not offer a medication cell.

- Psychotherapy studies typically last longer, which, on the one hand, increases the chances of a spontaneous remission and prolongs exposure to treatment but, on the other hand, increases the opportunity for dropout.
- The pill placebo controls used in medication studies are not equivalent to the wait-list controls employed in psychotherapy trials. The pill placebo controls receive the same support and case management that the active medication group receives. Many medication trials contain such a pill placebo arm. What is the appropriate control for a talking therapy? Only one psychotherapy trial containing a pill placebo control has been conducted to date (Elkin, Shea, Watkins, et al., 1989). More commonly, patients kept on a wait-list constitute the control group. Most proponents of talking therapies would argue that it is not just the talking, but the content of the talking, that makes the therapy effective. Therefore, the appropriate control should be some type of nonspecific talking that is devoid of the "active" content of the therapy in question so that controls still receive the support and case management that active psychotherapy patients receive. The appropriateness of the placebo becomes important in attempting to compare the treatment-placebo difference across treatment types. A medication that is 30 percent better than its pill placebo control may be more effective, less effective, or equally effective than a psychotherapy that is 40 percent better than its wait-list control. However, one must suspect that those in the pill placebo group received more support, guidance, and reassurance than did those placed on a wait-list, making the comparison between medication and placebo more stringent than that between psychotherapy and wait-list.
- The BDI and other self-reports commonly used in psychotherapy trials may be less sensitive (or slower to show improvement) than the clinician ratings (i.e., HAM-D, CGI) typically used in medication trials.
- Medication trials usually require greater symptom severity for study entry than do psychotherapy trials. Thus, less severely ill patients are typically studied with psychotherapy, while more severely ill patients are studied in medication trials.

Given these limitations, comparisons of medication and psychotherapy trials should not be given undue importance and should be considered hypothesis generating rather than hypothesis-testing.

Generalizability Issues. Although randomized trials provide the best evidence for the efficacy of a treatment in a specific type of patient, their applicability to the community at large may be limited by the trials' stringent enrollment criteria, unique treatment settings, and unrepresentative clinical procedures. While researchers are working to design methods that address this problem (see *Cross Design Synthesis: A New Strategy for Medical Effectiveness Research*, US GAO B244808, 1992), these methods were not yet sufficiently developed for use in this project. For these reasons, the panel restricted its analysis to clinical trials.

Two caveats must be emphasized, however, one related to patient populations and the other related to treatment quality.

The purpose of these guidelines is to make recommendations regarding the treatment of major depressive disorder in primary care settings. Analyses rely on the results of clinical trials that were typically performed in academic psychiatric settings and involved patients without other medical problems. This methodology raises concerns. First, clinical trials require patient consent and participation. Many patients decline a protocol for various reasons (e.g., too severely ill to accept the additional measurement procedures, fear of being placed on a placebo or wait-list, desire for medication, desire for psychotherapy). Thus, patients who enroll in trials may not be representative of the population of interest. Second, clinical trials of medications are often sponsored by pharmaceutical companies seeking Food and Drug Administration (FDA) approval for their products. To optimize the chances of a good result and to avoid problems with human subject protection committees, these studies typically exclude patients with important medical co-morbidities. Because many patients treated in primary care settings have such co-morbidities, the population of interest is different from the population summarized by the meta-analysis. It is not possible to determine, from the available evidence, how depressed patients with medical co-morbidities will respond to the various therapies. While the few studies done in primary care settings demonstrate response rates similar to those found in psychiatric settings, they are few in number, and they, too, have generally excluded patients with medical co-morbidities.

Randomized controlled trials are often conducted in research settings and always follow a prespecified protocol. Psychotherapy is often specified in a written "manual," with therapists restricted to particular procedures in research trials. For these reasons, the type of treatment provided as part of a clinical trial may differ substantially from that provided in routine practice. Thus, inferences from research trials to day-to-day practice remain tentative, as protocol-driven treatments may perform better or worse than do their community practice counterparts.

Potential Problems with Meta-Analysis Interpretation. Any time a new method for generating numerical output—in this case, meta-analysis —becomes available, there is potential for misunderstanding and abuse of the numbers. The panel offers some warnings regarding the meta-analysis presented in this *Clinical Practice Guideline*.

It is important not to attach undue significance to small differences. Figure 3 depicts the results of two meta-analyses, one for treatment A, with a success rate of 34 percent (SD 12), and one for treatment B, with a success rate of 28 percent (SD 11). While comparison of the means reveals that A is 6 percent better than B, there is about a 34 percent chance that B is actually better than A. Therefore, it would be improper to conclude with any certainty that A is superior.

Figure 3. Comparison of meta-analysis results for treatments A and B

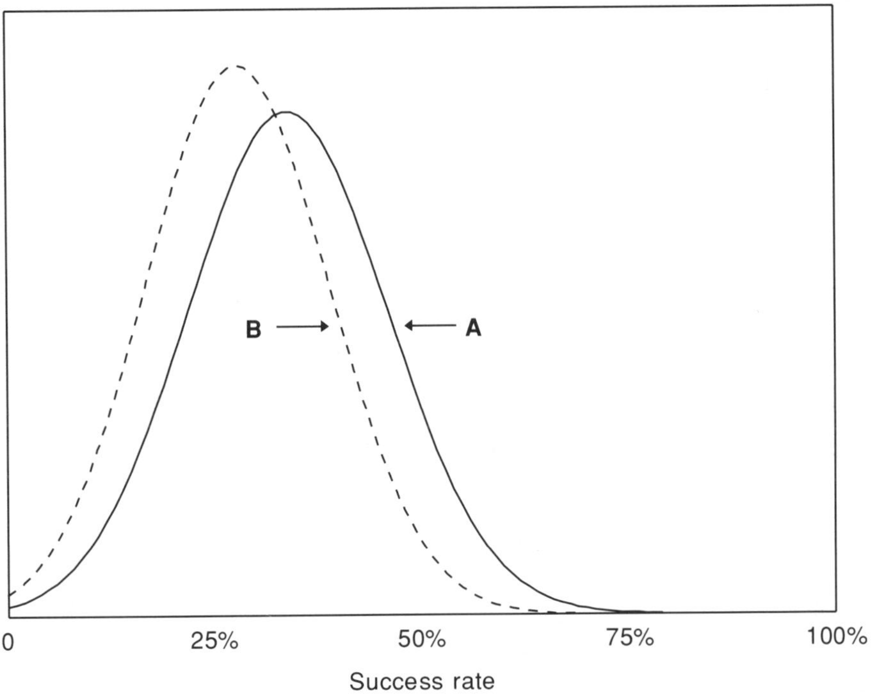

It is also important not to make improper inferences regarding numbers that are the same. In many cases, the data show that several treatments have similar response rates. These data could lead to the assertion that it is necessary only to use the least expensive agent. This assertion is true if the same patients respond to each treatment. However, there is strong evidence for biologic and psychological heterogeneity among patients with major depressive disorder, which is evident in the differential response of patients to medication (Goodwin and Jamison, 1990; Rush, Cain, Raese, et al., 1991). Thus, for a particular patient, drug A may be ineffective, while drug B may be quite effective; in another patient, the opposite may be true. Furthermore, some research suggests that certain medications may be effective earlier in the longitudinal course of recurrent mood disorders, while others may be better in more longstanding cases (Post, 1992). Similarly, clinical pharmacology studies and clinical experience provide evidence that patients differ in the nature, likelihood, and severity of the side effects that they experience with a medication. One patient may become sedated on a drug, another may develop insomnia, while others have no sleep difficulties. This heterogeneity suggests that more than one agent must be available to ensure adequate treatment of all patients.

2 Guideline: Aims of Treatment

Guideline: Once major depressive disorder is diagnosed, interventions that predictably decrease symptoms and morbidity earlier than would occur naturally in the course of the illness are logically tried first. The key initial objectives of treatment, in order of priority, are (1) to reduce and ultimately to remove all signs and symptoms of the depressive syndrome, (2) to restore occupational and psychosocial function to that of the asymptomatic state, and (3) to reduce the likelihood of relapse and recurrence. (Strength of Evidence = A.)

Acute treatment refers to formally defined procedures used to reduce symptoms and restore psychosocial function. All treatments are administered in the context of clinical management, which refers to the education of and discussion with patients (and families, when appropriate) about the nature of depression, its course, and the relative costs and benefits of treatment options. Clinical management is distinct from supportive therapy, which itself is a "formal" therapy or which can be combined with medication. Supportive therapy goes beyond clinical management and focuses on the management and resolution of current difficulties and life decisions through the use of the patient's strengths and available resources. In some milder, less chronic, nonrecurrent, nonpsychotic cases, an extended evaluation (one or two additional visits), when clinically safe, may help to differentiate those with major depression that requires formal treatment from those with depressive symptoms (not major depression) that may resolve with only time, support, explanation, and reassurance.

The certainty of treatment response is weighed against the likelihood and severity of potential adverse treatment effects. Treatment selection is based on an evaluation of the potential benefits and harms of each alternative. Second- and third-line treatments are considered if first-line treatments are contraindicated, ineffective, or inappropriate in particular cases.

The optimal treatment is highly acceptable to patients, predictably effective, and associated with minimal adverse effects. It results in the complete removal of symptoms and the restoration of psychosocial and occupational functioning. Potential adverse effects include:

- Side effects.
- Medical complications.
- Exacerbation of the underlying condition.
- Extraordinary monetary cost in relation to benefit.
- Excessive time requirement (inconvenience) at the expense of social, occupational, and family responsibilities in relation to benefit.

Effective treatment results in symptom remission; improved interpersonal, marital, and occupational functioning (DiMascio, Weissman, Prusoff, et al., 1979; Wells, 1985); reduced potential for suicide; reduction in excess health care utilization and cost (McDonnell-Douglas, 1989, 1990); as well as reduced disability from concurrent general medical conditions and improved long-term outcome (von Korff, Ormel, Katon, et al., 1992).

Benefits and Harms of Treatment

Formal treatments for major depressive disorder fall into four broad domains: medication, psychotherapy, the combination of medication and psychotherapy, and ECT. (Light therapy is also a treatment option for mild to moderate seasonal depressions.) Each domain has benefits and risks that must be weighed carefully in the selection of a treatment option for a given patient.

Medications

Medications have several clear benefits. They are easy to administer; are effective in mild, moderate, and severe forms of major depressive disorder; and require little patient time. Medications also have some disadvantages:

- Need for repeated medical visits to monitor response and adjust dosage.
- Unwanted side effects.
- More severe (but infrequent) medical reactions, such as allergic reactions.
- Potential use in suicide attempts.
- Failure of many patients (10 to 30 percent) to complete treatment.
- Lack of efficacy in some cases of major depressive disorder.
- Need for strict adherence to the medication schedule.
- Need for continuation phase treatment (see Chapter 9).

Side effects from antidepressants range from relatively minor, annoying, but fairly frequent, problems (e.g., dry mouth or constipation) to more significant, but less frequent, side effects (e.g., orthostatic hypotension) to substantial side effects (e.g., cardiovascular conduction abnormalities with classic tricyclic antidepressants [TCAs]). Most side effects are dose-dependent, requiring dosage adjustments in many cases. For most patients, the benefits of treatment far outweigh the risks.

Psychotherapy

The advantages of psychotherapy are:

- Lack of physiologic side effects, such as those found with medication or ECT.

- Logical possibility (not empirically documented) that psychotherapy is effective for some patients for whom medications are not effective.
- Theoretical possibility (with some empirical, but as yet inconclusive, evidence) that psychotherapy may make the depression less likely to recur once treatment stops because patients learn to cope with or avoid factors contributing to recurrence (Hollon, Shelton, and Loosen, 1991).

Although psychotherapy does not have the physiologic side effects found with medications, unrecognized disadvantages may occur when psychotherapy is chosen as the sole therapy:

- Psychotherapy has rarely been tested in patients with severe or psychotic depressions.
- Many patients (10 to 40 percent) fail to follow through with the full treatment (Persons, Burns, and Perloff, 1988).
- Many time-limited forms of psychotherapy, as well as all forms of longer term psychotherapy, have not been tested for efficacy in randomized controlled trials.
- The efficacy of the psychotherapies tested is defined with less certainty, since few studies have used a placebo or nonspecific therapy contrast group. Those on the wait-list commonly constitute the contrast group, and the more severely ill may refuse placement on the wait-list.
- Psychotherapy is not effective for all patients with major depressive disorder.
- Some therapies may differ from others in overall efficacy or in specific effects. For example, marital therapy may be more likely than therapy not focused on the marriage to improve marital function (Friedman, 1975).
- The quality of the therapy affects outcome, suggesting that the availability of trained therapists is pivotal (Shaw, Elkin, Vallis, et al., unpublished manuscript, 1993; Shaw and Olmsted, 1989; Woody, Luborsky, McLellan, et al., 1983).
- While psychotherapy, in theory, should reduce the likelihood of recurrence, available data do not support this idea for already established recurrent depressions (Frank, Kupfer, Perel, et al., 1990; Shea, Elkin, Imber, et al., 1992).
- Therapy sessions are time-consuming and may be inconvenient.
- Some patients and therapists are reluctant to consider somatic treatment alternatives (e.g., medication, ECT) when the psychotherapy has been ineffective after a reasonable time.
- Psychotherapy may be expensive, depending on the type of therapy and the provider.
- Treatment effect is usually measurable later (6 to 8 weeks) than with medication (4 to 6 weeks).

Combination of Medication and Psychotherapy

Although the routine use of both medication and a formal psychotherapy is not recommended as the initial treatment for most patients, panel consensus, logic, and some research suggest that combined treatment may be specifically useful in the following instances:

- Either treatment alone, optimally given, is only partially effective.
- The clinical circumstances suggest two discrete targets of therapy (e.g., symptom reduction addressed by medication and psychological/social/occupational problems addressed by psychotherapy).
- The prior course of illness is chronic (episodic with poor interepisode recovery or prolonged current episode greater than 2 years [Weissman, Jarrett, and Rush, 1987]).

In these cases, the advantages of combined treatment may include a higher probability of response, a greater degree of response for individual patients, or a lower attrition rate from treatment.

The disadvantages of combined treatment include the disadvantages of each alone. Those patients with milder, transient depressions may not require, respond to, or be able to tolerate medication. Those whose illness would have remitted with medication plus clinical management would have spent unnecessary time and money for a formal psychotherapy. Moreover, if the depression recurs, both treatments may again be indicated, since it will be unclear whether one alone would have been sufficient. There is no evidence, however, that the combination of medications and psychotherapy has a worse outcome than either treatment alone (see Depression Guideline Panel, forthcoming).

Electroconvulsive Therapy

Because of its proven efficacy in severely symptomatic patients who have failed to respond to one or more medication trials, ECT has an important role in the treatment of major depressive disorder. Electroconvulsive therapy is appropriate for patients with severe and/or psychotic depressions who have not responded to other forms of treatment or who have serious general medical conditions and severe depression for which ECT may be safer than medication. Although hospitalization is indicated for acutely suicidal or dangerously delusional patients, some practitioners believe that ECT results in more rapid resolution of these life-threatening features than does medication. However, ECT should be considered cautiously and used only after consultation with a psychiatrist, because ECT:

- Has not been tested in milder forms of illness.
- Is costly when it entails hospitalization.
- Has specific and significant side effects (e.g., short-term retrograde and anterograde amnesia).

- Includes the risks of general anesthesia.
- Carries substantial social stigma.
- Can be contraindicated when certain other medical conditions are present.
- Usually requires prophylaxis with antidepressant medication, even if a complete, acute phase response to ECT is attained.

Clinical Management

Treatment for major depressive disorder may include three phases: acute, continuation, and maintenance. The overall aim of all three phases is the attainment of a stable, fully asymptomatic state and full restoration of psychosocial function (a remission). Acute treatment aims at removing all depressive symptoms. If the patient improves with treatment, a response is declared. A remission may occur either spontaneously or with treatment. If the symptoms return and are severe enough to meet syndromal criteria within 6 months following remission, a relapse (return of symptoms of the current episode) is declared. Continuation treatment aims at preventing this relapse. Once the patient is asymptomatic for at least 6 months following an episode, recovery from the episode is declared. At recovery, continuation treatment may be stopped. For those with recurrent depressions, however, a new episode (recurrence) may occur months or years later. Maintenance treatment aims at preventing a recurrence. Recurrences are expected in 50 percent of cases within 2 years after continuation treatment (NIMH, 1985). For well established, recurrent depressions, the rate may approach 75 percent (Frank, Kupfer, Perel, et al., 1990).

Figure 4 illustrates the phases of treatment and the possible course of a depressive episode (Kupfer, 1991). The initially symptomatic patient begins to develop symptoms that ultimately (in days, weeks, or months) increase in number and severity until the full syndrome of major depressive disorder is present. It is useful to conceptualize treatment as having three phases (Frank, Prien, Jarrett, et al., 1991) because:

- A patient's full treatment plan must be based on his or her history of illness.
- The simple attainment of remission following acute treatment may be followed by relapse if continuation treatment is not provided.
- Not all, but a selected subgroup of patients, will require maintenance treatment to prevent recurrences.

It is reasonably well established that patients who have only a partial response to acute treatment will have more symptoms during continuation treatment. Furthermore, those with poor symptom control during continuation treatment have a higher chance of earlier relapse, as well as recurrence once treatment is discontinued (Prien and Kupfer, 1986). Figure 5 offers a schematic overview of treatment for depression.

Figure 4. Phases of treatment

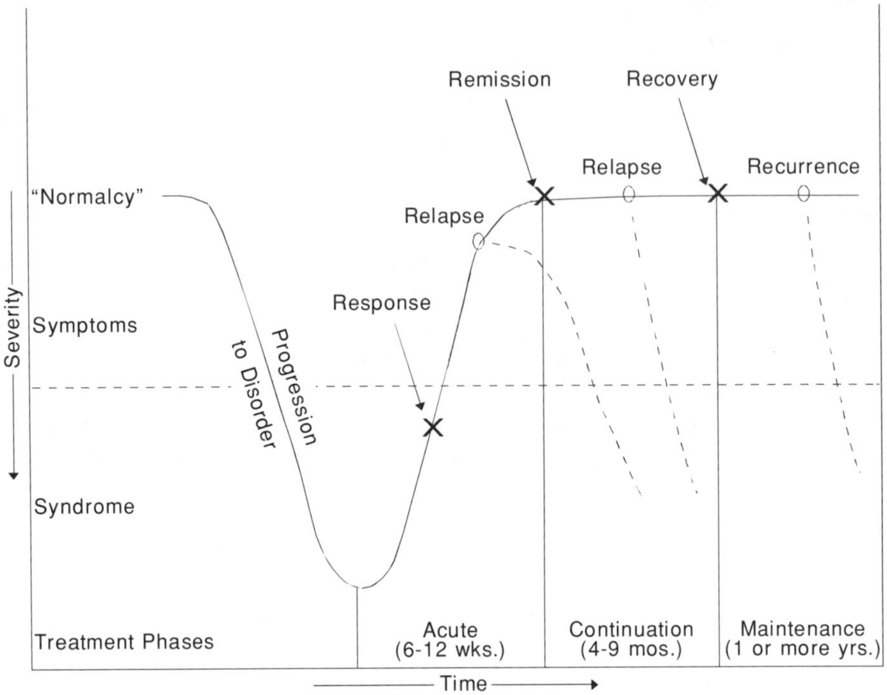

Source: Kupfer DJ. Long-term treatment of depression. J Clin Psychiatry 1991; 52(Suppl 5):28-34. Copyright © 1991, Physicians Postgraduate Press. Adapted and reprinted with permission.

For virtually all patients, the practitioner who provides the medication (or other treatment) also provides support, advice, reassurance, and hope as well as side-effect monitoring (including vital signs for those on medication), and dosage adjustments. This "clinical management" is exceptionally important, especially with depressed patients, whose pessimism, low motivation and energy, and sense of social isolation or guilt may lead them to give up, not adhere to treatment, or even to drop out of treatment.

Improving Adherence to Treatment

Guideline: A depressed outpatient's adherence to treatment can be improved by educating the patient and, in many cases, the family about the treatment, its potential side effects, and its likelihood of success. (Strength of Evidence = A.)

Adherence to treatment is a significant problem in the management of all patients, whether they have clinical depressions or other medical conditions. Compliance rates have been estimated from as low as 4 percent

Figure 5. Overview of treatment for depression

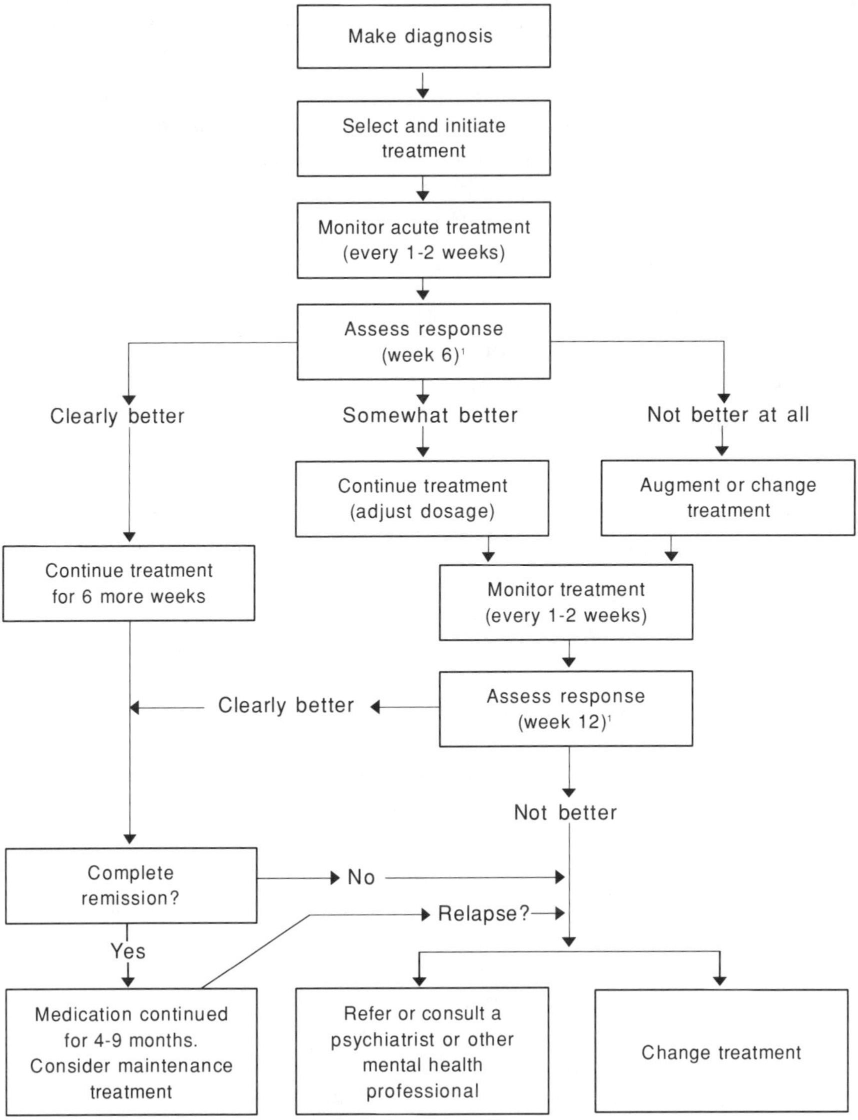

[1]Times of assessment (weeks 6 and 12) rest on very modest data. It may be necessary to revise the treatment plan earlier for patients failing to respond at all.

to as high as 90 percent in patients with mood disorders, depending on the methods of assessment (e.g., blood drug concentrations, pill counts, number of appointments kept). Adherence includes following prescribed activities, such as keeping appointments, taking medication, and completing assignments. Adherence can be evaluated directly by interviewing the patient.

In depressed patients, the presence of a personality disorder or concurrent substance abuse, a patient's lack of acceptance of the diagnosis or treatment plan, and troublesome treatment side effects are all associated with poorer treatment compliance (Depression Guideline Panel, forthcoming). Variables not consistently correlated with adherence include age, education, marital status, employment status, socioeconomic status, intelligence, gender, social adjustment, and life events.

At least seven studies have found that patient education helps to ensure treatment adherence in depressed outpatients (Altamura and Mauri, 1985; Anderson, Griffin, Rossi, et al., 1986; Myers and Calvert, 1984; Peet and Harvey, 1991; Seltzer, Roncari, and Garfinkel, 1980; van Gent and Zwart, 1991; Youssel, 1983). For this reason, clinical management for all depressed patients, regardless of the type of treatment that they receive, should include patient and, where appropriate, family education about depression. Appropriate information includes descriptions of:

- The cause, symptoms, and natural history of the illness.
- Treatment options, including indications, mechanisms of action, costs, risks, and benefits.
- Anticipated outcomes in terms of symptom relief, functional ability, and quality of life.
- Potential difficulties in complying with treatment and strategies to handle these problems.
- Early warning signs of relapse or recurrence.

It is helpful for the practitioner to give patients explicit instructions, offer them an opportunity to ask questions and discuss common difficulties in complying with the proposed treatment, and encourage them to report problems with adherence (Goodwin and Jamison, 1990). Information exchange can be enhanced by providing patients with educational materials. For some, one or two extra appointments designed specifically to provide information are useful. Practitioners may sometimes find it advisable to educate others in the patient's life (e.g., employers, spouses, children, licensing authorities), with the patient's permission, as well. Patients taking medication may initially need particularly close follow-up to ensure adherence, assess symptom response, minimize side effects, and find the optimal medication dosage. Medications that can be taken once daily may be preferable, as better adherence has been shown with once-a-day regimens than with medications that require multiple daily doses.

While it is essential that all patients be provided with information about their disorder and its treatment, the practitioner may want to consider specific adherence counseling for patients who demonstrate:

- A previous history of poor adherence.
- Unfounded negative attitudes toward the selected treatment.
- Significant lack of information or understanding about depression.
- Potential need for maintenance therapy based on history of illness.

A variety of useful educational materials are available from the D/ART (Depression/Awareness, Recognition, Treatment) Program of the National Institute of Mental Health (NIMH). Other organizations that provide support and information include the National Depressive and Manic-Depressive Association, the National Alliance for the Mentally Ill, the National Mental Health Association, and the National Foundation for Depressive Illness. Many diverse self-help groups are also available. These support groups provide an accepting, caring environment for people who share similar problems and life experiences. It is important, however, that patients with formal mood syndromes not rely solely on self-help as treatment for their conditions, since no data support the efficacy of such groups as sole "treatments." In fact, most of these groups provide medical information to patients, often assisting practitioners and patients with adherence problems, especially over the longer term.

Measuring Outcome

The initial evaluation includes asking the patient about the nine criterion symptoms of a major depressive episode, as well as the current level of interpersonal and occupational functioning. In addition to the clinical interview, patient self-report or clinician symptom-rating scales may permit a rapid assessment of the nature and severity of depressive symptoms. Interviewing a spouse or close friend about the patient's day-to-day functioning and specific symptoms is also helpful in determining the course of the illness, current symptoms, and level of functioning.

Follow-up visits during acute treatment are used to evaluate the level of symptom relief and restoration of function. Symptom evaluation (whether by interview alone or combined with the use of a symptom-rating scale) allows both practitioner and patient to assess response to treatment, determine whether the medication dosage should be adjusted, and clarify whether and when alternative treatments are needed.

Declaring a Treatment Response or Failure

Guideline: A 4- to 6-week trial of medication or a 6- to 8-week trial of psychotherapy usually results in at least a partial remission (50 percent symptom reduction), and a 10- to 12-week trial usually results in a nearly full response (minimal or no symptoms) to treatment. However, full restoration of psychosocial function often takes longer. (Strength of Evidence = B.)

Once selected, the initial treatment should be applied for a sufficient length of time to allow a reasonable assessment of the patient's response. Switching treatment too early provides no benefit, inappropriately discourages the patient, or leads to an erroneous conclusion that the treatment is ineffective. On the other hand, persisting over a prolonged period without any response is costly in pain and suffering and may unnecessarily prolong the episode.

The basis for this guideline rests on a careful review of 528 randomized controlled trials of medication (Table 4, page 47) and the 46 randomized controlled trials of psychotherapy (Table 11, page 75) in adult and geriatric out patients (Depression Guideline Panel, forthcoming). A partial response at 6 weeks may indicate the need for further medication dosage adjustments or a longer trial of the same treatment (i.e., medication, psychotherapy, or the combination, see pages 113-115). After 12 weeks, a partial response suggests the need for adjunctive psychotherapy, adjunctive medication, a switch to a different treatment, or consultation/referral.

Switching Versus Augmenting Treatments

Guideline: If a patient shows a partial response to treatment by 5 to 6 weeks, the same treatment is continued for 5 or 6 more weeks. (Strength of Evidence = A.) If the patient does not respond at all by 6 weeks or responds only partially by 12 weeks, it is appropriate to consider other treatment options. (Strength of Evidence = B.)

There are insufficient randomized controlled trials with medication, psychotherapy, or the combination to provide a scientifically sound basis for any conclusion about the "next best step" if the initial treatment is ineffective or only partially successful. However, it is well-known that patients differ from one another in the timing of treatment response (2 to 8 weeks for medication, 2 to 12 weeks for psychotherapy); therefore, a partial response by 5 to 6 weeks suggests that it is appropriate to continue the same treatment for 5 to 6 more weeks (optimizing dosage when medication is used). If the patient does not respond by 6 weeks or only partially responds by 12 weeks, the practitioner should consider the options of seeking consultation or referral, switching treatments altogether, or adding a second treatment to the first.

If the initial treatment is an antidepressant medication, there is evidence from sequential open trials to indicate that both partial responders and nonresponders will benefit from either adding a second medication to the first or augmenting or switching to a different medication class (Depression Guideline Panel, forthcoming). Switching or augmenting medications is an option for nonresponders at 6 weeks or for partial responders at 12 weeks.

If psychotherapy alone is the initial treatment and it produces no response by 6 weeks or only a partial response by 12 weeks, clinical experience and logic suggest a trial of medication, given the strong evidence for the specific efficacy of medication. The advisability of continuing formal psychotherapy in these situations has not been studied. However, some trials reveal that a subset of patients who are not responding to psychotherapy by 6 weeks will do so by 12 weeks (Elkin, Shea, Watkins, et al., 1989).

If the initial acute treatment is combined treatment (antidepressant medication administered optimally and formal psychotherapy) and it produces no response by 6 weeks, switching to another medication is a strong consideration. For some patients, especially those who have had previous medication trials, medication augmentation may be preferable to switching. For partial responders to the combination at week 12, no clear-cut data for the next best step are available, although logic and efficacy data indicate that augmenting or switching medication are reasonable options (Depression Guideline Panel, forthcoming).

3 Guideline: Strategic Planning for Acute Phase Treatment

Objectives of Acute Phase Treatment

Guideline: The objectives of acute phase treatment with medication, psychotherapy, the combination, or ECT are, in order of priority, (1) reduction and, wherever possible, removal of all signs and symptoms of the depressive syndrome, and (2) restoration of occupational and other psychosocial functioning to that of the asymptomatic state. (Strength of Evidence = A.)

A secondary, hoped-for consequence of acute treatment is prevention of relapse and recurrence. Table 1 shows the four most common acute phase treatment options and the suspected mechanisms by which each treatment is thought to achieve its objectives. Relapse/recurrence may occur once medication is discontinued. Theoretically, psychotherapy may prevent relapse/recurrence if patients have learned new skills or if situations have been modified. This latter notion is not fully tested or supported with evidence to date in those with recurrent major depressive disorders. One study (Frank, Kupfer, Perel, et al., 1990) indicates that recurrence may be delayed, but not prevented, with psychotherapy.

Table 1. Objectives and effects of different treatments

	Treatment			
Objective	**Medication**	**Psychotherapy**	**Combined**	**ECT**
Symptom reduction	Direct effect	Direct effect (cognitive) (behavioral) (interpersonal)	Direct effect	Direct impact
Improved function	Indirect effect (secondary to less depression)	Direct effect (marital)	Indirect and direct effects	Indirect effect (secondary to less depression)
Recurrence prevention	Direct effect (maintenance medication)	Direct effect (continued therapy) Indirect effect (learned skills following therapy)	Direct effect (maintenance medication or psychotherapy)	Direct effect (maintenance medication after ECT)

Note: ECT = Electroconvulsive therapy.

Indications for Acute Phase Treatment

Guideline: The practitioner must distinguish between major depression, which is sufficiently severe to require intervention, and the sadness or distress that is a normal part of the human experience. If a formal mood syndrome is present, treatment is indicated. (Strength of Evidence = A.)

Effective treatment rests on accurate diagnosis. The practitioner must first determine whether the patient has a clinical depression or is simply suffering normal sadness and distress. This distinction is analogous to others made in general medicine. When the patient's condition is primarily sadness, supportive discussions and/or the passage of time may be all that is necessary to resolve the symptoms. On the other hand, if a formal mood syndrome is present, specific treatments are usually indicated because there is clear evidence for their efficacy, because untreated major depressive episodes exact a high cost in pain and disability, and because the long-term prognosis for untreated major depressive disorder is poor (NIMH, 1985; Prien and Kupfer, 1986).

For patients who have very mild cases of major depression or whose diagnosis is unclear (e.g., major depression versus adjustment reaction with depressed mood) and who are not in immediate danger or are not suffering significant functional impairment, the practitioner may want to schedule one to two additional weekly evaluation visits to determine whether symptoms will abate without formal treatment or to discuss treatment options with the patient. There is evidence that clinical management leads to remission in 20 to 30 percent of cases (Elkin, Shea, Watkins, et al., 1989). However, several cautions are in order regarding extended evaluations:

- If the patient has a history of previous major depressive episodes, early intervention is recommended to prevent pain and suffering, once the presence of an episode has been clearly established (NIMH, 1985; Prien and Kupfer, 1986).
- Extended evaluations are not recommended for moderate, severe, or psychotic patients or for those with significant functional impairment.
- Although a reduction in symptoms often occurs with extended evaluation, this does not indicate that no treatment is needed. A full remission is the objective of both nonspecific and formal treatments.
- All patients who remit completely with clinical management (extended evaluation) alone should be followed up carefully (roughly two to three visits over the next 6 to 12 months), as evidence suggests that a large percentage may suffer a recurrence (Shea, Elkin, Imber, et al., 1992).

Given the evidence to date, it is appropriate to treat patients with moderate to severe major depressive disorder with medication whether or not formal psychotherapy is also used. For milder cases of major depressive disorder, there is some (albeit less clear-cut) evidence for the efficacy of medication versus placebo. Medication is administered in dosages shown to alleviate symptoms. The specific medication choice is based on side-effect profiles, history of prior response, family history of response, and type of depression. Typically, no one antidepressant medication exceeds the others in efficacy; some patients respond well to one, while others respond to a different treatment.

In general, the objectives of the formal psychotherapies in the treatment of major depressive disorder are similar to those of medication: symptom remission, improved psychosocial functioning, and prevention of relapse/recurrence. Most of the limited available data (see Table 12, page 76) have established that formal psychotherapy as the sole acute treatment for major depressive disorder is more effective than a wait-list control in outpatients with mild to moderate, nonpsychotic major depressive episodes.

Most psychotherapy efficacy studies have focused on symptom amelioration either by direct, time-limited, symptom-targeted psychological treatments, such as cognitive or behavioral therapy, or by time-limited treatments targeted at resolution of current interpersonal difficulties (interpersonal psychotherapy) or psychological conflicts (brief dynamic psychotherapy) assumed to act as vulnerability or precipitating factors or to maintain the syndrome once it has been established.

Preferred psychotherapeutic approaches are those shown to benefit patients in research trials, such as interpersonal, cognitive, behavioral, brief dynamic, and marital therapies. Because untested therapies are not, by definition, known empirically to be either effective or ineffective, these guidelines recommend choosing tested therapies over untested therapies, when available. The therapy should be limited to 20 sessions, since efficacy research on longer forms of therapy is not available and since strong evidence for the efficacy of medication with clinical management is available.

A second objective of formal psychotherapies is to address the patient's associated psychosocial problems, even if symptom control is largely accomplished with medication. In these patients, it is important to identify the objectives of therapy before selecting the specific treatment. Often, these associated problems are consequences of the depressive episode itself. If the depressive episode is effectively relieved with medication alone, the associated psychosocial problems often abate without additional psychotherapy (Mintz, Mintz, Arruda, et al., 1992). Thus, a reassessment of the patient's condition is advisable once symptom relief has been obtained with medication. The continued presence of associated psychosocial problems provides a reasonably strong rationale for augmenting treatment with formal psychotherapy aimed at the residual problems, even though sequential, randomized trials to support this stepwise approach are largely lacking to date.

Treatment Selection

Several general principles guide the selection of the first acute treatment:

- The patient and, where appropriate, the family need to be explicitly informed of the nature of the illness, all relevant treatment options, prognosis, and overall treatment plan.
- The ultimate selection of the first and subsequent treatments should, whenever possible, be a collaborative decision between practitioner and patient. Such shared decision making is likely to increase adherence and, therefore, treatment effectiveness.
- Treatments with established efficacy are preferred initially over less well tested or untested interventions.
- The initial treatment must be used in optimal fashion for a sufficient length of time to determine whether it is effective for the specific patient.
- Visits should be sufficiently frequent to optimize adherence.
- Outcome should be carefully assessed by interview for criterion signs and symptoms of depression. (This may be facilitated, but not replaced, with a self-report rating scale.)
- If the patient does not respond, it is logical to switch to a second treatment, as a wide range of effective treatments is available and no one treatment is effective for every patient.
- If the initial one or two treatments fail, a consultation with or referral to a psychiatrist or other mental health care professional trained in the diagnosis and treatment of depression is indicated.
- Consultation, if needed, must not be overly delayed, since longer episodes of major depressive disorder are more difficult to treat with either medication or psychotherapy (Bielski and Friedel, 1976; Goodwin and Jamison, 1990; Rush, Hollon, Beck, et al., 1978) and those with more recurrent forms of the illness may require more complex pharmacologic treatment (Post, 1992).
- The presence of a competent practitioner is a prerequisite for the selection of a specific treatment. It has been shown, for example, that the competency of the psychotherapist affects treatment efficacy (Shaw, Elkin, Vallis, et al., unpublished manuscript, 1993; Shaw and Olmsted, 1989). There is variability in the quality of administration of all treatments, and the quality of administration affects outcome for both medication and formal psychotherapies.
- For those with milder, less chronic, less recurrent, nonpsychotic major depressions, an extended evaluation (two to three visits) during which symptoms are monitored may usefully identify those who will remit fully with clinical management alone. However, careful followup is called for even in these patients since, in many, symptoms will return.

Table 2 shows the four main acute treatment choices for major depressive disorder and factors to be considered in their selection. The advantages and disadvantages of each should be evaluated by the practitioner and patient. Brief discussions of these treatment options are found in the sections that follow, and detailed descriptions appear in the chapters on each option. (The empirical evidence for these recommendations is found in the *Depression Guideline Report.*)

Table 2. Strategic choices in the acute treatment of major depressive disorder

Define Treatment Phases, Objectives, and Options with Patient (and Family, Where Appropriate)			
Medication[1]	**Formal Psychotherapy**	**Combined Treatment**	**ECT**[4]
More severe Chronic Recurrent Psychotic Melancholic Prior positive response Family history Patient preference Failure to respond to psychotherapy	Less severe Less chronic Nonpsychotic Prior positive response Availability Medical contraindication to medications Patient preference[2]	More severe Chronic Partial response to either alone Availability Personality disorder[3] Patient preference	Psychotic Severe or extremely severe Prior positive response Failure on several medications or combined treatment trials Need for rapid response Medical contraindication to medications

[1]Medication is always combined with clinical management.
[2]Patient preference applies more if depression is milder, nonpsychotic.
[3]This recommendation has not been empirically tested. It rests solely on clinical experience.
[4]Electroconvulsive therapy (ECT) is very rarely required for patients seen in primary care settings. It is reserved nearly always for those who have severe, often chronic, often psychotic depressions that have not responded to several trials of different standard medications.

Selection of Medication

Guideline: Patients with moderate to severe major depressive disorder are appropriately treated with medication, whether or not formal psychotherapy is also used. Medication is administered in dosages shown to alleviate symptoms. The specific medication choice is based on side-effect profiles, history of prior response, family history of response, type of depression, concurrent general medical or psychiatric illnesses, and concurrently prescribed medications. (Strength of Evidence = A.)

Most randomized controlled trials on the efficacy of medication were performed with the goal of obtaining FDA approval for these drugs. Therefore, data documenting efficacy apply most directly to patients who have moderate to severe depression, are free of other psychiatric and general medical conditions, and are seen in psychiatric settings. Only 24 studies have tested the efficacy of medication for major depressive disorder in primary care settings. Although, to date, efficacy is the same or slightly higher in primary care settings than in psychiatric settings, the placebo response rate may also be slightly greater. Most randomized controlled trials include a 7- to 10-day "washout" or "placebo run-in" period. Such a period includes at least two visits to ensure that the major depressive disorder does not remit either spontaneously or with the nonspecific aspects of treatment and to allow patients time to weigh the treatment options. A similar procedure in routine practice for patients who are not severely ill, psychotic, or acutely suicidal is a reasonable option since, in the psychiatric setting, substantial improvement may be seen in 15 to 25 percent of such patients without medication (Fairchild, Rush, Vasavada, et al., 1986); the improvement rate may be even higher in general medical settings (Kathol and Wenzel, 1992).

The decision to use medication depends on the patient's physical capacity and willingness to risk the possibility of and to tolerate the potential side effects of antidepressant medications. Patients with milder forms of major depressive disorder may be unwilling to tolerate side effects. Those with certain coexisting general medical conditions may be physically unable to tolerate these drugs.

Selection of Psychotherapy Alone

Guideline: Patients with mild to moderate major depression who prefer psychotherapy alone as the initial acute treatment choice may be treated with this option. Psychotherapy alone is not recommended for the acute treatment of patients with severe and/or psychotic major depressive disorders. (Strength of Evidence = B.)

Randomized controlled trials of psychotherapy have been largely limited to a number of short-term, structured forms, including cognitive, interpersonal, behavioral, brief dynamic, and marital psychotherapy. These trials have generally enrolled patients with less severe forms of major depressive disorder than those in medication trials. In general, the formal, time-limited psychotherapies are equivalent to each other and are significantly better than wait-list comparisons. In trials comparing therapy alone to standard antidepressant medication, the therapy and medication have often been equal, though only one trial has used a pill placebo contrast cell (Elkin, Shea, Watkins, et al., 1989).

Many forms of psychotherapy have not been subjected to clinical trials. Without data, scientifically based recommendations for or against these as first-line single or adjunctive treatments for major depressive disorder cannot be provided. The general absence of randomized controlled trials evaluating the efficacy of psychotherapy alone for patients with severe major depressive disorder also precludes a definitive statement regarding this option. Nevertheless, clinical experience clearly indicates that patients whose conditions have psychotic features or severe vegetative symptoms are less able to engage in the activities thought essential to the psychotherapeutic process. Given evidence for the efficacy of medication and the lack of information regarding the efficacy of formal psychotherapy alone, the panel does not advise practitioners to treat severe and/or psychotic major depressive disorders with psychotherapy alone.

The decision to use medication or a proven form of psychotherapy is best made with the patient. It should take into consideration the severity of the depression, the urgency of successful treatment, and the probability of and tolerance for potential harms of treatment.

Selection of Combined Treatment

Guideline: Combined treatment may have an advantage for patients with partial responses to either treatment alone (if adequately administered) and for those with a more chronic history or poor interepisode recovery. However, combined treatment may provide no unique advantage for patients with uncomplicated, nonchronic major depressive disorder. (Strength of Evidence = B.)

Randomized trials of the combination of medication and psychotherapy compared to medication or psychotherapy alone reveal only a modest advantage at best for the combination, especially regarding symptom reduction. On the other hand, there is some evidence that combined treatment may have a broader effect than does medication alone (Friedman, 1975; Weissman, 1979; Weissman, Kasl, and Klerman, 1976; Weissman, Klerman, Prusoff, et al., 1981). One study is consistent with the widely held clinical belief that combined treatment has a particular advantage for complicated, chronic major depressions (Blackburn, Bishop, Glen, et al., 1981).

Selection of ECT

Guideline: Electroconvulsive therapy is a first-line treatment option only for patients with more severe or psychotic forms of major depressive disorder, those who have failed to respond to other therapies, those with medical conditions precluding the use of medications, and those with an essential need for rapid response. (Strength of Evidence = A.)

Electroconvulsive therapy is not recommended as first-line therapy for uncomplicated, nonpsychotic cases in primary care since effective treatments that are less invasive and less expensive are available (Electroconvulsive Therapy, 1991).

Treatment Refusal

Some patients may refuse any formal treatment. For those who are not severely depressed, psychotic, or suicidal, selected therapeutically oriented reading materials may be more effective than no treatment at all in reducing symptoms (Scogin, Jamison, and Davis, 1989; Scogin, Jamison, and Gochneaur, 1989). Furthermore, such information may help those who are in need of treatment to accept it. For those who are suicidal or psychotic, or who pose a substantial danger to themselves or others, involuntary commitment procedures may be necessary.

4 Guideline: Acute Phase Management with Medication

Indications for Acute Phase Medication

Guideline: Medications have been shown to be effective in all forms of major depressive disorder. Barring contraindications to these agents, antidepressant medications are first-line treatments for major depressive disorder when:

- **The depression is moderate to severe.**
- **There are psychotic, melancholic, or atypical (overeating, oversleeping, weight gain) symptom features.**
- **The patient requests medication.**
- **Psychotherapy by a trained, competent psychotherapist is not available.**
- **The patient has shown a prior positive response to medication.**
- **Maintenance treatment is planned.**

Absence of these indicators does not predict medication failure. However, when these indications are present, there is high likelihood of a beneficial response to medication. (Strength of Evidence = A.)

Individual patient considerations for acute phase medication are summarized in Table 3. The rationale for these recommendations is as follows:

- For severe and psychotic depressions, there is strong evidence for the efficacy of medication and little or none for the efficacy of psychotherapy alone.
- There have been no randomized controlled trials of psychotherapy in patients with major depressive disorder with atypical symptom features, but placebo-controlled randomized controlled trials do indicate that antidepressant medications are effective (especially the monoamine oxidase inhibitors [MAOIs]).
- Maintenance medication clearly prevents recurrences, while, to date, maintenance psychotherapy does not (Frank, Kupfer, Perel, et al., 1990).

For virtually all patients, the practitioner who provides the medication also provides support, advice, reassurance, and hope, as well as monitoring side-effects (including monitoring of vital signs), adjusting the dosage, or switching the medication, if needed. This "clinical management" is critical with depressed patients, whose pessimism, low motivation, low energy, and sense of social isolation or guilt may lead them to give up, not adhere to treatment, or drop out of treatment. Clinical management of medication has been detailed in the form of a manual (Fawcett, Scheftner, Clark,

Table 3. Considerations for acute phase medication

Indication	Strength of Indication
Melancholic symptoms	Very strongly recommended
Psychotic symptoms	Very strongly recommended
Severe symptoms	Very strongly recommended
Moderate symptoms	Strongly recommended
Maintenance treatment planned	Very strongly recommended
Previous positive response to medications	Strongly recommended
Recurrent (>three episodes)	Very strongly recommended
At least two episodes with:	
Poor interepisode recovery	Strongly recommended[1]
Family history of depression	Strongly recommended[1]
Atypical symptoms	Recommended[2]

[1]Because a recurrent form of depression is likely (and, therefore, the need for maintenance medication).
[2]Because there are several randomized controlled trials indicating medication is more effective than placebo, but psychotherapy has not been studied to date by such a trial in this group.

et al., 1987) and may well be effective, either alone or with a placebo, in mildly to moderately depressed outpatients with major depressive disorder. For this reason, clinical management is viewed not only as a method to optimize dosage and patient adherence to medication, but also as a treatment, albeit nonspecific, in its own right. Common sense and a body of studies on adherence suggest that appropriate clinical management improves adherence and, therefore, patient response. In addition to routine clinical management, specific sessions aimed at increasing adherence (adherence counseling) may be indicated in the situations noted in Chapter 2.

Evidence for Efficacy

The search for randomized controlled trials evaluating the efficacy of medication treatment for adult and geriatric patients with major depressive disorder was restricted to English language literature published from 1975 to the present, as the diagnostic taxonomies in use before that time are incompatible with the present system. However, studies of MAOIs carried out between 1960 and 1975 were included because they represent an important body of work and used sufficiently well defined patient groups to make inferences to the present system. The vast majority of studies were conducted on outpatients with moderate to severe, nonpsychotic major depressive disorder seen in non-primary care settings.

Table 4 shows the number of randomized controlled trials for each medication in adult and geriatric patients with major depressive disorder. The largest number of randomized controlled trials is found for acute phase treatment. Studies of anxiolytic medications are included because these drugs are sometimes used for patients with milder forms of depression, for patients with both anxiety and depressive symptoms, and for depressed patients with complex associated medical conditions that make standard antidepressants risky to use. (Only acute phase studies were available for anxiolytic medications.) Unstudied treatments are, by definition, neither effective nor ineffective.

Intent-to-treat meta-analyses for acute phase treatment indicate that, in general, most antidepressant medications have comparable efficacy (Table 5). The drug-placebo comparisons are relatively equivalent across medications. Most reports focus on those with adequate treatment exposure (3 to 4 weeks of medication), an experimental condition that favors a higher response rate (65 to 70 percent) than that found with an intent-to-treat sample (50 percent), because patients unable to take medication because of the side effects or who decide to discontinue treatment often do so early in the course of treatment. In general, the percentage of responders expected for each drug (drug efficacy) for outpatients is larger than that for inpatients—a finding that appears to result from a greater placebo response in outpatients. The drug-placebo differences often appear larger for inpatients than for outpatients, which may result from both lower attrition and lower placebo response rates for inpatients.

Other highlights of Table 5 include the following:

- The oldest tricyclic medications are the most extensively studied, largely as a result of industry-sponsored studies that use older drugs as standards. In general, medications with the largest number of randomized controlled trials have efficacy equal to those with fewer studies.
- The efficacy of medications studied to date in geriatric patients is similar to that seen in younger adults (nearly all geriatric patient studies have been conducted on depressed, but otherwise medically fit, patients with major depressive disorder).
- The MAOIs have a larger number of studies reported, in part because of the longer period of research reviewed compared to that of other compounds.

Over 30 randomized controlled trials of antianxiety agents used for patients with depression were found to fulfill the panel's inclusion/exclusion criteria. Of these, 22 investigated alprazolam; 11, diazepam; and 4, chlordiazepoxide. Two additional studies of the non-benzodiazepine anxiolytic, buspirone, were also found. Diazepam, alprazolam, and chlordiazepoxide are not FDA-approved as antidepressant medications, although they are occasionally used in patients whose general medical conditions represent a special risk for the use of FDA-approved antidepressant medications.

Most of the 22 studies with alprazolam showed it to be more effective than a placebo or as effective as an established TCA. However, 3 studies in the more severely depressed patients failed to support this finding. Half of the studies examining diazepam alone showed it to be worse than another active standard antidepressant or no better than a placebo. Of the 4 studies reporting on antidepressant effects of chlordiazepoxide, 2 showed it to be superior to a placebo or equivalent to an antidepressant, while 2 did not. Table 5 shows that by meta-analysis of the drug-placebo differences, the anxiolytics differ in their comparative antidepressant efficacy.

A few studies that were not included in the evidence table merit comment. Several studies performed about 20 years ago using the combination of chlordiazepoxide and amitriptyline (Limbitrol, an FDA-approved antidepressant) suggested a faster onset of action, but no greater overall efficacy than amitriptyline alone (Feighner, Brauzer, Gelenberg, et al., 1979; Rickels, Gordon, Jenkins, et al., 1970). These studies were suggestive, but generally did not use sufficiently rigorous methodology or sufficiently high medication dosages to be clearly interpretable.

Two recent studies, however, have addressed the issue of combining an anxiolytic and an antidepressant (Feet, Larsen, and Robak, 1985; Kravitz, Fogg, Fawcett, et al., 1990.) A double-blind comparison of imipramine and the combination of imipramine plus 10 mg of diazepam per day in outpatients with nonagitated depression did not demonstrate any benefit from the addition of diazepam to imipramine (Feet, Larsen, and Robak, 1985). One study found that the combination of desipramine and alprazolam was associated with a more rapid response than was desipramine alone (Kravitz, Fogg, Fawcett, et al., 1990). In fact, this study, as well as several studies of alprazolam alone in the treatment of depressed outpatients, suggests that most of the clinical benefit derived in depressed patients who respond at all to alprazolam occurs during the initial 7 to 14 days of treatment (Overall, Biggs, Jacobs, et al. 1987; Rush, Erman, Schlesser, et al., 1985). Whether this finding applies to other benzodiazepines is unstudied.

In summary, these data suggest that benzodiazepines, with the exception of the triazolo-benzodiazepine, alprazolam, should generally not be used to treat major depressive disorder, even in combination with other antidepressants. Moreover, alprazolam is not recommended for routine clinical use because no continuation or maintenance phase trials have been published and because problems associated with discontinuing this compound in remitted, depressed patients have not been fully studied. However, the presence of certain concurrent general medical conditions for which standard antidepressants are contraindicated may necessitate consideration of this agent in selected patients because of its cardiovascular safety, quick onset of action, and generally low side-effect profile.

Table 4. Number of randomized controlled trials of medication in patients with major depressive disorder[1,2]

Medication	Adult			Geriatric		
	Acute	Cont	Maint	Acute	Cont	Maint
Tricyclic Antidepressants (TCAs)						
Amitriptyline	101 [45]	3 (2)	3	8 [3]	0	0
Desipramine	22 [7]	0	0	0	0	0
Doxepin	19 [7]	0	0	8 [4]	(1)	0
Imipramine	115 [66]	(5)	2	11 [7]	(1)	0
Nortriptyline	6 [5]	0	0	5 [2]	(1)	1
Protriptyline	1 [0]	0	0	0	0	0
Trimipramine	12 [5]	0	0	0	0	0
Heterocyclic Antidepressants						
Amoxapine	19 [11]	0	0	1 [0]	0	0
Bupropion	16 [10]	(4)	0	2 [0]	0	0
Maprotiline	28 [14]	(1)	0	1 [1]	0	0
Trazodone	25 [13]	(3)	0	4 [3]	0	0
Selective Serotonin Reuptake Inhibitors (SSRIs)						
Fluoxetine	32 [28]	(4)	1	3 [2]	(1)	0
Fluvoxamine[3]	18 [12]	0	0	1 [1]	0	0
Paroxetine	10 [5]	0	1[4]	1 [1]	0	0
Sertraline	2 [2]	0	1[4]	1 [1]	0	0
Monoamine Oxidase Inhibitors (MAOIs)						
Isocarboxazid	14 [9]	0	0	0	0	0
Phenelzine	30 [20]	(2)	1	1 [1]	(1)	1
Tranylcypromine	11 [6]	0	0	0	0	0
Anxiolytics						
Alprazolam[5]	22 [9]	0	0	0	0	0
Buspirone[5]	2 [2]	0	0	0	0	0
Chlordiazepoxide[5]	4 [2]	0	0	0	0	0
Diazepam[5]	11 [2]	0	0	0	0	0

[1]Numbers in brackets show the number of cells that were meta-analyzed for each drug.
[2]Numbers in parentheses indicate the number of double-blind, nonrandomized, extension trials within continuation or maintenance phases.
[3]Not FDA-approved for use in the United States.
[4]Completed after 1990.
[5]Not FDA-approved as an antidepressant medication.
Note: Cont = Continuation. Maint = Maintenance.

Table 5. Meta-analyses of antidepressant medications for patients with major depressive disorder (intent-to-treat samples)

	Adult					
	Drug Efficacy		Drug-Placebo		Drug-Drug	
Drug	Inpt	Outpt	Inpt	Outpt	Inpt	Outpt
Tricyclics						
Amitriptyline	54.0% (12.7) [13]	60.1% (14.1) [32]	31.3% (15.5) [2]	21.8% (5.7) [9]	1.3% (11.3) [11]	-0.2% (4.2) [32]
Desipramine	47.5% (10.7) [1]	52.1% (7.7) [6]	N/A	33.5% (19.5) [2]	-26.0% (15.1) [1]	-7.3% (15.4) [2]
Doxepin	37.5% (13.4) [1]	54.2% (11.6) [6]	N/A	28.9% (5.7) [1]	-25.0% (19.0) [1]	0.1% (6.1) [7]
Imipramine	45.4% (10.7) [13]	47.7% (9.0) [53]	21.3% (10.8) [6]	18.0% (6.9) [33]	0.0% (10.3) [13]	-3.0% (7.2) [48]
Nortriptyline	50.6% (19.4) [3]	44.5% (9.9) [2]	N/A	8.6% (8.6) [1]	-1.6% (21.4) [4]	1.5% (11.6) [2]
Protriptyline	N/A	N/A	N/A	N/A	N/A	N/A
Trimipramine	9.6% (12.9) [2]	63.2% (17.2) [3]	N/A	N/A	20.1% (17.8) [2]	0.3% (13.6) [1]
Total	50.0% (6.5) [33]	51.5% (5.2) [102]	25.1% (11.5) [8]	21.3% (3.9) [46]	-4.0% (7.4) [32]	-0.8% (3.4) [92]
Heterocyclics						
Amoxapine	54.8% (14.2) [3]	58.9% (11.6) [8]	N/A	27.5% (9.5) [1]	4.3% (14.9) [3]	-1.4% (6.9) [8]
Bupropion	51.9% (9.7) [4]	66.6% (15.3) [6]	39.5% (10.2) [3]	16.8% (6.6) [1]	N/A	-5.0% (7.3) [5]
Maprotiline	62.8% (12.5) [2]	63.2% (6.0) [12]	N/A	-5.9% (29.1) [2]	19.2% (19.9) [2]	4.7% (5.3) [12]
Trazodone	60.2% (11.8) [4]	59.8% (10.0) [9]	38.0% (13.5) [4]	23.6% (16.9) [3]	7.0% (19.4) [4]	7.9% (10.4) [9]
Total	55.1% (4.8) [13]	62.3% (11.0) [35]	39.3% (8.3) [7]	16.5% (9.9) [7]	8.7% (9.7) [9]	2.1% (4.5) [34]

See notes at end of table.

Table 5. Meta-analyses of antidepressant medications for patients with major depressive disorder (intent-to-treat samples), continued

	Geriatric					
	Drug Efficacy		Drug-Placebo		Drug-Drug	
Drug	**Inpt**	**Outpt**	**Inpt**	**Outpt**	**Inpt**	**Outpt**
Tricyclics						
Amitriptyline	N/A	44.4% (11.3) [3]	N/A	N/A	N/A	2.4% (10.9) [3]
Desipramine	N/A	N/A	N/A	N/A	N/A	N/A
Doxepin	80.0% (12.1) [2]	31.7% (10.0) [3]	46.7% (19.2) [1]	26.7% (16.0) [1]	-10.0% (15.1) [1]	-7.9% (8.3) [3]
Imipramine	94.4% (7.2) [1]	40.7% (9.2) [6]	63.2% (17.1) [1]	17.4% (15.4) [5]	11.1% (13.8) [1]	-10.7% (15.3) [4]
Nortriptyline	N/A	50.2% (16.6) [2]	N/A	37.5% (18.7) [2]	N/A	0.9% (13.8) [1]
Protriptyline	N/A	N/A	N/A	N/A	N/A	N/A
Trimipramine	N/A	N/A	N/A	N/A	N/A	N/A
Total	83.2% (14.3) [2]	40.4% (6.7) [14]	53.5% (21.9) [2]	22.0% (14.0) [6]	1.0% (20.7) [2]	-3.9% (6.8) [11]
Heterocyclics						
Amoxapine	N/A	N/A	N/A	N/A	N/A	N/A
Bupropion	N/A	N/A	N/A	N/A	N/A	N/A
Maprotiline	N/A	58.0% (9.7) [1]	N/A	N/A	N/A	25.3% (13.2) [1]
Trazodone	13.3% (8.5) [1]	36.7% (8.8) [2]	N/A	19.9% (13.1) [1]	-42.9% (14.7) [1]	10.9% (10.6) [3]
Total	13.3% (8.5) [1]	43.3% (12.1) [3]	N/A	19.9% (13.1) [1]	-42.9% (14.7) [1]	13.4% (11.8) [4]

See notes at end of table.

Table 5. Meta-analyses of antidepressant medications for patients with major depressive disorder (intent-to-treat samples), continued

	Adult					
	Drug Efficacy		Drug-Placebo		Drug-Drug	
Drug	Inpt	Outpt	Inpt	Outpt	Inpt	Outpt
Selective Serotonin Reuptake Inhibitors (SSRIs)						
Fluoxetine	67.2% (8.2) [1]	46.6% (11.7) [27]	N/A	21.7% (9.7) [16]	0.0% (11.6) [1]	2.7% (9.2) [14]
Fluvoxamine	51.3% (12.1) [6]	42.5% (14.1) [6]	36.9% (13.6) [1]	14.0% (7.4) [4]	4.4% (11.2) [6]	-1.5% (5.6) [6]
Paroxetine	N/A	59.2% (23.1) [5]	N/A	21.3% (23.6) [2]	N/A	8.0% (11.9) [5]
Sertraline	55.9% (11.7) [1]	51.7% (4.1) [1]	14.2% (16.3) [1]	18.9% (5.6) [1]	-27.5% (15.0) [1]	-6.0% (5.7) [1]
Total	54.0% (10.1) [8]	47.4% (12.5) [39]	25.5% (21.7) [2]	20.1% (7.8) [23]	0.5% (10.4) [8]	1.7% (6.8) [26]
Monoamine Oxidase Inhibitors (MAOIs)						
Isocarboxazid	56.7% (10.5) [4]	60.1% (7.1) [5]	15.3% (12.6) [4]	41.3% (18.0) [3]	-14.1% (27.5) [2]	1.9% (10.0) [2]
Phenelzine	49.5% (14.0) [7]	57.8% (7.4) [13]	22.3% (30.7) [5]	29.5% (14.6) [7]	-24.1% (16.6) [6]	7.2% (9.0) [11]
Tranylcypromine	58.6% (10.8) [3]	52.8% (13.4) [3]	N/A	21.1% (25.4) [3]	33.3% (23.5) [3]	10.1% (23.6) [2]
Total	52.7% (9.7) [14]	57.4% (5.5) [21]	18.4% (22.6) [9]	30.9% (17.1) [13]	-3.1% (26.1) [11]	6.2% (7.4) [15]

See notes at end of table.

Table 5. Meta-analyses of antidepressant medications for patients with major depressive disorder (intent-to-treat samples), continued

Drug	Geriatric					
	Drug Efficacy		Drug-Placebo		Drug-Drug	
	Inpt	Outpt	Inpt	Outpt	Inpt	Outpt
Selective Serotonin Reuptake Inhibitors (SSRIs)						
Fluoxetine	56.7% (12.4) [1]	48.7% (5.6) [1]	N/A	N/A	46.0% (14.7) [1]	0.6% (7.9) [1]
Fluvoxamine	N/A	57.4% (8.4) [1]	N/A	34.0% (13.5) [1]	N/A	19.0% (12.1) [1]
Paroxetine	N/A	64.6% (7.4) [1]	N/A	N/A	N/A	-6.6% (10.2) [1]
Sertraline	N/A	52.2% (3.9) [1]	N/A	N/A	N/A	2.2% (6.8) [1]
Total	56.7% (12.4) [1]	54.2% (6.7) [4]	N/A	34.0% (13.5) [1]	46.0% (14.7) [1]	2.4% (8.4) [4]
Monoamine Oxidase Inhibitors (MAOIs)						
Isocarboxazid	N/A	N/A	N/A	N/A	N/A	N/A
Phenelzine	N/A	57.7% (9.5) [1]	N/A	50.4% (10.3) [1]	N/A	0.9% (13.1) [1]
Tranylcypromine	N/A	N/A	N/A	N/A	N/A	N/A
Total	N/A	57.4% (9.5) [1]	N/A	50.4% (10.3) [1]	N/A	0.9% (13.1) [1]

See notes at end of table.

Table 5. Meta-analyses of antidepressant medications for patients with major depressive disorder (intent-to-treat samples), continued

Drug	Adult					
	Drug Efficacy		Drug-Placebo		Drug-Drug	
	Inpt	Outpt	Inpt	Outpt	Inpt	Outpt
Anxiolytics						
Alprazolam	-5.0% (13.1) [1]	56.6% (9.0) [10]	N/A	27.2% (6.1) [6]	N/A	2.6% (6.2) [12]
Buspirone	N/A	59.7% (5.2) [2]	N/A	21.4% (14.1) [2]	N/A	N/A
Chlordiazepoxide	N/A	46.6% (8.5) [2]	N/A	11.7% (28.2) [2]	N/A	-1.6% (16.3) [2]
Diazepam	N/A	42.4% (9.8) [2]	N/A	4.3% (8.3) [1]	N/A	-9.3% (14.4) [4]
Total	-5.0% (13.1) [1]	54.3% (8.4) [16]	N/A	20.8% (4.0) [11]	N/A	-0.4% (7.1) [18]

Note: The percentage shown in the Drug Efficacy column is the anticipated percentage of patients provided the treatment shown who will respond. The Drug-Placebo column shows the expected percentage difference in drug versus placebo in patients, based on direct drug-placebo comparisons in trials that included at least these two cells. The Drug-Drug column shows the percentage difference between the named compound and all other listed antidepressant medications studied in randomized controlled trials that included at least these two cells. A negative (-) sign before the percentage means the named compound fared less well than did the "other" to which it was compared. The numbers in parentheses are the

To compare acute phase medication efficacy for major depressive disorder in psychiatric versus primary care settings, the panel identified 24 randomized controlled trials conducted in primary care settings (Depression Guideline Panel, forthcoming). It was possible to meta-analyze 13 cells (3 placebo and 10 medication) in 7 of the 24 studies (Table 6). (These primary care settings were included within the outpatient studies in Table 4 and, where possible, in the outpatient meta-analysis in Table 5.) The overall drug efficacy in the 10 medication cells was 57.8 percent, and the placebo response rate (3 studies) was 35.6 percent. The efficacy data for

Table 5. Meta-analyses of antidepressant medications for patients with major depressive disorder (intent-to-treat samples), continued

	Geriatric					
	Drug Efficacy		Drug-Placebo		Drug-Drug	
Drug	Inpt	Outpt	Inpt	Outpt	Inpt	Outpt
Anxiolytics						
Alprazolam	N/A	N/A	N/A	N/A	N/A	N/A
Buspirone	N/A	N/A	N/A	N/A	N/A	N/A
Chlordiazepoxide	N/A	N/A	N/A	N/A	N/A	N/A
Diazepam	N/A	15.3% (5.1) [1]	N/A	N/A	N/A	-17.6% (9.7) [2]
Total	N/A	15.3% (5.1) [1]	N/A	N/A	N/A	-17.6% (9.7) [2]

standard deviations of the estimated percentage responders. The bracketed numbers are the number of studies on which these estimates are calculated. However, the Drug Efficacy calculations include all cells in all studies for which meta-analysis was feasible (i.e., if a study had two cells of the drug at two different dosages, efficacy trials included both cells). For drug-placebo comparisons, only those trials that contained both of these cells and that reported outcome in a manner that allowed for an estimate of the percentage of randomized patients who responded were included. N/A means no information that allowed for this type of meta-analysis was available. Inpt = Inpatient. Outpt = Outpatient.

various antidepressant medications (and placebo) found in psychiatric settings generally apply to primary care patients with major depressive disorder, though the placebo response rate may be slightly higher in primary care settings (Rickels and Case, 1982; Rickels, Chung, Csanalosi, et al., 1987). (While some studies suggest that, for severely depressed inpatients, the standard TCAs may exceed the efficacy of the newer selective serotonin reuptake inhibitors [SSRIs], meta-analyses [see Table 5] did not reveal meaningful differences in efficacy between SSRIs and TCAs in inpatient or outpatient populations.)

Table 6. Meta-analyses of primary care antidepressant medication trials

Drug	Drug Efficacy	Drug-Placebo	Drug-Drug
Tricyclics			
Mindham (1977) (amitriptyline) (versus maprotiline)	66.2% (7.7)	N/A	13.2% (11.0)
Rickels and Case (1982) (amitriptyline) (versus trazodone)	52.9% (6.0)	25.7% (7.9)	2.8% (8.4)
Rickels, Chung, Csanalosi, et al. (1987) (imipramine) (versus alprazolam)	45.2% (6.8)	3.7% (9.9)	2.2% (9.7)
Winsauer and O'Hair (1984) (doxepin) (versus amoxapine)	62.5%	N/A	-13.3%
Total	55.5% (8.2) [4]	15.0% (19.0) [2]	1.5% (9.3) [4]
Heterocyclics			
Mindham (1977) (maprotiline) (versus amitriptyline)	52.7% (8.1)	N/A	-13.5% (11.2)
Moon and Davey (1988) (trazodone) (versus mianserin)	90.5% (6.3)	N/A	-0.4% (8.6)
Richards, Midha, and Miller (1982) (trazodone) (versus mianserin, diazepam)	60.0% (7.2)	N/A	24.6% (11.7)[1]
Rickels and Case (1982) (trazodone) (versus amitriptyline)	50.0% (6.0)	22.9% (8.0)	-2.8% (8.4)
Winsauer and O'Hair (1984) (amoxapine) (versus doxepin)	76.6% (7.4)	N/A	13.7% (11.3)
Total	62.8% (13.9) [5]	22.9% (8.0) [1]	7.0% (11.8) [6]
Selective Serotonin Reuptake Inhibitors			
Corne and Hall (1989) (fluoxetine) (versus dothiepin)	51.0% (7.0) [1]	N/A	-21.1% (9.3) [1]
Grand Total	57.8% (8.9) [10]	18.2% (12.1) [3]	2.2% (8.5) [11]

[1]Two cells.

Note: The numbers in parentheses are the standard deviations of the estimated percentage of responders. The bracketed numbers are the numbers of studies on which these estimates are calculated.

Antidepressant Medication Selection

Guideline: No one antidepressant medication is clearly more effective than another. No single medication results in remission for all patients. The selection of a particular medication for a particular patient depends on a variety of factors: short-term and long-term side effects (Strength of Evidence = A); prior positive/negative response to the medication (Strength of Evidence = A); history of first-degree relatives responding to a medication (Strength of Evidence = B); concurrent, nonpsychiatric medical illnesses that may make selected medications more or less risky or noxious (Strength of Evidence = A); the concomitant use of other nonpsychotropic medications that may alter the metabolism or increase the side effects of the antidepressant medication (Strength of Evidence = A); likelihood of adherence based on patient's history (Strength of Evidence = B); type of depression (Strength of Evidence = B); effectiveness when given once a day (Strength of Evidence = B); degree of interference in life style expected from treatment (Strength of Evidence = B); cost of the medication; the practitioner's experience with the agent (Strength of Evidence = C); patient preference (Strength of Evidence = C); and other considerations. While these factors may point toward one or another medication, none is sufficiently predictive to allow selection for treatment with certainty. Therefore, an empirical trial and careful evaluation of outcome, with subsequent revision if response is insufficient, is recommended.

Side effects occur in a selected number of patients taking any medication and are typically dependent on dosage and blood level. Many side effects are more likely to occur at the initiation of treatment or within a short time following dosage increases, and patients often adapt to side effects over time. The reader is urged to review current publications for data on the actual incidence of various specific side effects of each medication (AMA, 1990; *Physician's Desk Reference*, 1992; USP, 1992).

A drug's short- and long-term side effects are critical factors to consider in treatment selection. In general, of the tricyclics, the secondary amines (e.g., desipramine, nortriptyline) have equal efficacy, but fewer side effects than do the parent tertiary amines (e.g., imipramine, amitriptyline) (Table 7). The secondary amines are especially preferred in the elderly, in whom the anticholinergic side effects of the tertiary amines may reduce adherence or be particularly severe. If the patient is a candidate for maintenance therapy, the long-term side effects are key considerations in maximizing adherence, and they should be minimal. The newer antidepressants (e.g., bupropion, fluoxetine, paroxetine, sertraline, trazodone) are associated with fewer long-term side effects, such as weight gain, than are the older tricyclic medications. The presence of certain nonpsychiatric medical conditions may favor some agents over others

Table 7. Side-effect profiles of antidepressant medications

Drug	Side Effect[1]						
		Central Nervous System		Cardiovascular		Other	
	Anti-cholinergic[2]	Drowsi-ness	Insomnia/Agitation	Orthostatic Hypo-tension	Cardiac Arrhyth-mia	Gastro-intestinal Distress	Weight Gain (Over 6 kg)
Amitriptyline	4+	4+	0	4+	3+	0	4+
Desipramine	1+	1+	1+	2+	2+	0	1+
Doxepin	3+	4+	0	2+	2+	0	3+
Imipramine	3+	3+	1+	4+	3+	1+	3+
Nortriptyline	1+	1+	0	2+	2+	0	1+
Protriptyline	2+	1+	1+	2+	2+	0	0
Trimipramine	1+	4+	0	2+	2+	0	3+
Amoxapine	2+	2+	2+	2+	3+	0	1+
Maprotiline	2+	4+	0	0	1+	0	2+
Trazodone	0	4+	0	1+	1+	1+	1+
Bupropion	0	0	2+	0	1+	1+	0
Fluoxetine	0	0	2+	0	0	3+	0
Paroxetine	0	0	2+	0	0	3+	0
Sertraline	0	0	2+	0	0	3+	0
Monoamine oxidase inhibitors (MAOIs)	1	1+	2+	2+	0	1+	2+

[1]0 = absent or rare
1+
2+ = in between
3+
4+ = relatively common.
[2]Dry mouth, blurred vision, urinary hesitancy, constipation.

because of their side-effect profiles. For example, for patients with coronary artery disease, drugs that do not lower blood pressure or are associated with no cardiac conduction changes (e.g., bupropion, fluoxetine) may be preferable.

Guideline: If the patient has a concurrent, non-mood psychiatric disorder, then medications that are effective in both depression and the associated psychiatric condition are preferred. (Strength of Evidence = B.)

If a patient suffers concurrently from both major depressive and obsessive-compulsive disorder, for example, the practitioner may be well advised to choose a medication, such as clomipramine or fluoxetine, that has demonstrated efficacy for both conditions.

Specific symptom clusters may suggest the appropriateness of a particular drug class for treatment. For example, patients whose conditions have atypical features appear to fare better on MAOIs (Liebowitz, Quitkin, Stewart, et al., 1988; Quitkin, Harrison, Stewart, et al., 1991; Quitkin, McGrath, Stewart, et al., 1990; Quitkin, Stewart, McGrath, et al., 1988; Thase, Carpenter, Kupfer, et al., 1991) or SSRIs (Reimherr, Wood, Byerley, et al., 1984) than on standard TCAs. Similarly, given the available data, the presence of psychotic features points more strongly toward TCAs combined with neuroleptics (three open trials or retrospective analyses [Charney and Nelson, 1981; Frances, Brown, Kocsis, et al., 1981; Minter and Mandel, 1979b] and five prospective randomized controlled trials [Kaskey, Nasr, and Meltzer, 1980; Minter and Mandel, 1979a,b; Moradi, Muniz, and Belar, 1979; Nelson and Bowers, 1978; Spiker, Weiss, Dealy, et al., 1985]), ECT (Avery and Lubrano, 1979; Avery and Winokur, 1977; Brown, Frances, Kocsis, et al., 1982; Charney and Nelson, 1981; Davidson, McLeod, Kurland, et al., 1977; DeCarolis, Gilberti, Roccatagliata, et al., 1964; Frances, Brown, Kocsis, et al., 1981; Glassman, Kantor, and Shostak, 1975; Lykouras, Malliaras, Christodoulou, et al., 1986a,b; Minter and Mandel, 1979a,b; Moradi, Muniz, and Belar, 1979), or possibly, based on one study, amoxapine (Anton and Burch, 1990; Anton and Sexauer, 1983).

If the patient is considered likely to take an overdose, the practitioner is advised to dispense only 1 week's supply of potentially lethal antidepressants (e.g., the tricyclics or MAOIs), to see the patient at least weekly, and to be readily available by telephone. In such situations, certain heterocyclic agents (bupropion or trazodone) or SSRIs, which appear safer in cases of potential overdose, may be preferred.

The likelihood that it will be necessary to monitor therapeutic blood levels of the drug is also a consideration in the selection of an antidepressant. In a patient who is older, who has other medical conditions, or who is taking medications that affect the metabolism of antidepressants, determining the blood level of the medication to gauge the minimal therapeutic dosage for that patient may be particularly helpful. Similarly, patients with complex general medical conditions that put them at particular risk for side effects from standard antidepressant medications may need blood level monitoring to ensure that the lowest possible dosage is used. Thus, an antidepressant with better established therapeutic and toxic levels, such as nortriptyline, may be preferred over another for which such levels are less well studied.

Guideline: If the patient previously failed to respond to an adequate trial of or could not tolerate the side effects of a particular compound, that agent is generally avoided. Similarly, if the patient has previously responded well to and has had minimal side effects with a particular drug, that agent is to be preferred. (Strength of Evidence = A.)

There is evidence, although not randomized controlled trials, that response to different classes of medication may run in families. (For a review, see Stern, Rush, and Mendels, 1980.) Thus, if the patient has a first-degree relative who responded well to a compound, a drug from the same class may be preferred. Whether this suggestion applies to the newer compounds, such as the SSRIs, has not been studied.

A history of failure to respond to a truly adequate trial of a drug in one class, such as the TCAs, strongly suggests that it would be appropriate to try a medication from a different class rather than another drug from the same class. The evidence for this recommendation is strongest for switching patients who have failed to respond to a TCA or an MAOI. Evidence is suggestive for switches among other classes of antidepressant medications (Depression Guideline Panel, forthcoming).

If the medication is ineffective or not tolerated, then the dosage can be adjusted or the medication changed. In milder cases, medication may be stopped and a trial of time-limited psychotherapy substituted. For patients with partial responses to medication, the dosage is adjusted or the blood level monitored to ensure that it is adequate. In some patients, adjunctive psychotherapy may be indicated, depending on the medication type. In others, a switch to another medication is logical. In yet others, adjunctive medication (augmentation) with agents such as lithium may be preferable.

Table 8 provides an overview of the pharmacology of the various antidepressants, the usual therapeutic dosages, half-lives, and potentially fatal drug interactions. The suggested therapeutic blood levels for various antidepressant medications are as follows:

Well Established Therapeutic Ranges

- Nortriptyline—50-150 ng/mL.
- Amitriptyline—80-250 ng/mL of amitriptyline plus nortriptyline.
- Desipramine—125-300 ng/mL.
- Imipramine—150-250 ng/mL of imipramine plus desipramine.

Less Well Established Therapeutic Ranges

- Clomipramine—Up to 700 ng/mL of clomipramine plus desmethylclomipramine.
- Doxepin—150-250 ng/mL of doxepin plus desmethyldoxepin.
- Fluoxetine—200-700 ng/mL of fluoxetine plus norfluoxetine.
- Trimipramine—150-250 ng/mL.
- Amoxapine—200-600 ng/mL of amoxapine plus 8-hydroxyamoxapine.
- Maprotiline—200-600 ng/mL.

Therapeutic ranges have generally not been established by randomized controlled trials with patients on predesigned fixed medication levels in which group efficacy was measured. Rather, the suggested ranges are derived from laboratory/clinical interaction such that most patients who responded did so with dosages that produced the therapeutic levels indicated. Furthermore, most of these levels were established on inpatients. Their applicability to primary care outpatients is largely unstudied.

Table 8. Pharmacology of antidepressant medications

Drug	Therapeutic Dosage Range (mg/day)	Average (Range) of Elimination Half-Lives (Hours)[1]	Potentially Fatal Drug Interactions
Tricyclics			
Amitriptyline (Elavil, Endep)	75-300	24 (16-46)	Antiarrhythmics, MAOIs
Clomipramine (Anafranil)	75-300	24 (20-40)	Antiarrhythmics, MAOIs
Desipramine (Norpramin, Pertofrane)	75-300	18 (12-50)	Antiarrhythmics, MAOIs
Doxepin (Adapin, Sinequan)	75-300	17 (10-47)	Antiarrhythmics, MAOIs
Imipramine (Janimine, Tofranil)	75-300	22 (12-34)	Antiarrhythmics, MAOIs
Nortriptyline (Aventyl, Pamelor)	40-200	26 (18-88)	Antiarrhythmics, MAOIs
Protriptyline (Vivactil)	20- 60	76 (54-124)	Antiarrhythmics, MAOIs
Trimipramine (Surmontil)	75-300	12 (8-30)	Antiarrhythmics, MAOIs
Heterocyclics			
Amoxapine (Asendin)	100-600	10 (8-14)	MAOIs
Bupropion (Wellbutrin)	225-450	14 (8-24)	MAOIs (possibly)
Maprotiline (Ludiomil)	100-225	43 (27-58)	MAOIs
Trazodone (Desyrel)	150-600	8 (4-14)	--
Selective Serotonin Reuptake Inhibitors (SSRIs)			
Fluoxetine (Prozac)	10- 40	168 (72-360)[2]	MAOIs
Paroxetine (Paxil)	20- 50	24 (3-65)	MAOIs[3]
Sertraline (Zoloft)	50-150	24 (10-30)	MAOIs[3]
Monoamine Oxidase Inhibitors (MAOIs)[4]			For all 3 MAOIs: Vasoconstrictors,[5] decongestants,[5] meperidine, and possibly other narcotics
Isocarboxazid (Marplan)	30- 50	Unknown	
Phenelzine (Nardil)	45- 90	2 (1.5-4.0)	
Tranylcypromine (Parnate)	20- 60	2 (1.5-3.0)	

[1]Half-lives are affected by age, sex, race, concurrent medications, and length of drug exposure.
[2]Includes both fluoxetine and norfluoxetine.
[3]By extrapolation from fluoxetine data.
[4]MAO inhibition lasts longer (7 days) than drug half-life.
[5]Including pseudoephedrine, phenylephrine, phenylpropanolamine, epinephrine, norepinephrine, and others.

Nortriptyline has the best defined therapeutic window (upper and lower limits). The lower limits for the remaining medications are reasonably well established; upper limits are far less well established. The routine use of therapeutic blood level determinations generally is not needed, although their selected use in particular clinical instances can be of value.

Table 9 suggests options for first- and second-line treatments. Because there is no strong evidence for differential efficacy of the various medications, selection rests on other factors. Assuming that a patient has had no prior treatment, that the depression is of moderate or greater severity and not associated with psychotic symptoms, and that the patient has no other associated general medical disorders, side effects become a significant consideration. The secondary amines are listed as first- and second-line choices because they have fewer side effects than do the

Table 9. Selecting among antidepressant medications for depressed outpatients

I. First- and second-line choices:

A. Secondary amine tricyclics (e.g., nortriptyline, desipramine).[1]

B. Bupropion.

C. Fluoxetine.

D. Paroxetine.

E. Sertraline.

F. Trazodone.

II. Alternative agents for patients with special presentations or needs:

A. Tertiary amine tricyclics (e.g., amitriptyline, imipramine):

Special considerations:

Absence of serious medical illnesses, including cardiac disease, that preclude use.

Need for rapid sedation.

B. Monoamine Oxidase Inhibitors (MAOIs):

Special considerations:

Nonresponse or intolerance to at least one tricyclic and one heterocyclic.

Family or personal history of MAOI response.

Atypical symptom features.

C. Selected Anxiolytic Medications:[2]

Special considerations:

Medical contraindications to FDA-approved antidepressant medications.

No adverse cardiovascular effects.

Low side-effect profile.

Substantial withdrawal with long-term use.

Limited exposure time expected (<3 months).

Patient has no history of substance abuse.

Quick action needed.

[1]Other first- and second-line choices are recommended for patients with arrhythmias, cardiac conduction defects, ischemic heart disease, cardiomyopathy, or cardiac valve disease.

[2]Evidence is clearest for alprazolam. Not recommended in severe depressions as studies reveal reduced efficacy. Not recommended for prolonged care as no studies longer than 12 weeks are available. Not recommended when FDA-approved antidepressant medications can be used safely. For buspirone, efficacy is suggested in those with primary anxiety disorders and mild associated depressive symptoms.

Note: Evidence for efficacy with severely depressed inpatients is more abundant for the standard tricyclics than for newer agents.

tertiary amine tricyclics (as do the newer heterocyclics). The available MAOIs require significant dietary restrictions and are, therefore, alternatives. Anxiolytics, particularly alprazolam, have some evidence for efficacy, but have substantial disadvantages. Therefore, alprazolam is an option only in very selected situations.

Although their efficacy is equal to that of other standard antidepressant medications, the MAOIs are usually not first-line treatments because of the required dietary restrictions and potentially fatal interactions with other medications. However, patients who have major depressive disorder with atypical features may optimally benefit from such agents. As for second-line treatments, there is substantial evidence that patients who fail to respond fully or partially to tricyclic medications may benefit substantially from MAOIs and modest evidence that these patients may benefit from the newer SSRIs.

Frequency of Visits

Since providing patient support and education optimizes adherence, facilitates dosage adjustments, minimizes side effects, and allows monitoring of clinical response, careful followup is essential. The panel recommends that patients with more severe depressions be seen weekly for the first 6 to 8 weeks of acute treatment. Once the depression has resolved, visits every 4 to 12 weeks are reasonable. Patients with less severe illness may be seen every 10 to 14 days for the first 6 to 8 weeks or more frequently if required to ensure adherence.

Medication Dosage Adjustments

Several suggestions can be made concerning dosage adjustments for frequently prescribed medications in primary care. For TCAs, patients generally begin with a low dosage (e.g., 25 to 50 mg/day of desipramine) administered at bedtime. The dosage may be increased in increments to the full therapeutic dosage over 1 to 3 weeks. There is no pharmacologic rationale for prescribing most TCAs in divided doses since most have half-lives approximating 24 hours. Once-daily dosing, usually at bedtime, often minimizes side effects. The full therapeutic dosage is maintained until the patient has either responded or clearly failed to respond. The major consideration in dosage increases is the emergence of side effects. Because side effects decrease with time, the patient should be told that they may occur, but are likely to decrease within several weeks of beginning medication.

Fluoxetine may be initiated at 20 mg/day, usually given in the morning, and should be maintained at a full therapeutic dosage (20 mg/day) for at least 4 to 8 weeks before the dosage is increased. Some patients may require less than 20 mg/day, while others may require more. Some patients feel restless or hyperalert with fluoxetine or develop initial insomnia. If significant side effects occur within 7 days, the dosage should be lowered or the medication changed, as the drug at a fixed oral dosage will continue to increase in plasma concentration for 4 weeks (until steady state is reached). Bupropion must be given in divided doses up to 450 mg/day. Dosages above 450 mg/day are associated with an increased risk of seizure.

Figure 6 outlines the general steps in the medication management of depression with or without psychotherapy.

Figure 6. Steps in medication management of major depressive disorder

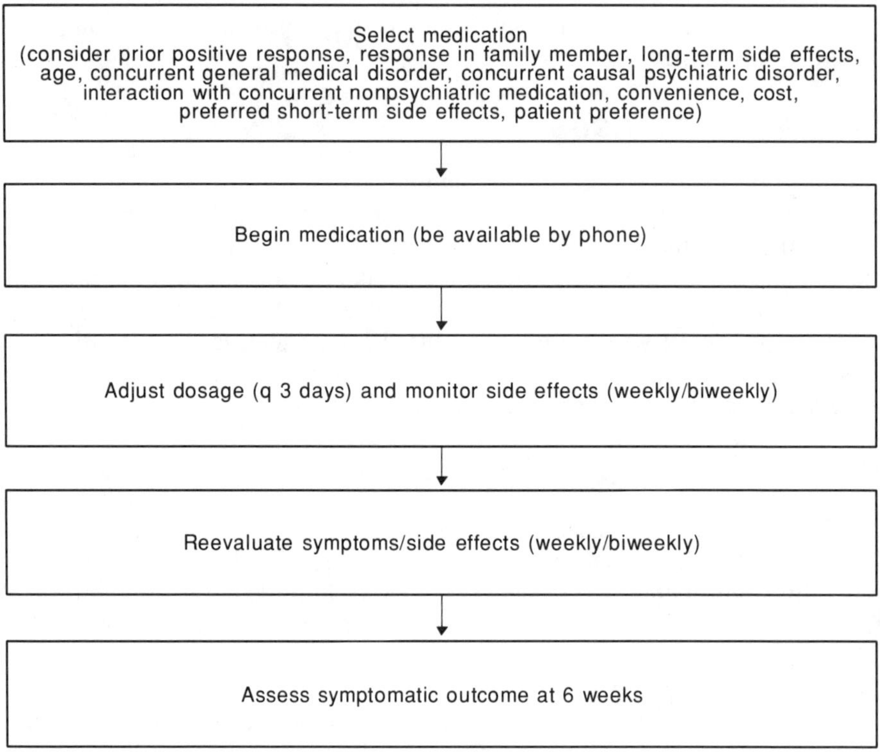

Note: Not all medications (e.g., fluoxetine) require frequent, early dosage adjustment.

Antidepressant Drug Blood Levels

Determinations of antidepressant drug blood levels can establish that patients are receiving a therapeutic dosage, help in the evaluation of adherence, or exclude toxicity. Logically, patients cannot be declared to be nonresponsive to a treatment unless the steady-state serum level is within the therapeutic range for at least 2 to 4 weeks. While the presence or absence of side effects can be helpful indicators of trial adequacy, serum levels are more accurate; patients differ widely in their individual side-effect sensitivity and in the blood levels achieved with a fixed oral dosage. Blood level determinations also enable clinicians to adjust the oral medication dosage for differences in metabolism due to age, race, drug interactions, concurrent medical conditions, or erratic adherence (Amsterdam, Brunswick, and Mendels, 1980; Bourin, Kergueris, and Lapierre, 1989; Glassman, Schildkraut, Orsulak, et al., 1985; Preskorn, Dorey, and Jerkovich, 1988; Preskorn and Kent, 1984; Voris, Morin, and Kiel, 1983).

Four antidepressant medications—nortriptyline, desipramine, imipramine, and amitriptyline—have more consistent evidence of a minimal therapeutic blood levels. Most have established toxic ranges, and a few have established upper therapeutic ranges. The best established therapeutic blood levels are for nortriptyline.

Toxic blood levels can occur in patients who initially exhibit no clinical signs of tricyclic toxicity (Tamayo, Fernandez de Gatta, Gutierrez, et al., 1988). Similarities between depressive and toxic symptoms in patients with deteriorating clinical status often make it difficult for clinicians to assess a patient's condition correctly without quantitative blood level information (Appelbaum, Russell, Orsulak, et al., 1979; Preskorn and Simpson, 1982; Preskorn, Weller, Jerkovich, et al., 1988). In addition to high antidepressant medication dosages, risk factors for developing toxic levels include advanced age and serious concurrent, general medical illnesses. For these high-risk patients, determinations of medication blood levels provide a safe, effective method of attaining an optimal dosage while avoiding toxicity.

Patients for whom blood level monitoring may be particularly helpful include the following:

- Nonresponders or partial responders to therapeutic dosages of medication.
- Those who show symptom breakthrough following full response to medication.
- Those with symptoms of medication toxicity.
- Elderly or pregnant patients (because of altered metabolism).
- Those of African or Asian descent (because of slower metabolism).
- Those who are likely to take overdoses.
- Those who are potential nonadherers.
- Those with general medical illnesses that either alter metabolism or necessitate minimal, but therapeutic, levels of medication.
- Those taking medications that affect antidepressant drug metabolism.
- Those requiring quick assurance of an adequate medication trial.
- Those with particular medical risks for antidepressant side effects such that minimal effective levels are highly desirable.
- Those who develop new medical conditions or are prescribed additional medications that may change called-for blood levels.

These situations are most pertinent for patients taking a medication for which therapeutic levels are well established.

Failure to Respond

Guideline: If the patient has not responded at all or has only a minimal symptomatic response to medication by 6 weeks, two steps are needed: (1) reassessment of the adequacy of the diagnosis and (2) reassessment of the adequacy of treatment. (Strength of Evidence = A.)

Ongoing (but undisclosed) substance abuse or underlying general medical conditions causing the depression are two common diagnostic pitfalls. If either is found, treatment focuses on the relevant potential cause. In cases of substance abuse, a substance-free state for 6 to 8 weeks is usually sufficient to determine whether the depressive syndrome will remit without additional formal treatment for the depression. In some cases, however, the abusive and depressive disorders may require treatment simultaneously. Furthermore, some patients may have another psychiatric condition not initially disclosed to the practitioner, so reevaluation for both psychiatric and nonpsychiatric illnesses should be strongly considered for partial responders.

In addition to reassessment of the diagnosis, reevaluation of the adequacy of treatment is indicated. Medication underdosing is a common cause of nonresponse. Increasing dosages should be given in the first few weeks for most antidepressants. The major exception is fluoxetine, for which the starting dosage (20 mg/day) is often the full therapeutic dosage.

At 6 weeks (range, 4 to 8 weeks), if medically safe, a further dosage increase may be called for, especially in those without significant side effects. In selected clinical situations and with selected medications, a blood level determination may reveal suboptimal antidepressant levels in poor adherers, rapid metabolizers, or those concurrently taking medications that alter the metabolism of antidepressants (e.g., anticonvulsants). If the therapeutic range is well established, and the patient's blood levels are not within that range, adjust the dosage appropriately.

Some evidence from randomized controlled trials suggests a poorer response to TCAs alone in patients with the following conditions:

- Depression with atypical features (Davidson and Pelton, 1986; Liebowitz, Quitkin, Stewart, et al., 1984; Liebowitz, Quitkin, Stewart, et al., 1988; Quitkin, Stewart, McGrath, et al., 1988; Thase, Carpenter, Kupfer, et al., 1991).
- Depression with psychotic features (Chan, Janicak, Davis, et al., 1987; Charney and Nelson, 1981; Glassman, Kantor, and Shostak, 1975; Kroessler, 1985; Kupfer and Spiker, 1981; Nelson and Bowers, 1978; Scott, 1989; Spiker, Weiss, Dealy, et al., 1985).

- Depressions complicated by severe personality disorder (Akiskal, 1985; Frank and Kupfer, 1990; Soloff, George, Nathan, et al., 1987).
- Severe (melancholic) depressions in the elderly (Abou-Saleh and Coppen, 1983; Brown, Sweeney, Frances, et al., 1983).

While these conditions may be associated with a lower response rate to standard tricyclic medications in some studies, the response rates are still nearly always greater than those obtained with placebo. Typically, the initial strategy is to use a single standard antidepressant medication before moving to more complex regimens, even for these subgroups. The exception is for psychotic depression, where the combination of a neuroleptic and an antidepressant or ECT may be optimal initial treatments.

Guideline: By 6 weeks, patients will have responded fully, partially, or not at all. For those with a full symptomatic response, psychosocial function may either have returned to normal or still be impaired. For full responders, continuation phase treatment should begin with visits every 1 to 3 months. For those who still have impaired psychosocial function, many are likely to improve over the next 6 weeks. Therefore, neither the dosage nor the medication type need be changed, but the patient's condition should be reevaluated in 6 weeks to determine whether normal function has returned. If so, continuation treatment is begun. For patients with continued impairment, psychotherapy focused on the residual psychosocial difficulties may be beneficial. (Strength of Evidence = B.)

The algorithms shown in Figures 7 and 8 for the management of patients initially treated with medication alone are based on the patients' level of response. Depressive symptoms remit with the first medication in 40 to 60 percent of patients. These patients usually return to their previous level of psychosocial function, although sometimes weeks to months after full symptom remission. Whether or not residual psychosocial problems are present, patients should be maintained on the same dosage of medication found effective in acute phase treatment for 4 to 9 months of continuation treatment. For patients with recurrent depressive episodes, maintenance medication is an option (see Chapter 9).

If the patient continues to have psychosocial problems following a good symptomatic response to medication, psychotherapy may be added. The rationale for delaying the use of formal psychotherapies to ameliorate associated psychosocial problems rests on recent evidence that, for outpatients with major depressive disorder who respond to medication, psychotherapy, or the combination during acute treatment, return to the premorbid level of psychosocial function often occurs, but is delayed by weeks to months following significant symptomatic improvement (Mintz, Mintz, Arruda, et al., 1992).

Figure 7. Six-week evaluation: responders to medication[1]

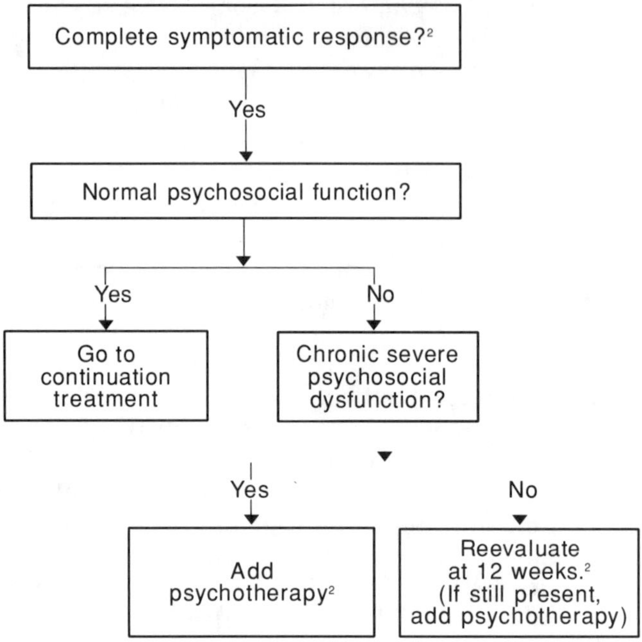

[1]Complete response—with no or very few symptoms.
[2]These suggestions are based on indirectly relevant data, logical inference, and clinical experience.

Guideline: For those with no meaningful symptom response by 6 weeks (or by 4 weeks in the severely ill), there are five possible options (Strength of Evidence = A):

- **Continue medication at corrected dosage.**
- **Discontinue the first medication and begin a second.**
- **Add an adjunctive treatment (augment with a second medication).**
- **Add psychotherapy to the initial medication.**
- **Obtain a consultation/referral.**

Figure 8 provides a flow chart for the management of those with a partial or poor symptomatic response at 6 weeks. (As noted earlier, the symptomatic response should be assessed during the first 6 weeks as well.)

Continue Medication

Guideline: Before changing a patient's treatment, the practitioner is advised to evaluate the adequacy of the medication dosage. (Strength of Evidence = A.)

Medication underdosing is the most common problem in the partially responsive patient in primary care (Baumann, 1986). Thus, strong

Figure 8. Six-week evaluation: partial responders or nonresponders to medication

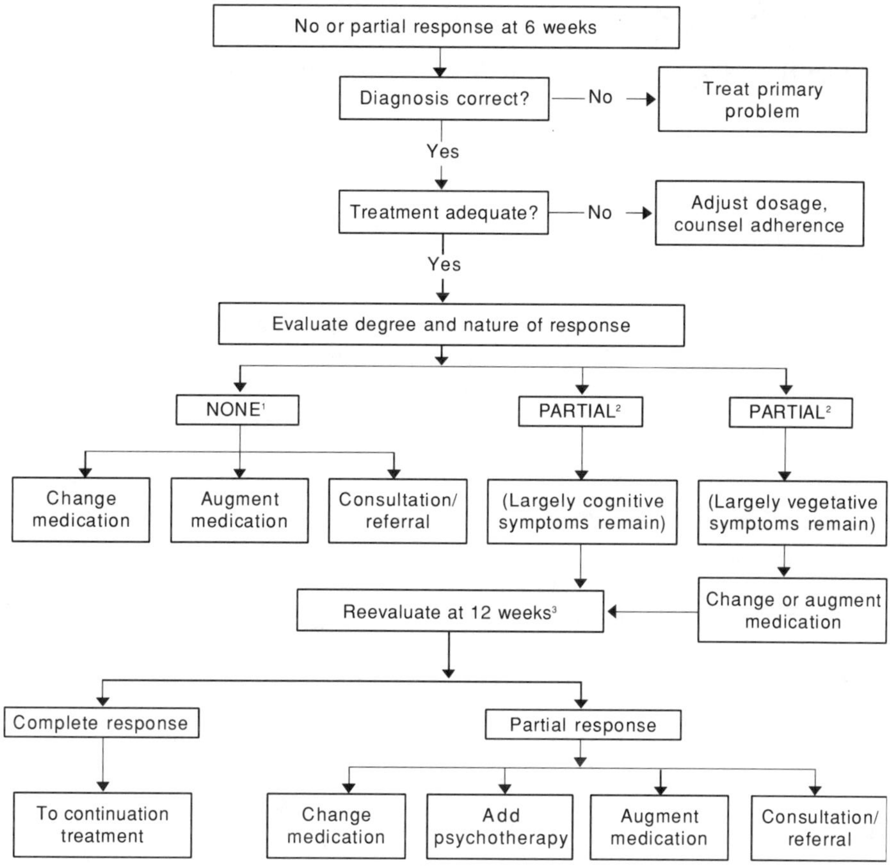

[1]No response—patient is nearly as symptomatic as at pretreatment.
[2]Partial response—patient is clearly better than at pretreatment, but still has significant symptoms. Consultation or referral may be valuable before proceeding further.
[3]Suggestions for management are based on some indirectly relevant studies. logic, and clinical experience.

consideration should be given to either empirically raising the dosage or determining the blood level.

In addition, response to fluoxetine and other standard antidepressants at the typical "adequate" dosages may continue to improve between weeks 4 and 8 of treatment (Dornseif, Dunlop, Potvin, et al., 1989; Schweizer, Rickels, Amsterdam, et al., 1990). Thus, even for those with a partial response by week 6, a longer trial at the therapeutic dosage is a logical option.

Switch Medication

Guideline: Switching to a new medication is an option after an adequate trial of the first treatment. A general medical principle is that a combination of two drugs should not be used when one drug will suffice. Thus, switching medications is often preferred over augmentation as an initial strategy. (Strength of Evidence = A.)

An adequate medication trial likely will include:

- Increasing the dosage when medically safe beyond the minimal therapeutic dosage.
- Checking blood levels (only if relevant).
- Checking for adherence.

Several reports describe patients who did not respond to traditionally adequate dosages of TCAs, but who were "converted" to responders when the TCA dosage was adjusted to higher than normal dosages (Amsterdam, Brunswick, and Mendels, 1979; Schuckit and Feighner, 1972; Simpson, Lee, Cuculic, et al., 1976). However, nortriptyline has been shown to have a therapeutic window for plasma levels. Therefore, nortriptyline dosages may need to be titrated downward in nonresponders with high plasma levels.

The tricyclic, heterocyclic, and SSRI antidepressants differ considerably in both pharmacologic actions and side effects. Therefore, it is reasonable to expect that an alternate antidepressant may prove effective in some patients who either do not respond to or cannot tolerate adequate dosages of a standard TCA. Three studies document tricyclic response rates of approximately 10 to 30 percent in patients with a history of nonresponse to another TCA (Beasley, Sayler, Cunningham, et al., 1990; Charney, Price, and Heninger, 1986; Reimherr, Wood, Byerley, et al., 1984).

The literature is replete with case reports of patients who failed to respond to multiple trials of standard agents, but who nevertheless responded to newer antidepressants, such as bupropion, fluoxetine, paroxetine, or sertraline. The efficacy of crossover treatment with bupropion in tricyclic nonresponders has been described in a report including both a small double-blind study of inpatients and a larger, open-label outpatient study (Stern, Harto-Truax, and Bauer, 1983). The utility of fluoxetine in patients with a history of tricyclic nonresponse has been demonstrated in two controlled trials (Beasley, Sayler, Cunningham, et al., 1990; Reimherr, Wood, Byerley, et al., 1984). Open-label treatment with trazodone was reported to be effective in 56 percent of a diverse group of 25 TCA nonresponders (Cole, Schatzberg, Sniffin, et al., 1981).

In addition, MAOIs may be effective for patients who do not respond to TCAs. Nine open-label reports provide evidence that 40 to 60 percent of patients who have not responded to at least one TCA respond to an MAOI. For example, 50 percent of highly refractory patients in one study responded to tranylcypromine (Nolen, Van De Putte, Dijken, et al., 1985, 1988). Four double-blind crossover studies of MAOI efficacy in patients who did not respond to a TCA revealed similar results (Lipper, Murphy, Slater, et al., 1979; McGrath, Stewart, Harrison, et al., 1987; Potter, Murphy, Wehr, et al., 1982; Thase, Mallinger, McKnight, et al., 1992). In an open-label crossover study, MAOI response was found to be both statistically and clinically significant (57 percent response rate) in patients who had been vigorously treated with imipramine (mean dosage: 257 mg/day) and psychotherapy (Thase, Frank, Mallinger, et al., 1992). These studies suggest that it would be appropriate to switch a patient who fails to respond to a TCA to an MAOI. Whether such a switch would be as strongly indicated had the patient also failed to respond to a nontricyclic agent (e.g., fluoxetine, trazodone, or bupropion) is not known.

In summary, based on these data, one may expect a 30 to 60 percent response when a tricyclic is "crossed over" to a nontricyclic. Similar data have not been presented for amoxapine, maprotiline, or alprazolam. The timing of a switch to a new medication depends on the patient's treatment history and the length and adequacy of the current treatment. For nonresponders at 6 weeks (assuming that the trial has been at an adequate dosage and the diagnosis is correct), a switch is a reasonable option. For partial responders at weeks 8 to 12 (again assuming an adequate trial and correct diagnosis), a switch is also logical. Some clinicians believe a switch (or augmentation with another medication) is particularly advisable for patients with residual vegetative symptoms. When switching medications, the practitioner should be well informed of drug-drug interactions (fluoxetine raises the blood levels of TCAs); pharmacokinetics (shorter versus longer half lives); and untoward effects of combination medication (TCAs plus MAOIs). The specific steps in switching or augmenting depend on application of such knowledge.

Augment Medication

Guideline: Augmentation of the initial medication with a second one is not advised until the initial trial has been adequate in time and dosage. (Strength of Evidence = A.)

There is evidence from tertiary care studies that, for both partial responders and nonresponders, augmentation, particularly with lithium, can be helpful in 20 to 50 percent of patients (Depression Guideline Panel, forthcoming). Augmentation carries the additional risks of more side effects, greater expense, and potentially complex drug-drug interactions. A history of nonresponse to adequate trials of other individually prescribed antidepressants increases the likelihood that augmentation may be required. Because augmentation strategies are an evolving specialized area of knowledge requiring substantial sophistication in psychopharmacology, as well as greater risk to patients, the panel recommends that, where feasible, primary care practitioners consider consultation (at a minimum) or referral before embarking on this option.

Add Psychotherapy

Guideline: For patients with a partial response at week 12 whose residual symptoms are largely psychological rather than vegetative, psychotherapy may be added and the medication remain unchanged. If the residual symptoms at 6 or 12 weeks are largely somatic or vegetative, either adjunctive medication or a new, different medication may be indicated. (Strength of Evidence = C.)

Both of these options are based on clinical experience, logic, and panel consensus. They have not been empirically tested.

Obtain a Consultation

Guideline: In any case in which the practitioner feels that he or she lacks sufficient knowledge and/or experience to manage a patient's medication or if two or more attempts at acute phase medication treatment have failed or resulted in only partial response, the practitioner is advised to seek a consultation from or refer the patient to a psychiatrist well trained in psychopharmacology. In addition, if drug-drug interactions are anticipated (for example, in patients taking nonpsychotropic medications that may interact with the antidepressants), consultation from a pharmacist or psychiatrist is advisable. (Strength of Evidence = C.)

5 Guideline: Acute Phase Management with Psychotherapy

Guideline: Psychotherapy alone to reduce the symptoms of major depressive disorder may be considered a first-line treatment if the major depressive episode is mild to moderate and the patient desires psychotherapy as the first-line therapy. (Strength of Evidence = B.)

Psychotherapy, a generic term, refers to a variety of verbal and nonverbal techniques, packages, and procedures that differ in their immediate, intermediate, and long-term objectives. More than 250 types of psychotherapy have been described (Parloff, 1982). Table 10 provides an overview of the various potential objectives of psychotherapy and examples of therapies aimed at each.

Table 10. Objectives of acute phase psychotherapy

Primary Objectives[1]	Examples
1. Symptom removal	1. Cognitive, behavioral, interpersonal therapies
2. Restoration of normal psychosocial and occupational functioning	2. Case management; cognitive, behavioral, psychoeducational, occupational, marital therapies
3. Prevention of relapse/recurrence	3. Maintenance therapy (cognitive, behavioral, interpersonal, other)
4. Correction of "causal" psychological problems with secondary symptom resolution	4. Marital, cognitive, interpersonal, brief dynamic, other therapies
5. Increased adherence to medication prescription	5. Clinical case management; specific cognitive, behavioral, or other psychoeducational techniques or packages
6. Correction of secondary consequences of the depression (e.g., marital discord, low self-esteem)	6. Occupational, marital, interpersonal, cognitive therapies; other therapies focused on specific problems

[1]While the tactics of a specific therapy package may change depending on the objectives (e.g., symptom removal versus adherence), the term (e.g., "cognitive therapy") is retained as it refers to the theoretical basis and broad strategies involved in the approach.

Objectives and Indications

Guideline: As the sole treatment for major depressive disorder, the initial objectives of acute phase psychotherapy are the same as for medication: symptom removal and restoration of normal social and occupational functioning. Acute phase psychotherapy may be considered as the sole treatment for major depressive disorder of mild to moderate severity that is not chronic, psychotic, or melancholic. This recommendation assumes the availability of a trained, competent therapist. (Strength of Evidence = B.)

Clinical experience and logic suggest that this recommendation may particularly apply if (a) the patient expresses a preference for psychotherapy as the initial treatment, (b) medication is contraindicated for the particular patient, or (c) the patient exhibits prominent psychosocial difficulties or evidence of a personality disorder.

Symptom removal and functional restoration are the goals of therapies targeted at symptom relief (e.g., cognitive or behavioral therapy) or current psychological problems (e.g., interpersonal or brief dynamic psychotherapy) that theoretically cause or maintain symptoms. It is hoped (though not established) that acute phase psychotherapy will prevent subsequent relapses and recurrences once treatment ends. (For recent reviews, see Hollon, DeRubeis, and Seligman, 1992; Persons, in press; Rehm, in press). Psychotherapies in combination with medication may also be used to augment symptom relief or to address collateral issues, such as adherence or secondary psychosocial problems (Rush, 1986).

Many commonly used forms of psychotherapy have not been subjected to randomized controlled trials in patients with major depressive disorder. That is, their efficacy has not been proven or disproven. Whether all psychotherapies are equally effective and whether they are differentially effective in different patient groups is unknown. The efficacy of psychotherapies studied to date is more similar than different, though only a few studies have included two psychotherapy cells to allow a direct comparison. In addition, most psychotherapies have many common features, although they may differ in specific procedures, tactics, or techniques. Whether these differences result in differential efficacy or whether they are of therapeutic value for some, but not other, patients is not known.

Randomized controlled trials of time-limited psychotherapies that have been codified in manuals reveal a significant benefit over wait-list controls for patients with mild to moderate forms of major depressive disorder (Depression Guideline Panel, forthcoming). However, there is minimal evidence that psychotherapy alone is effective in severe or psychotic forms of depression. There is strong evidence for the efficacy of medication (or ECT) for severe or psychotic depressions (Depression Guideline Panel, forthcoming).

A key problem in fully understanding the role of psychotherapy in major depressive disorder is identification of an adequate placebo control. Formal therapies nearly always exceed the effects of no treatment, minimal contact, or wait-list controls. Whether efficacy can uniquely, specifically, and with certainty be attributed to the particular therapy still remains an open question. That is, whether the beneficial outcome with therapy would have occurred with nonspecific interpersonal interactions of equal time and frequency has not been fully investigated.

On the other hand, studies directly comparing medication (as the "gold standard") to psychotherapy alone have generally found equal efficacy in acute phase treatment in mild to moderate depression (Beck, Hollon, Young, et al., 1985; Covi and Lipman, 1987; Hersen, Bellack, Himmelhoch, et al., 1984; Murphy, Simons, Wetzel, et al., 1984; Roth, Bielski, Jones, et al., 1982; Rush and Watkins, 1981). However, equivalent response rates do not imply that the same patient would have responded to these two different treatments. It is logical to consider that some would have responded to one, while others would preferentially respond to the alternative treatment. For this reason, a time-limited treatment trial is recommended for acute phase treatment with psychotherapy, just as it is for medication.

If some patients do respond to psychotherapy, while others respond to medication, then patients' recent treatment history will influence response rates. Yet, to date, only one study has attempted to evaluate this variable (Blackburn, Bishop, Glen, et al., 1981). This omission limits the utility of these studies in developing algorithms for which patients should receive which treatment. Furthermore, time-limited psychotherapies codified in manuals may not be particularly representative of actual clinical practice, which limits generalizability of the trials performed to date (Persons, 1991).

The psychotherapies that have been tested rarely differ from each other in efficacy. Failure to find that psychotherapies have different comparative response rates is not evidence that all are either ineffective or effective. In addition, most such studies have used small patient groups so that the ability to detect group differences is limited.

Guideline: As with a medication trial, if psychotherapy alone is selected as the initial treatment, the practitioner is advised to monitor symptom response. If the psychotherapy is completely ineffective by 6 weeks or if it does not result in nearly a full symptomatic remission within 12 weeks, a switch to medication may well be appropriate since there is clear evidence of its specific efficacy. (Strength of Evidence = A.)

During the course of therapy, criteria-based symptoms should be reviewed at 6 and 12 weeks to gauge response. Self-report or interviewer-rated symptom scales are useful in following patient progress.

The possibility that psychotherapy prevents relapse/recurrence deserves special comment. There is suggestive evidence from some post–acute treatment followup studies that those who respond to therapy, particularly cognitive therapy, as acute treatment have a lower relapse rate over the ensuing 6 months to 2 years than do those who respond to medication (see Hollon, DeRubeis, and Seligman, 1992; Depression Guideline Panel, forthcoming). However, methodological limitations make interpretation of these findings quite tentative. First, all studies to date are *naturalistic*, meaning that the patients' treatment in the followup period is not controlled. Second, it is possible that those who respond to medication have a poorer prognosis, if untreated, than do those who respond to therapy. Thus, there may be a sample bias favoring a better prognosis for responders to psychotherapy. (For a recent review, see Hollon, DeRubeis, and Seligman, 1992.) Third, not all these followup studies reveal a better prognosis in those receiving acute phase psychotherapy versus medication. Given these methodological limitations, interpretive difficulties, and inconsistent results, the panel concludes that acute phase psychotherapy has not yet been shown to be of prophylactic value for recurrent major depressive disorder.

Evidence for Efficacy

Peer-reviewed publications that report patient diagnoses using a specified descriptive system and a specified form of psychotherapy constitute the evidence for psychotherapeutic efficacy. Adult and geriatric studies were pooled for this synopsis because the number of geriatric studies that met criteria was small and there is no evidence yet for differences in adult and geriatric efficacy rates.

Table 11 summarizes the number of randomized controlled trials for each form of therapy found in the panel's literature review. To include the maximum number of studies in meta-analysis, the panel relied, whenever possible, on response as defined by the BDI (a self-report). The panel conducted analyses on intent-to-treat samples, which were calculated from the original reports. Most reports focused on completer samples (i.e., patients who completed the full trial), which likely biases the outcome in favor of the treatment studied. Thus, in a number of studies subjected to intent-to-treat meta-analysis, psychotherapy response rates are lower than those reported by the authors using either the completer sample or those with "adequate exposure." The panel's analysis includes no studies of partial therapy packages that attempted to isolate the "active" ingredients in a particular therapy. Also omitted are studies that added a psychotherapy to an otherwise unspecified "treatment as usual," since the specific efficacy of the therapy alone could not be inferred from this design.

Table 11. Number of randomized controlled psychotherapy trials in patients with major depressive disorder

	Adult			Geriatric		
Therapy	**Acute**	**Cont**	**Maint**	**Acute**	**Cont**	**Maint**
Cognitive	19 [10][2]	1[1] [0]	0	3 [2]	0	0
Behavioral	11 [8]	0	0	2 [1]	0	0
Interpersonal	2 [1]	1[3] [0]	1 [0]	0	0	0
Brief dynamic	5 [5]	0	0	3 [1]	0	0
Marital	1 [0]	0	0	0	0	0

[1]Not randomized (open trial of responders to acute phase).
[2]Number in brackets is the number of cells for which meta-analysis was possible. Studies published only as dissertations or in non-peer-reviewed sources were not included.
[3]Trial included responders to acute phase interpersonal psychotherapy plus imipramine.
Note: Cont = Continuation. Maint = Maintenance.

Cognitive Therapy

For depression, cognitive therapy aims at symptom removal by identification and correction of the patient's distorted, negatively biased, moment-to-moment thinking and theoretically aims at prevention of relapse/recurrence by identifying and correcting silent assumptions (personal beliefs or schemas) (Beck, Rush, Shaw, et al., 1979; Dobson, 1989; Shaw, 1989; Wilson, 1989).

Twenty-two acute phase randomized controlled trials were conducted with cognitive therapy alone in adult or geriatric patients (Beck, Hollon, Young, et al., 1985; Blackburn, Bishop, Glen, et al., 1981; Covi and Lipman, 1987; de Jong, Treiber, and Henrich, 1986; Elkin, Shea, Watkins, et al., 1989; Gallagher and Thompson, 1982; Hogg and Deffenbacher, 1988; Murphy, Simons, Wetzel, et al., 1984; Neimeyer and Feixas, 1990; Neimeyer, Heath, and Strauss, 1985; Neimeyer and Weiss, 1990; O'Leary and Beach, 1990; Pecheur and Edwards, 1984; Ross and Scott, 1985; Rush, Beck, Kovacs, et al., 1977; Rush and Watkins, 1981; Scott and Stradling, 1990 [two trials]; Selmi, Klein, Greist, et al., 1990; Steuer, Mintz, Hammen, et al., 1984; Thompson, Gallagher, and Breckenridge, 1987; Turner and Wehl, 1984). Nearly all were conducted on outpatients. Certain pivotal studies (e.g., Blackburn, Bishop, Glen, et al., 1981) could not be included in the meta-analysis because the number randomized to each cell was not reported. In other cases, outcome was not reported in a categorical form. When outcome was reported categorically by a measure other than the BDI, the panel included the study in the analysis. Based on analysis by means of the confidence profile method (CPM), the overall efficacy of cognitive therapy alone was 46.6 percent. For adult outpatients, efficacy was 46.9 percent; for geriatric outpatients, it was 51.3 percent. In the only inpatient study available for CPM meta-analysis, the response rate was 58.3 percent (de Jong, Treiber, and Henrich, 1986).

Table 12 shows a comparison of cognitive therapy alone and alternative acute phase treatments. Overall, cognitive therapy was similar in efficacy to all other psychotherapies taken together. Cognitive therapy exceeded pill placebo with clinical management by only 9.4 percent (Elkin, Shea, Watkins, et al., 1989). Compared to medication alone, cognitive therapy had a slight advantage.

Table 12. Meta-analyses of psychotherapy trials in outpatients with major depressive disorder

Therapy[1,2]	Overall Efficacy	Therapy vs. Wait List	Therapy vs. Placebo	Therapy vs. Other Therapy	Therapy vs. Drug Alone
Behavioral therapy alone[3]	55.3% (9.3)[4] [10][5]	17.1% (34.0) [5]	N/A	9.1% (19.9) [6]	23.9% (11.6) [2]
Brief dynamic psychotherapy alone	34.8% (17.8) [6]	N/A	N/A	-7.6% (14.6) [8]	8.4% (21.3) [2]
Cognitive psychotherapy alone	46.6% (6.9) [12]	30.1% (22.0) [2]	9.4% (8.3) [1]	-4.4% (16.9) [6]	15.3% (26.1) [3]
Interpersonal psychotherapy alone	52.3% (6.1) [1]	N/A	22.6% (8.4) [1]	13.3% (8.6) [1]	12.3% (8.6) [1]
Marital psychotherapy alone	N/A	N/A	N/A	N/A	N/A
Totals	50.0% (5.3) [29]	26.0% (23.5) [7]	15.7% (13.0) [2]	4.7% (8.5) [21]	14.0% (11.2) [8]

[1]Intent-to-treat sample.
[2]Adult and geriatric patient studies are combined.
[3]Behavioral therapy includes one cell with behavioral therapy plus placebo (Hersen, Bellack, Himmelhoch, et al., 1984).
[4]The numbers in parentheses are the standard deviations of the estimated percentage of responders.
[5]The bracketed numbers are the numbers of cells on which these estimates are calculated.

These analyses combined group and individual cognitive therapy. Separating these two treatment formats, the overall efficacy of group cognitive therapy was 39.2 percent, and the overall efficacy of individual cognitive therapy was 50.1 percent. However, these response rates come from different trials. The one small study that directly compared these two formats found both to have equal efficacy (Rush and Watkins, 1981). Whether the group format is less effective than is individual cognitive therapy remains an open question that is particularly germane to the issue of cost containment. Of special note is a study that showed the efficacy of computer-assisted cognitive therapy to equal that of standard individual cognitive therapy (Selmi, Klein, Greist, et al., 1990). Further research on this potentially cost-effective approach is needed.

The prophylactic effects of cognitive therapy once acute phase treatment has been discontinued have not been established. They have not yet been fully evaluated because of methodological problems, such as brief followup periods, lack of controls, difficulties in defining relapse/recurrence, inclusion of acute phase nonresponders in followup, naturalistic rather than controlled followup, and interpretive limitations. (For a recent review, see Hollon, DeRubeis, and Seligman, 1992.) Seven studies included a 1-year followup (Beck, Hollon, Young, et al., 1985; Gallagher and Thompson, 1982; Kovacs, Rush, Beck, et al., 1981; O'Leary and Beach, 1990; Ross and Scott, 1985; Scott and Stradling, 1990; Simons, Murphy, Levine, et al., 1986), one included a 2-year followup (Gallagher-Thompson, Hanley-Peterson, and Thompson, 1990), and one included an 18-month followup (Shea, Elkin, Imber, et al., 1992). All followups were naturalistic. Three studies showed that acute phase cognitive therapy was followed by fewer depressive symptoms at followup than was wait-list (Gallagher-Thompson, Hanley-Peterson, and Thompson, 1990; O'Leary and Beach, 1990; Ross and Scott, 1985). When compared to patients treated with acute phase pharmacotherapy without a formal continuation or maintenance medication phase, patients treated with cognitive therapy showed fewer self-reported depressive symptoms (Kovacs, Rush, Beck, et al., 1981) or a lower relapse rate (Simons, Murphy, Levine, et al., 1986) at followup. In the 18-month followup of patients treated in the multisite NIMH collaborative study, all four treatments tested (cognitive-behavioral therapy, interpersonal psychotherapy, imipramine, and placebo plus clinical management) were associated with relatively high relapse rates (Shea, Elkin, Imber, et al., 1992). No one acute phase treatment was associated with a better prognosis in this naturalistic followup. Of all patients who entered the acute study (intent-to-treat sample), only 15 to 28 percent suffered no further major depressive disorder and needed no further treatment in the 18-month followup period.

Behavioral Therapy

Several different treatment packages (manuals), all of which are based on a functional analysis of behavior (Ferster, 1973) and/or social learning theory (Bandura, 1977), are involved in behavioral therapy for depression. They include activity scheduling (Lewinsohn, Antonuccio, Steinmetz, et al., 1984; Lewinsohn and Clarke, 1984), self-control therapy (Rehm, 1979), social skills training (Bellack, Hersen, and Himmelhoch, 1983), and problem solving (Nezu, 1986).

In the panel's analysis, the overall efficacy of behavioral therapy was 55.3 percent. Compared to wait-list, behavioral therapy was 17.1 percent more effective; compared to all other forms of psychotherapy, behavioral therapy was 9.1 percent more effective. Compared to medication alone, it was 23.9 percent more effective. Behavioral therapy has not been compared to a pill placebo. Group behavioral therapy had a response rate of 51.1 percent, while individual behavioral therapy had a response rate of 57.7 percent. Thus, these two formats appear equally effective. In the one study that allowed for meta-analysis by providing a head-to-head comparison of group versus individual behavioral therapy (Brown and Lewinsohn, 1984), individual therapy had a response rate of 58.8 percent, while group therapy had a 52.9 percent response rate. The minimal contact group, however, had a higher response rate than did either "active" treatment (84.4 percent), as determined from the intent-to-treat sample.

Studies of the prophylactic value of acute phase behavioral therapy, once discontinued, are insufficient to draw firm conclusions. Only four studies involved a control or another formal acute phase treatment for depression (Brown and Lewinsohn, 1984; Gallagher and Thompson, 1982; Gallagher-Thompson, Hanley-Peterson, and Thompson, 1990; McLean and Hakstian, 1990). All four used naturalistic followup. In general, most between-group comparisons in these studies showed no difference in depressive symptoms for patients treated with behavioral therapy in the acute phase and those treated otherwise. One of the two comparisons that did reveal a difference found that only 11 percent of depressed elderly outpatients treated with either cognitive or behavioral therapy relapsed, compared to 44 percent of those treated with relational insight-oriented psychotherapy (Gallagher and Thompson, 1982); the other found that behavioral therapy was significantly more effective than was nonspecific treatment (relaxation training) on improving mood at followup (McLean and Hakstian, 1990). Rehm, Kaslow, and Rabin (1987) found that 87 percent of their depressed sample had subsequent episodes in a 6-month followup. Gonzales, Lewinsohn, and Clark (1985) found that 50 percent of their sample, who had been treated with group or individual behavioral therapy, relapsed within a 1- to 3-year period. Several previous depressive episodes, positive family history, poor health, greater dissatisfaction with major life roles, greater pretreatment severity, and younger age were all predictive of relapse.

Interpersonal Psychotherapy

The aims of interpersonal psychotherapy are the clarification and resolution of one or more of the following interpersonal difficulties: role dispute, social isolation, prolonged grief reaction, or role transition. The patient and therapist define the nature of the interpersonal difficulty and work to resolve it. Interpersonal difficulties are viewed as either causal, concomitant, or exacerbating/maintaining factors for depression. Initial treatment sessions focus on patient education about the nature and course of the depressive syndrome, while subsequent sessions aim at resolving interpersonal difficulties.

Interpersonal psychotherapy for depression (Klerman and Weissman, 1987; Klerman, Weissman, Rounsaville, et al., 1984) has been studied in two acute phase randomized trials in outpatients with nonpsychotic major depressive disorder (Elkin, Shea, Watkins, et al., 1989; Weissman, Prusoff, DiMascio, et al., 1979). It is reported to be more effective than nonscheduled supportive treatment over 12 weeks of acute treatment and as effective as amitriptyline alone and the combination of interpersonal psychotherapy plus amitriptyline in reducing depressive symptoms. Although amitriptyline improved vegetative symptoms earlier in treatment, interpersonal psychotherapy improved mood, suicidal ideation, work, and interest earlier (DiMascio, Klerman, Weissman, et al., 1979; DiMascio, Weissman, Prusoff, et al., 1979). Patients in combined treatment were least likely to refuse treatment or to drop out (Weissman, Prusoff, DiMascio, et al., 1979).

In the only study for which meta-analysis was feasible (Elkin, Shea, Watkins, et al., 1989), the efficacy of interpersonal psychotherapy exceeded that of cognitive therapy by 13.2 percent, that of placebo plus clinical management by 22.6 percent, and that of imipramine by 12.3 percent, based on the BDI as the outcome measure and the intent-to-treat sample.

In a comparison of interpersonal psychotherapy with and without involvement of the spouse, the two approaches reduced depressive symptoms equally, but interpersonal psychotherapy with addition of the spouse was more effective in improving marital satisfaction (Foley, Rounsaville, Weissman, et al., 1987; cited in Jacobson, Holtzworth-Munroe, and Schmaling, 1989).

The initial naturalistic study of the potential prophylactic effects of acute/continuation phase interpersonal psychotherapy, once stopped, found no difference at 1-year followup between interpersonal psychotherapy, amitriptyline, the combination of interpersonal psychotherapy and amitriptyline, and nonscheduled treatment in reducing relapse/recurrence (Weissman, Klerman, Prusoff, et al., 1981). Interpersonal psychotherapy did significantly improve social functioning. A more recent report also failed to find a lower relapse rate in interpersonal psychotherapy responders than in responders to the other three acute treatments in an 18-month followup (Shea, Elkin, Imber, et al., 1992).

Marital Therapy

One of several treatment paradigms that involve patients' significant others (Jacobson, Holtzworth-Munroe, Schmaling, 1989), marital therapy is believed to be indicated in the treatment of some patients with major depressive disorder because:

- About 20 percent of all married couples are distressed (Beach, Arias, and O'Leary, 1983).
- Within more than 50 percent of these distressed couples, at least one spouse suffers from depression (Beach, Jouriles, and O'Leary, 1985).
- Marital conflict/disruption is a common stressful life event preceding the onset of a depressive episode (Paykel, Myers, Dienelt, et al., 1969).
- Marital discord often persists after the depression has remitted (Bothwell and Weissman, 1977; Hinchliffe, Hooper, and Roberts, 1978).
- Relapses/recurrences are frequently preceded by marital discord or disruption (Brown and Harris, 1978; Hooley, Orley, and Teasdale, 1986).

The only randomized controlled trial of behavioral marital therapy (BMT) for depression reported that BMT reduced depressive symptoms significantly more than did a wait-list control and as well as did cognitive therapy in women with major depressive disorder or dysthymia (O'Leary and Beach, 1990). Both BMT and cognitive therapy reduced depressive symptoms significantly more than did wait-list, but only BMT increased marital satisfaction. Meta-analysis was not feasible, because outcome was not reported categorically.

In a preliminary report of a randomized trial of depressed married women assigned to marital therapy alone, cognitive therapy alone, or individual cognitive therapy with conjoint marital therapy, individual treatments effectively reduced depressive symptoms in those without marital discord (Jacobson, Schmaling, Salusky, et al., 1987). However, for those with marital discord, marital therapy was more effective than was cognitive therapy in alleviating depressive symptoms.

Four other studies, while ineligible for meta-analysis, indicated that marital or couples therapy addresses broader domains of outcome than does medication. Friedman (1975) randomly assigned married depressed patients in a mixed sample of "neurotic" (80 percent), bipolar, and psychotic (DSM-II) depressed outpatients to four treatment groups (amitriptyline and marital therapy, amitriptyline and minimal contact, placebo and marital therapy, and placebo and minimal contact). The study found that amitriptyline produced significantly greater relief from depressive symptoms than marital therapy or placebo. Marital therapy was more effective than placebo plus minimal supportive contact in reducing depressive symptoms and improving family functioning. McLean, Ogston, and Grauer (1973) found that couples behavioral therapy reduced self-reported depressive symptoms and decreased negative verbal interactions and actions toward the significant other more than did a nonspecific comparison condition. Corney (1987) assigned 80 depressed women who were seeing their general practitioners either to treatment with the general practitioner alone or to this treatment plus social work intervention. Social work intervention reduced depressive symptoms in the sample overall and was specifically beneficial to patients with marital problems. Sher, Baucom, and Larus (1990) treated couples with marital distress by BMT alone, BMT plus cognitive restructuring, BMT plus emotional expressiveness training, BMT plus cognitive restructuring plus emotional expressiveness, or wait-list. All treatment conditions improved marital satisfaction more than did wait-list.

Brief Dynamic Psychotherapy

The goal of brief dynamic psychotherapy is to resolve core conflicts based on personality and situational variables, thereby, in theory, resolving depressive symptoms in depressed patients. Neither the theory nor the technique was designed specifically for depression. Several brief dynamic psychotherapy approaches have been described (Malan, 1976, 1979; Mann, 1973; Wolberg, 1967). Treatment manuals are available (Luborsky, 1984; Strupp and Binder, 1984).

The acute effects of brief dynamic psychotherapy were investigated in seven randomized controlled trials (Covi and Lipman, 1987; Gallagher and Thompson, 1982; Hersen, Bellack, Himmelhoch, et al., 1984; Kornblith, Rehm, O'Hara, et al., 1983; McLean and Hakstian, 1979; Steuer, Mintz, Hammen, et al., 1984; Thompson, Gallagher, and Breckenridge, 1987), of which six could be meta-analyzed. No studies have compared brief dynamic psychotherapy to a pill placebo.

The overall efficacy of brief dynamic psychotherapy in these six studies was 34.8 percent. Compared to other therapies, brief dynamic psychotherapy may be slightly less effective. Compared to medication, it was 8.4 percent more effective. No placebo-controlled comparisons are available. Only one study contrasted brief dynamic psychotherapy to a wait-list control, but the response rate for those in the wait-list group was not reported categorically (Thompson, Gallagher, and Breckenridge, 1987).

Of the therapies studied to date, brief dynamic psychotherapy may have a slightly weaker overall effect. While this finding may suggest that better effects can be obtained with more structured, directive, less exploratory therapies (such as cognitive therapy, behavioral therapy, and interpersonal psychotherapy) for those with major depressive disorder, present data have several key limitations. Five of the six studies used brief dynamic psychotherapy in the group format, while the individual format is typical practice. Second, the investigators were aligned in nearly every case with other forms of psychotherapy, which may have led to less than optimal implementation of brief dynamic psychotherapy. Third, it is conceivable that some patients respond to brief dynamic psychotherapy, while others respond to other forms of treatment. If so, comparisons across different forms of treatment will be dictated by the mix of such patients in any given sample.

All naturalistic studies of the prophylactic value of acute phase brief dynamic psychotherapy for major depression revealed no differences in depressive symptoms at followup between brief dynamic psychotherapy and nonspecific treatment (McLean and Hakstian, 1990), cognitive therapy (Gallagher-Thompson, Hanley-Peterson, and Thompson, 1990), behavioral therapy (Gallagher-Thompson, Hanley-Peterson, and Thompson, 1990; McLean and Hakstian, 1990), or the use of antidepressant medication (McLean and Hakstian, 1990). However, these studies have methodological problems that prohibit firm conclusions.

Factors Affecting Response to Psychotherapy

Guideline: Because psychotherapy alone has produced equivocal results in patients with melancholic (endogenous) symptom features, medication is recommended as the first-line treatment in these patients; medications have clear evidence of efficacy in placebo-controlled trials. (Strength of Evidence = A.)

Melancholic (endogenous) symptom features, such as pervasive anhedonia, unreactive mood, psychomotor disturbances, severe terminal insomnia, and weight and appetite loss, have been suggested as predictive of a poor response to psychotherapy for the acute treatment of major depressive disorder, but the strength of this possible association is unclear. Gallagher and Thompson (1982, 1983) found that elderly patients who had major depressive disorder without endogenous features responded more quickly to psychotherapy than did those who had the disorder with such features. Prusoff, Weissman, Klerman, and colleagues (1980) ascertained that patients with endogenous symptom features did not respond well to interpersonal psychotherapy alone, but this finding was not replicated (Sotsky, Glass, Shea, et al., 1991). Patients with situational depressions responded as well to amitriptyline as to interpersonal psychotherapy alone or to the combination (Prusoff, Weissman, Klerman, et al., 1980). On the other hand, two studies failed to find a relationship between response to cognitive therapy alone and the presence of endogenous symptom features in outpatients with major depressive disorder (Blackburn, Bishop, Glen, et al., 1981; Kovacs, Rush, Beck, et al., 1981). Finally, Persons, Burns, and Perloff (1988), in an open trial of cognitive therapy in routine practice, found that patients without endogenous symptoms and those with personality disorders were more likely to discontinue therapy prematurely.

However, those with endogenous symptoms who completed treatment fared less well than did those without endogenous symptoms.

The value of endogenous symptom features in predicting behavioral therapy response is unclear. Some found no difference in acute phase response to behavioral therapy between those with and those without endogenous symptoms (Thase, Hersen, Bellack, et al., 1983), but others did (Brown and Lewinsohn, 1984; Gallagher and Thompson, 1982; Kornblith, Rehm, O'Hara, et al., 1983; McLean and Hakstian, 1979; Nezu, 1986; Nezu and Perri, 1989; Rehm, Kornblith, O'Hara, et al., 1981; Robin and De Tissera, 1982; Roth, Bielski, Jones, et al., 1982; Rude, 1986; Steuer, Mintz, Hammen, et al., 1984; Thompson and Gallagher, 1984; Thompson, Gallagher, and Breckenridge, 1987; Usaf and Kavanagh, 1990). Outpatients with more severe pretreatment symptoms seem less likely to respond to behavioral therapy (Steinmetz, Lewinsohn, and Antonuccio, 1983; Teri and Lewinsohn, 1986) and more likely to drop out of treatment (Last, Thase, Hersen, et al., 1985).

By contrast, there is strong evidence in inpatients and some in outpatients that those with a disorder that has melancholic features will do especially well with medication alone (Rush and Weissenburger, in press). Given the positive findings for medication and the unresolved, conflicting findings for acute phase psychotherapy alone, logic dictates that medication should be the first-line treatment for patients with melancholic symptoms.

The presence of personality disorders may reduce or slow the response to cognitive, interpersonal, and other time-limited, symptom-focused psychotherapies alone, as well as to medication (Thompson, Gallagher, and Czirr, 1988; Depression Guideline Panel, forthcoming). For example, higher levels of neuroticism and personality pathology have generally been associated with a poorer response to interpersonal psychotherapy (Frank, Kupfer, Jacob, et al., 1987; Prusoff, Weissman, Klerman, et al., 1980; Shea, Pilkonis, Beckham, et al., 1990; Zuckerman, Prusoff, Weissman, et al., 1980) or cognitive therapy (Persons, Burns, and Perloff, 1988). A better response has been found in those without personality pathology (Pilkonis and Frank, 1988). Similarly, the therapist's judgment of emotional health and better pretreatment social adjustment may predict better outcome (Rounsaville, Weissman, and Prusoff, 1981).

Marital dissatisfaction may be associated with higher rates of relapse and recurrence following maintenance interpersonal psychotherapy (Rounsaville, Weissman, Prusoff, et al., 1979), which logically suggests that marital therapy may be indicated for patients who suffer from marital discord and depression. Thus, remediation of continued psychosocial difficulties by means of therapy may help in the long-term prognosis of some depressed patients.

Selection of a Psychotherapy

Guideline: In most cases, therapies that target depressive symptoms (cognitive or behavioral therapy) or specific interpersonal or current psychosocial problems related to the depression (interpersonal psychotherapy) are more similar than different in efficacy. (Strength of Evidence = B.) Long-term therapies are not currently indicated as first-line the acute phase treatments for patients with major depressive disorder. (Strength of Evidence = C.)

The exception to this guideline may be brief dynamic psychotherapy, which seems to have a lower overall response rate (34.8 percent, based on meta-analyses) in outpatients with major depressive disorder. However, different individuals may differentially benefit from one or another treatment (Persons, 1991), which mitigates strong inferences from the available data.

The evidence upon which to select among the several psychotherapies with efficacy suggested by randomized trials for the acute treatment of major depressive disorder is sparse (Table 12). Few studies have directly compared one psychotherapy to another. Furthermore, studies to date have been conducted largely at sites closely associated with the development or administration of one of these methods. Whether the comparison therapy(ies) was (were) administered with equal skill and enthusiasm (which could potentially bias findings) is unclear.

When formal psychotherapy is selected as the sole treatment for less severe episodes of major depression, the following general principles may be useful:

- The psychotherapy should generally be time-limited, focused on current problems, and aimed at symptom resolution rather than personality change as the initial target.
- Since it has not been established that all forms of psychotherapy are equally effective in major depressive disorder, if one is chosen as the sole treatment, it should have been studied in randomized controlled trials.
- The therapist should be experienced and trained in use of the therapy with patients who have major depressive disorder.
- Assessment of symptom response (as with medication trials) is very useful in planning the next steps, should the patient not respond fully.
- If the patient fails to show any improvement in depression by 6 weeks, or nearly full remission by roughly 12 weeks, a reevaluation and potential switch to, or addition of, medication should be considered.

Medication and formal, short-term therapies or the combination of both are effective treatments for major depression. Long-term therapies have not been studied in randomized controlled trials. Therefore, long-term therapies used alone are not recommended as acute phase treatments for major depressive disorder.

Some forms of short-term psychotherapy not specifically designed for treatment of depression (e.g., marital therapy) may contribute to symptom improvement if the psychosocial situation indicates that focused therapy would be helpful.

Only a few forms of therapy as solitary acute treatments for major depressive disorder have been studied. In these cases, the therapists were highly trained in the particular modality, followed a manual, and often received ongoing supervision. Therefore, the question of the effectiveness of these therapies in everyday practice has not yet been fully addressed.

Frequency of Visits

Guideline: At least once-a-week visits on a regular basis are recommended for formal psychotherapy. (Strength of Evidence = B.)

There are no randomized controlled trials comparing different psychotherapy session schedules. In nearly all of the published trials of psychotherapy, sessions occur once (most often) or sometimes twice a week (for cognitive therapy) (see Beck, Rush, Shaw, et al., 1979). In primary care settings, therapy is likely to be provided by a consultant/therapist who sees the patient one to two times a week. This schedule facilitates the assessment of the severity of depressive symptoms, seems sufficient to promote the therapeutic alliance between therapist and patient, and allows frequent enough visits to ensure adherence. Based on the available randomized controlled trials, at least a partial response is often present by 6 weeks, and remission occurs in most patients by 12 weeks.

Failure to Respond

Guideline: If psychotherapy alone is chosen as the acute treatment and there is no improvement of depression after 6 weeks or only partial improvement after 12 weeks, a consultation, referral, change in, or augmentation of the treatment plan is advised. Medication may appropriately be started in those who do not respond at all. (Strength of Evidence = B.)

No crossover trials to either another form of psychotherapy or medication have been conducted on patients who have not fully responded to psychotherapy alone. A switch to or addition of antidepressant medications, which are thought to work by different mechanisms of action and have been well demonstrated to be effective in major depressive disorder, should be considered. Medication should be started in those who do not respond at all. Formal psychotherapy may be continued or discontinued.

As with medications, a significant number of patients (20 to 50 percent) may drop out of psychotherapy shortly after its initiation for various reasons (Persons, Burns, and Perloff, 1988; Depression Guideline Panel, forthcoming). The primary care practitioner will find it helpful to provide the patient with the option of returning for consultation or alternative therapy if the patient remains depressed, even before the 6-week reassessment visit.

6 Guideline: Acute Phase Management with Medication and Psychotherapy

In providing medication, practitioners always provide some talking "therapy"—clinical management. This process includes educating the patient about the illness, medication or therapy options, side effects, prognosis, and treatment plan. Adjustments in treatment and adherence are also discussed. This clinical management is essential to optimal treatment (see Chapter 2).

Mental health care practitioners may engage in more formal therapies such as supportive therapy to provide advice, guidance on current problems, reinforcement of the patient's psychological strengths, and development of social supports. Modification of work schedules, reduction or management of current demands, and resolution of current interpersonal difficulties all are part of supportive therapy, which can take 15 to 50 minutes per session. Supportive psychotherapy has not been studied per se in randomized controlled trials. However, a closely related therapy, interpersonal psychotherapy, has been specifically designed for depressed patients and formally tested. In combination with medication, interpersonal psychotherapy seems both to reduce early termination and to result in better symptom relief and social adjustment than either treatment alone (Weissman, Prusoff, DiMascio, et al., 1979). By logical extension, supportive therapy may be particularly useful in those with complex social difficulties not resolved with medication or in those with adherence problems.

Other formal therapies, such as cognitive therapy and behavioral therapy, have been developed and tested with depressed patients alone or in combination with medication. When used alone, the targets are symptom reduction and restoration of psychosocial function. In combination with medication, the same targets apply; but, in addition, these treatments may be aimed more selectively at psychosocial difficulties, with medication as the mainstay of symptom amelioration. The term *combined treatment*, thus, refers to the combination of medication and a formal psychotherapy.

Objectives and Indications

Guideline: Combined treatment is a reasonable consideration for initial acute phase treatment if:

- **The prior course of illness is chronic or characterized by poor interepisode recovery. (Strength of Evidence = B.)**

- **Either treatment alone (optimally delivered) has been only partially effective. (Strength of Evidence = C.)**
- **The patient has a history of chronic psychosocial problems, both in and out of episodes of major depression. (Strength of Evidence = C.)**
- **The patient has a history of treatment adherence difficulties. (Strength of Evidence = B.)**

For other patients, psychotherapy may be added to acute phase medication once the patient has responded to an optimal medication regimen if significant psychological or interpersonal problems continue following symptom remission. (Strength of Evidence = C.)

It is recommended that medication be added to (or substituted for) acute phase psychotherapy if:

- There is no response at all to psychotherapy alone at approximately 6 weeks.
- There is only a partial response to an adequate 12-week trial of psychotherapy.
- The patient worsens with psychotherapy alone.
- The patient requests medication during or following psychotherapy and symptoms are appropriate and sufficient to warrant medication.

There are few data to guide clinicians in determining when to choose the combination of medication and a formal psychotherapy. While it is common *psychiatric* practice to use such a combination in the treatment of major depressive disorder, the need for this combination in *primary care patients* is not well established. Available research does not allow for strong recommendations in this area for several reasons:

- The efficacy of combined treatment has not been tested in primary care and has been infrequently tested in tertiary care settings.
- The evidence to date in tertiary care settings does not consistently support the notion that combined treatment is more effective than medication alone, at least in terms of symptom reduction, in many patients with major depressive disorder.
- There is evidence that effective treatment of major depression with medication and clinical management ameliorates associated psychosocial problems in many patients without formal psychotherapy to redress these problems (Mintz, Mintz, Arruda, et al., 1992).

On the other hand, some research supports the ideas that:

- Some patients either respond more completely or a larger number of patients respond when both psychotherapy and medication are used, especially in psychiatric, but not necessarily in primary care, settings (Blackburn, Bishop, Glen, et al., 1981).
- The combined approach addresses a wider domain of disabilities (symptoms plus psychosocial functioning) (Corney, 1987; Friedman, 1975; Weissman, Prusoff, DiMascio, et al., 1979).

- For some, exposure to formal therapy may improve the prognosis compared to that associated with medication plus clinical management, once treatment is stopped (Frank, Kupfer, Perel, et al., 1990). (See Chapter 5 of this guideline and Depression Guideline Panel, forthcoming.)

Guideline: Formal psychotherapy can be used in combination with medication with the objectives of rectifying ongoing psychosocial difficulties that contribute to some depressive symptoms, such as pessimism, low self-esteem, or marital difficulties. (Strength of Evidence = B.)

There are no well established predictors of which patients preferentially benefit from combined treatment. The following suggestions are based on logical inference from the few studies that have searched for predictors of who is best served by combined treatment, from the clinical experience of the panel, and from knowledge about the course and complications of major depressive disorder.

Psychotherapy as an adjunct to medication can be useful in addressing associated psychosocial problems, such as marital difficulties (Friedman, 1975). The structured psychotherapies also tend to be specific, targeted, and time-limited. Some practitioners believe and some evidence suggests that the therapies are more effective if patients are less severely symptomatic and, therefore, better able to participate in the therapy.

Guideline: The likelihood that adjunctive therapy is indicated may be better gauged once the depressive syndrome has largely resolved with medication, since medication alone improves psychosocial difficulties in many patients. (Strength of Evidence = B.)

Psychosocial difficulties may well improve during the 1 to 3 months following symptomatic improvement in depressed outpatients (Mintz, Mintz, Arruda, et al., 1992). For example, should marital problems persist well past the reduction of the depressive symptoms, marital therapy may be more clearly indicated.

One problem is to decide when the combined treatment should begin. In primary care settings, given the limited time and need to educate the patient (and family, where appropriate) about the treatment and prognosis of major depression, the likely optimal procedure in the treatment of patients who are to receive medication and a formal psychotherapy is to (1) begin medication, (2) provide support and education, (3) optimize adherence, (4) adjust the dosage, and (5) gain symptom relief and resolution of psychosocial problems before starting formal therapy. Once medication has reduced symptoms, a reassessment for continuing psychosocial or chronic interpersonal problems may identify those patients who may benefit by adding psychotherapy to the medication. This approach has the added advantage of allowing the practitioner time to develop a close alliance with the patient and to explore briefly in the course of general clinical management ongoing difficulties that may be exacerbating the depression.

Many practitioners recommend formal psychotherapy combined with medication for depressed patients with personality disorders. In these cases, the therapy is aimed at the personality disorder itself. The diagnosis of a personality disorder is complex, time-consuming, and generally impractical in primary care settings. However, evidence from clinical trials of medication and psychotherapy suggests that patients with personality disorders are more likely to exhibit partial responses to short-term, symptom-reducing therapies or to medication, to have stormy life histories with a variety of smoldering symptoms between episodes, and to terminate treatment prematurely. Treat the major depression first; a partial success or a lack of patient adherence raises the logical possibility of a personality disorder and, therefore, a consultation or referral. Specific considerations in selecting combined treatment and initiating it appropriately are shown in Table 13.

Table 13. Considerations for combined treatment

A. Consider combined treatment as an initial option more strongly if:
   (1) History reveals a partial response to a full trial of either treatment alone.
   (2) Current episode of major depression is longer than 2 years.
   (3) Patient has a history of two or more episodes with poor interepisode recovery.
   (4) Significant psychosocial difficulties are present that interfere with adherence *and* indications for medication are present.
   (5) Patient requests it.

B. Add medication to psychotherapy if:
   (1) Patient shows poor response to psychotherapy alone after 6 weeks or only a partial response after 12 weeks; if no response at all to psychotherapy, it may be discontinued and clinical management provided.

C. Add psychotherapy to medication (if medication has been used optimally) if:
   (1) Patient shows partial response to medication and residual symptoms are largely psychological (e.g., low self-esteem).
   (2) Patient shows partial or complete response to medication and psychosocial problems remain significant.
   (3) Patient has difficulty with adherence.

Evidence for Efficacy

Table 14 shows those studies of combined acute phase treatment for which meta-analyses were feasible. Altogether, seven acute phase randomized controlled trials compared the combination of formal psychotherapy and medication to one or the other treatment alone in depressed adult outpatients (six studies) (Beck, Hollon, Young, et al., 1985; Covi and Lipman, 1987; Hersen, Bellack, Himmelhoch, et al., 1984; Murphy, Simons, Wetzel, et al., 1984; Roth, Bielski, Jones, et al., 1982; Rush and Watkins, 1981) or inpatients (one study) (Bowers, 1990). No such geriatric randomized controlled trials were found. Of these seven, five included cognitive therapy plus medication, two included behavioral therapy plus medication, and one included interpersonal psychotherapy plus medication. None included marital therapy or brief dynamic psychotherapy combined with medication.

Table 14. Meta-analyses of combined treatment in outpatients with major depressive disorder

Combination[1]	Combination Efficacy	Combination vs. Wait-List or Placebo	Combination vs. Therapy[2] Alone	Combination vs. Other Therapy Alone[3]	Combination vs. Drug Alone
Behavioral therapy plus medication	34.6% (10.9)[4] [2][5]	N/A	-7.4% (22.3) [2]	-2.2% (11.5) [1]	6.2% (11.4) [1]
Brief dynamic psychotherapy plus medication	N/A	N/A	N/A	N/A	N/A
Cognitive therapy plus medication	53.7% (17.3) [5]	N/A	6.4% (15.3) [6]	35.4% (9.4) [1]	39.4% (32.9) [2]
Interpersonal therapy plus medication	N/A	N/A	N/A	N/A	N/A

[1]Intent-to-treat sample.
[2]Therapy contrast is that specified in the combination column (e.g., behavioral therapy).
[3]The combination indicated in the first column was compared to a different form of psychotherapy alone.
[4]Standard deviation is in parentheses.
[5]Number of cells in the meta-analysis is in brackets.

These intent-to-treat analyses lead to an interesting potential conclusion. The efficacy of the combination (column 2, Table 14) is roughly equal to the efficacy of medication alone. The combination versus therapy alone is roughly equal, but the number of studies is small (column 4, Table 14). However, in a study with a primary care and a tertiary care sample (not included in Table 14 because intent to treat could not be calculated) (Blackburn, Bishop, Glen, et al., 1981), the effects of the psychotherapy (cognitive therapy) exceeded those of combined treatment or medication alone (primary care); in contrast, combined treatment was better than either alone in the tertiary care setting. This study and the meta-analyses (column 6, Table 14) are consistent with the idea that some patients—perhaps those with milder, less chronic forms of depression or those who are earlier in the course of what may become a more recurrent illness (Post, 1992)—may not specifically benefit from combined treatment. On the other hand, those with more severe or chronic disease and partial responders to either treatment alone may benefit specifically from the combination.

One difficulty in the literature available is the lack of placebo-controlled, primary care psychotherapy, medication, and combined treatment randomized controlled trials. It is clear from the many available studies that some patients with major depressive disorder respond and some even remit fully with placebo and clinical management. Patients with less severe, less chronic forms of illness seem most responsive to such nonspecific treatment. It is logical to suspect that such patients are more likely to be found in primary care settings. For this reason, a two- to three-visit evaluation may be useful to determine which patients require formal treatment (see Chapter 3). There are no studies in primary care settings of less severely ill patients with major depressive disorder given several sessions of clinical management followed, for those who do not remit, by either psychotherapy, medication, or placebo with clinical management. Such information would provide a firmer basis for recommending treatment options for these less symptomatic, less chronic, and less recurrent forms of major depression.

For these reasons, routine use of the combination of medication and a formal psychotherapy as an initial treatment is not recommended for all patients. Some patients who actually need psychotherapy may be lost to treatment if they find the medication intolerable. For others, medication may be especially useful and therapy unneeded. Thus, initial therapy for less severely ill patients may be either a trial of medication or a trial of time-limited psychotherapy, as long as the outcome (symptom remission) is monitored. Should either trial fail to produce remission, the alternative treatment or a consultation are options.

Selection of a Combined Treatment

Guideline: Given the modest advantage for combined treatment and the suggestive evidence that some patients respond better (but others do not) to the combined treatment, clinical judgment remains the basis for deciding when to use combined treatment and which type of psychotherapy to use. (Strength of Evidence = C.)

Current evidence (Table 14) suggests the efficacy of medication combined with either cognitive, interpersonal psychotherapy (Weissman,

Prusoff, DiMascio, et al., 1979), or possibly behavioral therapy (Table 14), at least for some patients (Blackburn, Bishop, Glen, et al., 1981). Whether the efficacy of other forms of therapy combined with medication is greater than for either alone has not been studied.

Practically speaking, the type of psychotherapy used will be substantially dictated by the availability of trained and skilled practitioners. When psychotherapy is added to medication to assist patients with psychosocial problems that may be contributing to their symptoms, the selection of therapy should be based on the specific difficulties identified by the patient (e.g., marital or family therapy for such problems, vocational counseling for those with occupational skill deficits, cognitive or interpersonal psychotherapy for low self-esteem/interpersonal difficulties). Since short-term, targeted therapies in combination with medication have been studied to some degree, while longer term therapies have not, logic and parsimony suggest that psychotherapy be limited in focus and duration when used in combination with medication in acute treatment and that its effectiveness be monitored.

Frequency of Visits

Patients in combined treatment may require greater time for each session than do those receiving either medication or psychotherapy alone. The frequency of visits for medication and psychotherapy is dictated by the same forces as if either were being used alone, such as severity of illness, need for determinations of blood levels, and type of psychotherapy. As symptoms improve, the intervals between visits will also increase. When possible, appointments with the physician and therapist should be coordinated to minimize inconvenience, thereby maximizing adherence.

Dosage Adjustments

Full therapeutic dosages of medication should be prescribed for patients receiving combined treatment. Dosage adjustments follow suggestions in Chapter 4.

Failure to Respond

Guideline: If a patient given the combination of medication and formal psychotherapy has not responded at all by week 6 or only partially by week 12, the practitioner is advised to reevaluate the patient's condition to ensure that an alternative source for symptoms has not been overlooked. (Strength of Evidence = A.)

There is no evidence that changing the form of psychotherapy will alter the course of symptoms. However, changing or augmenting the medication is a strong consideration. For severely depressed patients who are unresponsive to combined treatment, a consultation or referral for alternative medication or ECT may be considered.

7 Guideline: Acute Phase Management with ECT

Guideline: The indications for ECT in the treatment of severe depression are a depressive episode in which symptoms are intense, prolonged, and associated with severe vegetative symptoms and/or a marked functional impairment, the presence of psychotic symptoms, or failure to respond fully to several adequate trials of medication. (Strength of Evidence = A.)

The panel recognizes that very few patients will require ECT, that it must be conducted by a specialist, and that side effects can be significant. However, ECT is an important option in selected cases.

In acute phase treatment, seven well-controlled and six additional randomized controlled trials revealed that ECT was generally effective in the short run for inpatients with severe depressive disorders. Predictors of a good response to ECT are similar to those of a good response to TCA medication. The presence of melancholic symptoms appears predictive of a positive response to ECT. Depressions accompanied by psychotic features respond better to ECT than to antidepressants or neuroleptics alone. For psychotic depressions, either ECT or the combination of antidepressant with neuroleptic medications may be equally effective. Some studies indicate that ECT appears effective in patients who have not responded to TCAs. Thus, if patients with severe depressions or melancholic features do not respond fully to antidepressant medication and have continued vegetative symptoms, or if they have not responded at all, ECT is a treatment option.

Electroconvulsive therapy may be advantageous over other treatments in patients (Yudofsky, 1981):

- Who have severe major depressive disorder that has not responded to adequate trial(s) of antidepressant medications.
- Who have psychotic depression.
- For whom antidepressant or neuroleptic medications pose a particular medical risk.
- Who have severe psychomotor retardation, suicidal behavior, or any clinical situation that requires a rapid response.
- Who have had a previous good response to ECT.
- Who have mixed manic episodes.
- Who have schizoaffective disorder that responds only partially to medication.
- Who are catatonic.
- Who have melancholic symptoms and have previously failed to respond to medications.

Randomized sham-controlled trials of ECT have demonstrated that it is highly effective for inpatients with severe forms of major depressive disorder, especially those with psychotic symptoms (Brandon, Cowley, McDonald, et al., 1984; Freeman, Basson, and Creighton, 1978; Gangadhar, Kapur, and Kalyanasundaram, 1982; Gregory, Shawcross, and Gill, 1985; Johnstone, Lawler, Stevens, et al., 1980; Lambourn and Gill, 1978; West, 1981). The available evidence suggests that ECT may be less effective in those with less severe forms of depression, though it may be an option for some (Avery and Lubrano, 1979). Two retrospective chart reviews of medication-resistant patients later treated with ECT (Howarth and Grace, 1985; Perry, Morgan, Smith, et al., 1982) and eight prospective open trials of patients with documented (observed) medication failure (DeCarolis, Gilberti, Roccatagliata, et al., 1964; Hamilton, 1982; Lykouras, Malliaras, Christodoulou, et al., 1986b; Magni, Fisman, and Helmes, 1988; Mandel, Welch, Mieskie, et al., 1977; Medical Research Council, 1965; Paul, Extein, Calil, et al., 1981; Prudic, Sackeim, and Devanand, 1990) indicate that ECT is effective for 50 to 70 percent of inpatients who have not responded to adequate medication trials. While this response rate is significant, it is lower than the response rate to ECT in nonresistant cases (Sackeim, Prudic, and Devanand, 1990), and it is equal to (Dinan and Barry, 1989) or better than that found with lithium augmentation (roughly 50 percent) or MAOI augmentation (roughly 50 percent) (Davidson, McLeod, Law-Yone, et al., 1978) of TCAs (Depression Guideline Panel, forthcoming).

Those responding to ECT should receive continuation treatment with antidepressant medications, given the 30 to 60 percent likelihood of relapse/recurrence without such treatment. The use of continuation medication or maintenance ECT has not been subjected to randomized controlled trials.

8 Guideline: Special Situations

The Suicidal Patient

Guideline: The primary risk factor for suicide in both the general and clinical populations is a psychiatric diagnosis. An active or chronic general medical disease is also a significant risk factor. (Strength of Evidence = A.)

There are approximately seven suicide attempts for every completed suicide, and about 2 to 3 percent of those who attempt suicide go on to complete suicide. In the general population, the single most reliable risk factor for completed suicide is a psychiatric diagnosis. Other risk factors are being Caucasian, male, and elderly. Roughly 25 percent of all suicides occur in the elderly, though they constitute only 10 percent of the general population. Elderly men continue to have the highest suicide rates, even though the rates among male youths are increasing.

As in the general population, the primary risk factor for suicide in clinical populations is a psychiatric diagnosis. Male gender is less significant than in the general population, but being Caucasian remains an important risk factor. The middle years seem to have increased risk in patient populations, while higher rates are found in the elderly and youths in the general population. The period of highest risk is during hospitalization or immediately after discharge.

The suicide literature on both general and clinical populations consistently reveals the risk factors of depression, alcohol or drug abuse, and psychosis (psychotic depression, mania, or schizophrenia). The presence of general medical disorders is a risk factor in the general population, but is not always evaluated in clinical studies. Approximately 70 percent of suicide completers have one or more active or chronic medical illnesses at the time of death. Acquired immune deficiency syndrome (AIDS) has recently been reported to carry a high suicide risk as well. To summarize, the following risk factors have been empirically related to suicide:

- Hopelessness.
- General medical illnesses.
- Family history of substance abuse.
- Depression.
- Substance abuse.
- Male gender.
- Caucasian race.
- Psychotic symptoms.
- Living alone.
- Prior suicide attempts.

Many patients with suicidal ideation can be managed as outpatients if they are not psychotic, if they do not abuse substances to a significant extent, and if they themselves feel that they can control their suicidal ideations or impulses, based on direct discussions about their thoughts of suicide. A few general principles for managing the patient with suicidal ideation are suggested by the panel, based on current clinical practice, logic, panel consensus, and knowledge of risk factors.

The practitioner is advised to:

- Evaluate the patient's condition for relevant risk factors.
- Suspect suicidal ideation in most depressed patients and others with risk factors.
- Inquire directly about the frequency and content of suicidal ideation during both diagnostic and treatment visits.
- Ask the patient about factors that argue against and for attempting suicide.
- Evaluate the patient's access to means of suicide.

The practitioner is advised to consider hospitalization for suicidal patients if:

- Psychosis is present.
- Suicidal ideation is present with significant substance abuse, severe hopelessness, strong impulses to act on the ideas, or specific suicide plans.
- The patient lacks sufficient social support to execute effective outpatient treatment.
- Concurrent general medical conditions make outpatient medication treatment unsafe.
- The patient lacks the ability to participate in outpatient care.

For outpatient management, the practitioner is advised to:

- Explain the nature of depression, its prognosis, and treatment, thereby raising hope; explain that depression itself is often associated with a feeling of hopelessness and thoughts of suicide and that, as the depressive syndrome resolves, so should the hopelessness and suicidal ideation.
- Develop either a formal contract (patient to call practitioner if suicidal feelings become strong) or be very easily available to patients if suicidal ideation or impulses increase.
- Strongly advise patients to discontinue all alcohol and drug use immediately.
- See patients at least weekly while suicidal ideation is significant.
- Avoid prescriptions for more than 1 week of medication until suicidal risk is lower.
- Explain to family members, when appropriate, how to respond to suicidal ideas (e.g., provide reassurance, call the practitioner).

- Advise patients, when appropriate, to remove easily available instruments of suicide (e.g., guns) from the house.
- Provide supportive interactions with the patient in 15- to 20-minute visits in acute phase treatment until suicidal ideation resolves.
- Provide reassurance and support the patient's reasons to live.
- Reassess the patient's condition for hopelessness, suicidal ideation, and substance abuse at each treatment visit.

Geriatric Depression

Guideline: Depression in the elderly should not routinely be ascribed to demoralization or "normal sadness" over financial barriers, medical problems, or other concerns. The general principles for treatment of adults with major depressive disorder apply as well to elderly patients. (Strength of Evidence = A.)

The diagnosis of late-life depression must be given particular attention. The prevalence of major depressive disorder may be lower in the elderly than in nonelderly adults, which suggests that aging per se is not an etiological factor in depression. In elderly patients with recurrent depression, the possibility of bipolar disorder must be considered. Other psychiatric disorders to be considered in the differential diagnosis include early dementia, delusional disorders, organic (secondary) disorders, and substance-induced mood disorders. Finally, the first onset of primary major depressive disorder past the age of 50 is uncommon and often related to a specific medical etiology. A particularly careful medical evaluation is often needed in these patients.

The efficacy of the various treatments for depression in the elderly is, by and large, equal to that found in adults in general. The differences in dealing with the elderly are the particular practical problems that they and the treatments confront. These problems require more strategic planning and somewhat different tactics (e.g., more likely use of blood level determinations, particular care in minimizing side effects). Treatment of late-life major depressive disorder was reviewed by an NIMH Consensus Development Conference (1991), the general conclusions of which are entirely consistent with these guidelines. The consequences of unrecognized and untreated depression in the elderly include increased health services utilization, longer hospital stays, poor treatment compliance, and increased morbidity and mortality from medical illness and suicide. The costs of treatment are relatively modest and can be minimized by careful monitoring of the patient's clinical status.

In general, major depressive disorder in late life is a treatable illness. The evidence for the specific efficacy of medication is strongly based on randomized placebo-controlled trials. The evidence for the efficacy of psychotherapy alone as a treatment for less severely ill, nonpsychotic outpatients is beginning to accumulate, though this area remains understudied. Electroconvulsive therapy appears to be as effective in geriatric patients with severe or psychotic major depressive disorder as in nongeriatric groups. Evidence for or against the efficacy of combined acute phase treatment is generally lacking in geriatric patients, but studies are currently under way. One preliminary analysis (based on intent-to-treat samples) found that interpersonal psychotherapy and nortriptyline, within the context of a supportive, psychoeducationally oriented milieu, achieved a treatment success rate of around 75 percent in acute phase treatment (Reynolds, Frank, Perel, et al., 1992). Finally, the utility of maintenance phase medication is suggested by a few studies.

Nearly all randomized controlled treatment trials in elderly depressed individuals to date have been conducted in the otherwise medically healthy. These patients are not representative of all depressed elderly. In fact, other nonpsychiatric medical conditions are risk factors for depression. Thus, in recommending treatments, the panel is assuming that those treatments effective in the depressed, but otherwise healthy, elderly will be effective in those with other concurrent medical conditions. However, the presence of such medical conditions appears to be a risk factor for a poorer prognosis in younger depressed patients (Keitner, Ryan, Miller, et al., 1991).

The problems of treating depression in the elderly can be complex and challenging, particularly with the high rate of co-morbid medical disorders. Although treatment appears helpful for the depressed elderly, a pressing need remains for further controlled intervention research for depressions late in life, especially in patients with depressive disorders occurring in association with other nonpsychiatric medical and neurologic disorders.

Several obstacles or special risks confound treatment of the elderly (Table 15). Pharmacotherapy in elderly depressed patients is complicated by:

- Poor adherence, due to greater sensitivity to side effects.
- Medically significant side effects.
- Inadequate family support to continue taking medication properly.
- Intercurrent medical disease that interferes with proper antidepressant dosing.
- Occult self-medication with drugs such as alcohol.
- The need for education of the patient and family about depression and its treatment.
- The risk of death from suicide.

To provide optimal pharmacotherapy in elderly patients taking other medications or who have other nonpsychiatric medical disorders, the practitioner may need to rely on repeated plasma antidepressant drug level determinations, as the other medications and/or disorders can alter antidepressant absorption or metabolism. Because of the natural metabolic slowing that accompanies aging, blood level monitoring may be advisable in otherwise healthy elderly patients, particularly where therapeutic ranges are better established.

Table 15. Confounds in the diagnosis and treatment of depression in the elderly

A. Concurrent nonpsychotropic medications may:
   (1) Cause depression.
   (2) Change antidepressant blood levels.
   (3) Increase antidepressant side effects.
   (4) Biochemically block antidepressant effects.
   (5) Call for modifying the oral dosage.

B. Concurrent medical illnesses may:
   (1) Cause depression biologically.
   (2) Reduce the efficacy of antidepressant medication or psychotherapy.
   (3) Change antidepressant drug metabolism.
   (4) Impair ability to participate in psychotherapy.
   (5) Create disability contributing to both chronicity and reduced treatment efficacy.
   (6) Increase the need for simplified medication dosing schedules (e.g., once daily).

C. Concurrent nonmood psychiatric conditions may:
   (1) Cause depression (e.g., early Alzheimer's).
   (2) Call for different medications.
   (3) Impair participation in psychotherapy .
   (4) Reduce response to antidepressant medications (e.g., personality disorders).
   (5) Worsen prognosis of the depression (e.g., alcoholism).

D. Other issues:
   (1) Slower metabolism with age often requires lower dosages.
   (2) Transportation difficulties may restrict access to care.
   (3) Increased interview time needed.
   (4) Fixed income may limit availability of therapy and nongeneric antidepressant medications due to cost.

Psychosocial difficulties that may interfere with optimal treatment response include:

- Negative intercurrent life events.
- Ongoing severe interpersonal conflicts about dependency and role transitions.
- Prolonged or unresolved grief.
- Social isolation.

General clinical management or a formal psychotherapy may be equally helpful in addressing these psychosocial obstacles. Social casework, particularly during acute treatment, to remove or modify "real life" obstacles to recovery may be helpful. However, the efficacy of social casework in those with major depressive disorder has not been formally tested. Regular contacts with family members during periods of individual crisis may also be useful.

The use of stimulant medications in the elderly was recently reviewed by an NIMH Consensus Development Conference (1991). While no randomized controlled trials were available, 8 to 12 open trials conducted over the last 3 decades, as well as clinical experience of psychopharmacologists who are expert in the treatment of the depressed elderly, suggest some efficacy and a low abuse potential for stimulant medications (NIMH, 1991). The panel does not recommend the routine use of stimulants in depressed elderly patients, given the availability of antidepressants with more predictable and established efficacy and side-effect profiles. However, stimulants may be an option for highly selected elderly patients who have not responded to adequate trials of other treatments. A psychopharmacologic consultation is mandated before selection of this treatment.

Seasonal Depression

Guideline: Light therapy is a treatment consideration only for well-documented mild to moderate seasonal, nonpsychotic, winter depressive episodes in patients with recurrent major depressive or bipolar II disorders or milder seasonal episodes. (Strength of Evidence = B.)

Light therapy is a relatively new treatment that has been tested in randomized trials for up to 2 weeks in patients with seasonal mood disorders, nearly always those with winter depressions (Depression Guideline Panel, forthcoming). Its longer term efficacy has not been formally evaluated, though case reports and clinical experience suggest efficacy throughout the winter and in subsequent episodes. In addition, light therapy has not been tested against other potentially active treatments, such as medication, psychotherapy, or the combination, so whether seasonal depressions respond to these alternative treatments is unknown. Case reports suggest some efficacy for selected antidepressants. Since many patients with major depressive episodes occurring in a seasonal pattern have bipolar II or recurrent major depressive disorder, it is logical to believe that medication will be effective.

Given the current modest knowledge about light therapy and continuing research into the optimal method of administration, long-term safety, and other practical issues, the panel suggests the following principles:

- Light therapy is a logical consideration only for well documented seasonal, nonpsychotic, winter depressive episodes in patients with recurrent major depressive or bipolar II disorders or milder seasonal episodes.
- It should be administered by a professional with experience and training in its use who deems it suitable for the particular patient.
- It may be a second-line treatment option after the patient has failed to respond to an adequate medication trial.
- It may be a first-line treatment for these patients if they are not severely suicidal and if there are medical reasons to avoid antidepressants, if the patient has a history of a positive response to light therapy and no negative effects, if the patient requests it, or if an experienced practitioner deems it indicated.

Since the underlying mechanisms implicated in the seasonal pattern are not likely to be remedied by psychotherapy alone and there is no evidence to date for its efficacy, formal psychotherapy is not recommended as a first-line approach for truly seasonal depressions. Logically, light therapy should not be used as an adjunct to medication until either one alone has been optimally used. Light therapy can be useful to augment the response (if partial) to antidepressant medication and vice versa.

As with any treatment, the patient's response should be closely monitored. Response to light therapy can be rapid (4 to 7 days), but for some, response may be delayed to 2 weeks. However, the placebo response rate may be significant as well. Therefore, one or several "extended evaluation" visits may be useful in identifying those in whom symptoms persist. Caution is urged in the use of light therapy with patients with specific ophthalmologic or other conditions (Depression Guideline Panel, forthcoming). Since safety and efficacy have not been fully established beyond 2 weeks, consultation with a specialist may be helpful in determining specific risks and benefits for particular patients. Further information is available for interested practitioners (see Oren and Rosenthal, 1992; Terman, Williams, and Terman, 1991).

Depression and Other Nonpsychiatric Medical Disorders

Guideline: If a patient has a depressive episode thought to be biologically caused by a concurrent general medical disorder, the practitioner is advised to (1) treat optimally the associated general medical condition, (2) reevaluate the patient's condition, and (3) treat the major depression as an independent disorder if it is still present. In some cases, treatment of the major depression may need to proceed along with efforts to optimize treatment for the general medical disorder. (Strength of Evidence = B.)

As noted in Volume 1 of *Depression in Primary Care, Detection and Diagnosis*, the incidence of a major depressive episode at some time in the course of several other medical conditions (e.g., myocardial infarction, stroke, cancer, diabetes) is around 25 percent. Similar percentages may be expected for other nonpsychiatric medical conditions. The general strategy in such cases is to treat the medical condition first, since depression can be an unwanted direct effect of either the illness or its treatment, to reevaluate the patient's condition for continued depression, and to treat the major depression as an independent disorder if it is still present (Hall, Popkin, Devaul, et al., 1978) (Figure 9). However, in some cases, the major depression is sufficiently severe or disabling that treatment for it is indicated while the general medical condition is being treated.

There are insufficient studies to recommend one medication over another solely on the basis of efficacy data. The side-effect and pharmacologic profiles of the antidepressant, patient age, prior response to specific antidepressants, family history of response to an antidepressant, and drug-drug interactions are among the many factors that must be weighed by a clinician when choosing a particular medication. The efficacy of psychotherapy is suggested by some open studies (see Watson, 1983, for a review) and by 20 randomized controlled trials for patients with cancer and depression (Depression Guideline Panel, forthcoming), but predictors of response are not well defined. Those with low emotional support and pessimism who are widowed or divorced may particularly benefit from psychotherapy (Weisman and Worden, 1976-77). An empirical treatment trial with careful assessment of outcome (just as with major depressive disorder not associated with a general medical illness) is recommended. Further research in this area is sorely needed to determine which patients should be treated with which therapy and to establish with greater certainty the efficacy of various treatments.

Figure 9. Relationship between major depressive and other current general medical disorders

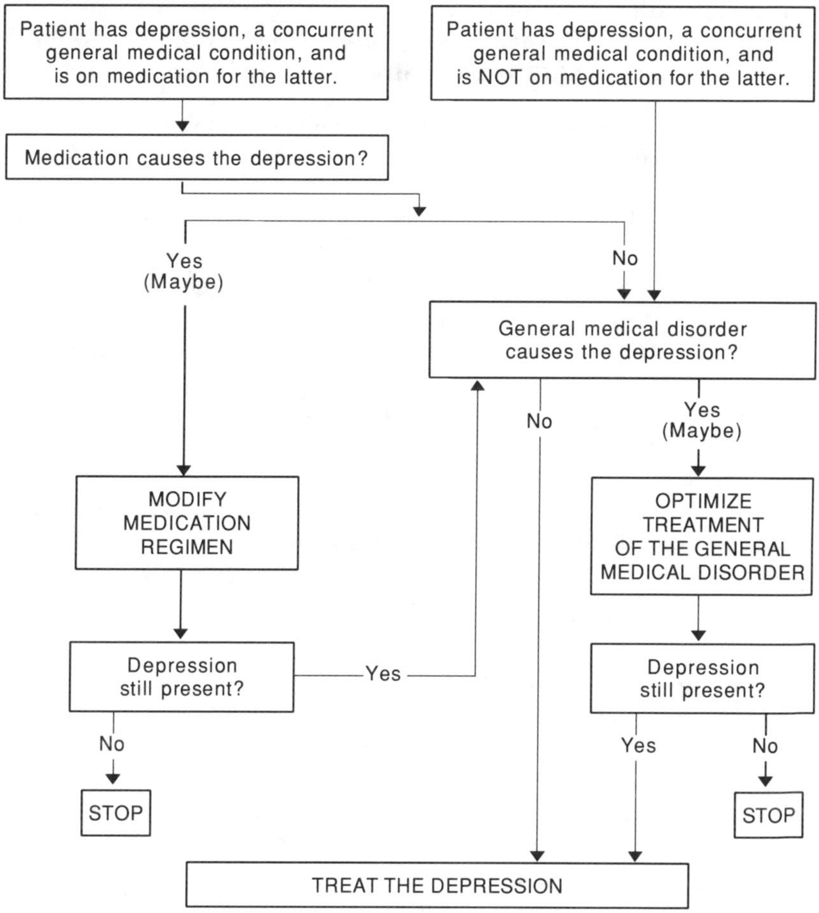

Note: In some clinical situations, treatment of the depression (e.g., if severe, incapacitating, or life-threatening) cannot be delayed until treatment for the general medical disorder has been optimized.

Depression and Other Psychiatric Disorders

Guideline: When major depressive disorder co-occurs with another psychiatric disorder, the practitioner has three options: (1) to treat the major depressive disorder as the primary target and reevaluate the patient's condition once he or she has responded to determine whether additional treatment is needed for the associated condition (e.g., as in major depressive disorder with personality disorder or generalized anxiety disorder), (2) to treat the associated condition as the initial treatment focus (e.g., as in concurrent major depression and anorexia

nervosa, bulimia nervosa, obsessive-compulsive disorder, or substance abuse), or (3) to attempt to decipher which condition is "primary" and select it as the initial treatment target (e.g., as in cases of major depressive and panic disorder). The option selected will depend on the nature of the concurrent disorder. (Strength of Evidence = B.)

Figure 10 provides an overview of the strategic choices that the practitioner confronts when depression occurs with other psychiatric or substance abuse problems.

The reasons to treat major depression as the primary target for those with concurrent generalized anxiety disorder (GAD) are:

- Randomized controlled trials of medication or psychotherapy have generally not excluded concurrent GAD.
- The presence of GAD has not been shown to reduce the efficacy of treatments for depression.
- Many patients with major depression have anxiety symptomatology of sufficient severity to be diagnosed as GAD, but the anxiety symptoms abate with remission of the depression.
- The *Diagnostic and Statistical Manual of Mental Disorders* (American Psychiatric Association, 1987) recommends that the diagnosis of GAD not be made if it occurs only in the presence of a mood disorder.

Available data on treating major depression when it is associated with a personality disorder suggest the following:

- Nearly all randomized controlled trials of treatment for major depressive disorder do not exclude personality diagnoses.
- It is difficult to assess personality disorders reliably in the presence of a major depressive episode.
- While a personality disorder may complicate treatment or slow response, it does not prevent a response in many patients.
- What may appear to be a "personality disorder" may actually be dysthymia concurrent with major depressive disorder, which, by its chronicity, affects interpersonal function. However, when the depression is specifically treated, the "personality disorder" abates.

The rationale for treating concomitant obsessive-compulsive disorder, bulimia, anorexia, or substance abuse as the primary treatment target includes the following:

- Randomized controlled trials indicate that, when these conditions are present with depressive symptoms or major depression and the conditions are effectively treated, the depression remits (Depression Guideline Panel, forthcoming).
- As a general principle, it is prudent when selecting a medication to consider initially those compounds for which efficacy is established or suggested for both conditions; for example, the compounds with established efficacy for obsessive-compulsive disorder also have established antidepressant efficacy.

Figure 10. Relationship between major depressive and other current psychiatric disorders

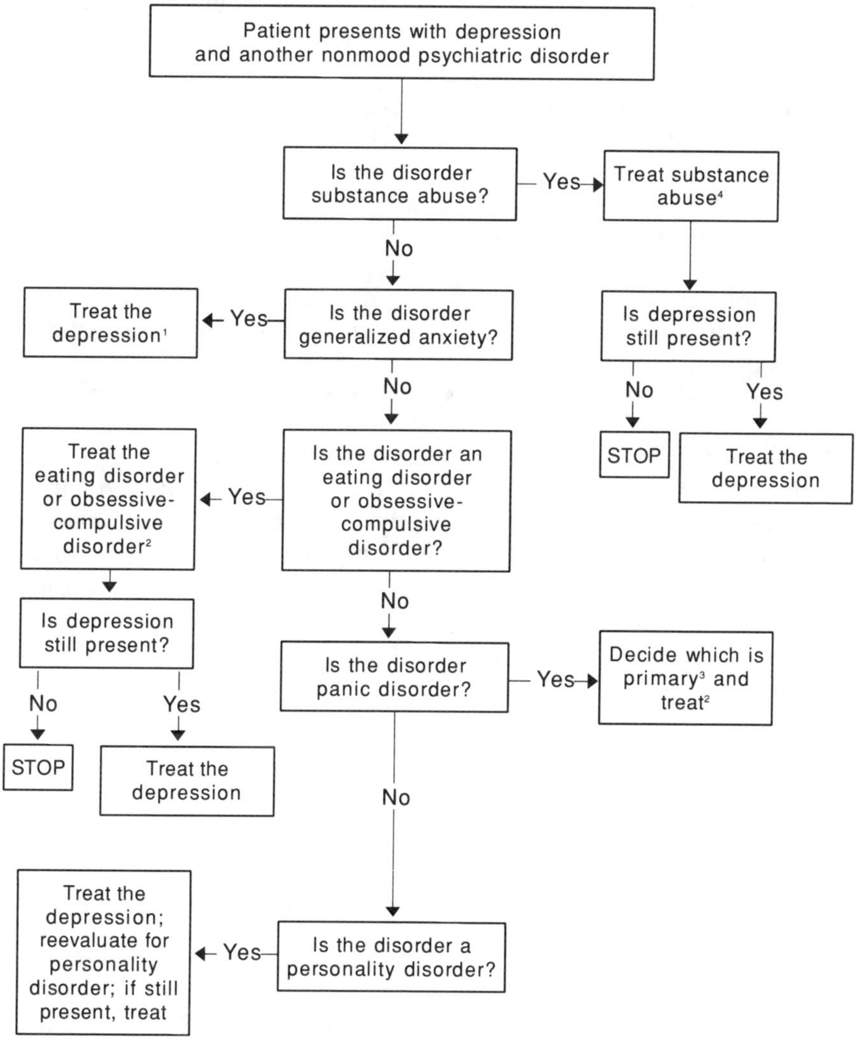

[1]When the depression is treated, the anxiety disorder should resolve as well.
[2]Choose medications known to be effective for both the depression and the other psychiatric disorder.
[3]Primary is the most severe, the longest standing by history, or the one that runs in the patient's family.
[4]In certain cases (based on history), major depression and substance abuse may require simultaneous treatment.

- As always, careful followup and repeat assessment are essential to producing the optimal result.

When panic disorder and major depression co-occur, the rationale for determining which disorder is to be the initial target of treatment rests on the following:

- Panic disorder often presents with depressive symptoms or even major depression but, when the panic disorder is treated effectively, the depressive symptoms may remit.
- Many patients with more severe depression have panic attacks, but only during the depressive episode. For these patients, the major depression is the primary target.
- The clinician can further gauge which disorder may be primary by determining which disorder causes the greatest disability and reviewing the patient's family history. If the family history is positive for depression, the practitioner treats depression; if positive for panic, the practitioner treats panic.
- Some antidepressant medications (e.g., TCAs and MAOIs) appear effective in panic disorder, especially if combined with behavioral therapy, in which case they may be the preferred medication options. Case reports and case series of SSRIs in panic disorder suggest that lower dosages than those used for major depressive disorder may be preferred.

9 Guideline: Continuation and Maintenance Treatment Options

Objectives and Indications for Continuation Treatment

Guideline: The objective of continuation treatment is to decrease the likelihood of relapse (a return of the current episode of depression). If patients respond to acute phase medication, it is generally continued at the same dosage for 4 to 9 months after return to the clinically well state. (Strength of Evidence = A.)

The recommendation for continuation medication treatment rests on a few randomized controlled trials with medication in continuation phase treatment, a substantial number of open continuation trials, and a more substantial number of such trials in maintenance phase studies. In general, it is preferred that acute phase response to medication be followed by continuation treatment with the same medication at the same dosage. Early discontinuation is followed by a roughly 25 percent relapse rate within 2 months (Maj, Veltro, Pirozzi, et al., 1992; NIMH, 1985).

Unless maintenance treatment is planned, antidepressant medication is discontinued at 4 to 9 months or tapered over several weeks (TCAs should be tapered). Patients are followed during the next several months to ensure that a new depressive episode (recurrence) does not occur. If a major depressive episode does return after discontinuation of medication, the patient is likely to respond to the same medication at the same dosage effective previously, which should then be continued for 4 to 9 months; in other words, the depression should be treated as a new episode. Thereafter, discontinuation may be attempted unless the patient has become a candidate for maintenance treatment.

Guideline: A decision to implement continuation phase psychotherapy depends on the patient's residual symptoms, psychosocial problems, history of psychological functioning between episodes, and the practitioner's and patient's judgment about the need for such treatment. Continuation psychotherapy can be added to continuation medication following acute phase response to either medication alone or the combination. (Strength of Evidence = C.)

No studies have evaluated acute response to medication followed by continuation phase psychotherapy or vice versa. In all cases, continuation phase treatment should be monitored for symptom breakthrough.

Continuation phase psychotherapy following acute treatment response to psychotherapy has not been studied in randomized controlled trials to date. Suggestive, albeit indirect, evidence for better, longer term outcome is available from two open continuation studies of cognitive therapy (Blackburn and Bishop, 1983; Jarrett, Ramanan, Eaves, et al., 1992) and one randomized controlled trial with interpersonal psychotherapy (Weissman, Prusoff, DiMascio, et al., 1979). Thus, there is only scant evidence to confirm or disconfirm the utility of continuation psychotherapy alone at once or twice a month for 6 to 8 months following acute treatment response.

Once the depressive symptoms have remitted with medication, therapy aimed at residual or persistent psychosocial problems is logical and reasonable. However, the efficacy of these types of intervention in this sequence has not been well studied. A notable exception is one controlled continuation/maintenance phase trial (32 weeks) of high versus lower contact with a focus on interpersonal function following response to acute phase medication alone (Weissman, Prusoff, DiMascio, et al., 1979). This study revealed that medication, but not placebo (with or without psychotherapy), prevented relapse/recurrence. This finding suggests that acute phase medication responders should be continued on medication and not switched to psychotherapy alone as a continuation/maintenance treatment. On the other hand, psychotherapy as opposed to no psychotherapy was associated with better social adjustment 1 year later.

Continuation medication treatment is also used following acute response to ECT and generally reduces the relapse/recurrence rate. By extrapolation from medication trials, patients should be followed up for relapse/recurrence of the disorder and should be maintained on antidepressant medication for at least 8 months. However, in some patients who have not responded to trials of many medications, but respond to ECT as acute treatment, continuation ECT is a treatment option; some of these ECT-responsive, medication-resistant patients will also not respond to continuation medication (Sackeim, Prudic, and Devanand, 1990; Sackeim, Prudic, Devanand, et al., 1990). There are no randomized trials of continuation ECT, but case reports suggest a potential role for this treatment. Psychotherapy alone following acute phase ECT has not been studied; given the apparent prophylactic efficacy of medication and continuation ECT in particularly refractory patients, continuation phase psychotherapy alone following acute phase ECT is not recommended.

Objectives and Indications for Maintenance Treatment

Guideline: Maintenance treatment is aimed at preventing a new episode of depression. Patients who have had three or more episodes of major depression are potential candidates for long-term maintenance

antidepressant medication. Maintenance medications are generally of the same type and dosage found effective in acute phase treatment. (Strength of Evidence = A.) Maintenance psychotherapy does not appear to be effective in preventing a recurrence, although it may delay the onset of the next episode. (Strength of Evidence = B.)

Patients who have had three episodes of major depression have a 90 percent chance of having another (NIMH, 1985). In fact, the World Health Organization (WHO) recommends considering maintenance treatment for patients who have experienced two depressive episodes within a 5-year period (Coppen, Mendelwicz, and Kielholz, 1986). Clinical issues that affect the decision for instituting maintenance medication include:

- Time between prior episodes.
- Severity of the episodes.
- Risk of suicide during the prior episodes.
- Acuteness of episode onset.
- Patient preference.
- Practitioner comfort in managing patients with recurrent depressions without maintenance medication.

Table 16 provides an overview of the considerations for maintenance medication based on the available maintenance phase studies, the NIMH Consensus Conference (NIMH, 1985) on maintenance treatments, and panel consensus. The appropriate length of maintenance treatment may vary from 1 year to a lifetime, depending on the patient's history (many, frequent episodes argue for longer periods); the likelihood of severe, precipitous recurrences; treatment side effects; and patient preference.

Table 16. Considerations for maintenance medication

Considerations	Strength of Indication
1. Three or more episodes of major depressive disorder	Very strongly recommended
2. Two episodes of major depressive disorder and	
(a) Family history[1] of bipolar disorder	Strongly recommended
(b) History of recurrence within 1 year after previously effective medication was discontinued	Strongly recommended
(c) A family history of recurrent major depression[1]	Strongly recommended
(d) Early onset (before age 20) of the first episode	Strongly recommended
(e) Both episodes were severe, sudden, or life-threatening in the past 3 years	Strongly recommended

[1]A family history is a positive, clear-cut history in one or more first-degree relatives.

The practitioner and patient should discuss the pros and cons of maintenance treatment before embarking on it. A consultation with a psychopharmacologist may be particularly useful when maintenance treatment is under consideration.

The panel's recommendations are based on the following considerations:

- Those with modest rather than full symptom control appear to have a poorer prognosis (Prien and Kupfer, 1986).
- Optimal symptom control requires optimal dosing.
- Lower imipramine maintenance dosages (roughly half the acute treatment dosage) are associated with poorer maintenance results (Prien, Balter, and Caffey, 1978) than is a full dosage (Frank, Kupfer, Perel, et al., 1990). However, the issue of maintenance dosing has not been fully evaluated for all antidepressants.
- Preferred maintenance medications are logically those with fewer long-term side effects, since adherence remains an issue.

Based on the evidence that patients with a family history of recurrent major depressive or bipolar I or II disorder are more likely themselves to have recurrent major depressive disorder (Winokur, 1991; Winokur and Kadrmas, 1989; Winokur and Wesner, 1987), it is logical to consider those with two episodes of major depressive disorder and such a family history as potential candidates for maintenance medication. Earlier age at onset of the initial episode of major depressive disorder is associated with a greater familial incidence of the disorder (Strober, 1984; Strober and Carlson, 1982; Winokur, 1979), as well as an earlier and more likely recurrence once treatment has ended (Giles, Jarrett, Biggs, et al., 1989; Giles, Jarrett, Roffwarg, et al., 1987).

Maintenance psychotherapy (at least in once-a-month sessions) does not appear to be effective in ultimately preventing a recurrence, though it may delay by months the onset of the next episode (Frank, Kupfer, Perel, et al., 1990). The efficacy of more frequent maintenance psychotherapy has not been evaluated. For selected patients with recurrent depression, such as those undergoing surgery; those who are pregnant or trying to become pregnant; and those in athletic competitions or occupational roles that preclude medication for a fixed, limited time period, maintenance psychotherapy may have an important role if the patient has had a thorough acute and continuation phase response to medication plus psychotherapy.

Continuation/Maintenance Phase Management with Medication

Guideline: There is very strong evidence that specific medications prevent relapse/recurrence in most patients with recurrent forms of major depressive disorder. Since the episode onset date may not be

readily determined, particularly in first-episode patients, most patients should receive the full therapeutic dosage of antidepressant drug for 4 to 9 months (the average duration of a major depressive episode) of continuation therapy after symptom remission is achieved. In those for whom the onset date is known, a somewhat shorter continuation phase may be attempted, but it should not be less than 4 months. For those with episodes of 2 years or more, it may be wise to pursue a continuation period of at least 9 months. Patients who have a recurrence shortly following continuation therapy withdrawal may require long-term maintenance medication. (Strength of Evidence = A.)

Evidence for Efficacy

Several double-blind extension trials for those who responded to acute phase amitriptyline are consistent with the notion that extended medication exposure following response to acute phase treatment is associated with a low relapse or recurrence rate (e.g., Mendels, Amin, Chouinard, et al., 1983; Othmer, Othmer, Stern, et al., 1983). However, to be certain that such exposure is in fact specifically benefiting patients, randomized, controlled continuation or maintenance trials are essential. These trials engage patients who have responded to acute phase treatment, and who are then randomly assigned and treated under double-blind conditions either with the medication to which they responded or with pill placebo. The relapse rates (if randomization occurs prior to continuation phase) or recurrence rates (if randomization occurs after continuation phase) are then compared between placebo and medication.

Mindham, Howland, and Shepherd (1973) established that continuation treatment with either amitriptyline or imipramine for 6 months was more beneficial (22 percent relapsed) than placebo (50 percent relapsed) for acute phase responders to these medications. Similar results were reported by Stein, Rickels, and Weise (1980), who randomly assigned acute phase amitriptyline responders to either amitriptyline (28 percent relapsed) or placebo (69 percent relapsed) for 6 months of continuation treatment.

In a randomized, double-blind controlled continuation maintenance trial reported in various publications (DiMascio, Klerman, Prusoff, 1975; Klerman, DiMascio, Weissman, et al., 1974; Paykel, DiMascio, Haskell, et al., 1975; Paykel, DiMascio, Klerman, et al., 1976), responders to acute phase amitriptyline (6 weeks) were randomly assigned to high- or low-contact case management psychotherapy while continuing amitriptyline. Two months later, while continuing high or low contact psychotherapy, patients were randomly assigned to (a) continued amitriptyline, (b) pill placebo, or (c) no medication for the next 8 months (largely a maintenance trial). Results revealed relapse/recurrence rates of 12.2 percent (amitriptyline) versus 29.2 percent (placebo) versus 26.6 percent (no medication) over the next 8 months. Psychotherapy had no effect on the relapse/recurrence rate.

Glen, Johnson, and Shepherd (1984) reported the multisite Medical Research Council Study involving 136 patients who, having responded to acute phase medication (practitioner's choice, median duration 8.5 weeks), were randomized to and treated under double-blind conditions for up to 3 years with lithium, amitriptyline, or placebo. Recurrence rates for amitriptyline were 30 percent (at 6 months postrandomization), 53 percent (at 12 months), 63 percent (at 24 months), and 69 percent (at 36 months). The corresponding rates for placebo were 66 percent, 67 percent, 78 percent, and 89 percent. Coppen, Ghose, Montgomery, et al. (1978) randomly assigned patients with major depression who responded to acute phase amitriptyline to either placebo or continued amitriptyline at the beginning of continuation treatment and followed them for 1 year. Again, a lower relapse/recurrence rate was associated with amitriptyline. Giller, Bialos, Harkness, et al. (1985) (see also Bialos, Giller, Jatlow, et al., 1982) randomly assigned outpatients with major depression who had recovered and been stabilized for at least 6 months to either continued amitriptyline or placebo. Eleven of 15 (73 percent) on placebo, compared with 1 of 9 (11 percent) on continued amitriptyline, had a recurrence within 1 year. Most patients in this study had been stable while in maintenance therapy for several years prior to the study.

For imipramine, double-blind extensions of acute phase treatment (from 6 to 12 weeks) also revealed that (1) those who responded by 6 weeks continued to respond to imipramine, and (2) some who partially responded by 6 weeks fully responded by 12 weeks (Liebowitz, Quitkin, Stewart, et al., 1988; Mann, Georgotas, Newton, et al., 1981; Peselow, Filippi, Goodnick, et al., 1989a,b; Quitkin, Stewart, McGrath, et al., 1988).

In a randomized, placebo-controlled double-blind 2-year maintenance trial, Prien, Klett, and Caffey (1973) found a distinct and significant advantage of imipramine over placebo for recurrent depression. Recurrence rate was 29 percent for imipramine versus 85 percent for placebo.

Randomized, double-blind placebo-controlled maintenance trials in mixed samples (bipolar plus unipolar, recurrent major depressive disorders) (Kane, Quitkin, Rifkin, et al., 1982; Prien, Kupfer, Mansky, et al., 1984) or bipolar patients only (Shapiro, Quitkin, and Fleiss, 1989) revealed similar prophylactic effects for imipramine as for amitriptyline. For example, in the unipolar group, Prien, Kupfer, Mansky, et al. (1984) found that 55 percent remained well after both 1 and 2 years of maintenance imipramine, compared with 30 percent and 25 percent, respectively, for placebo.

In the most definitive maintenance study to date (Frank, Kupfer, Perel, et al., 1990), a 22.6 percent recurrence rate was found for imipramine, compared with 78.2 percent for placebo over 3 years. Those in maintenance psychotherapy (with or without a placebo) suffered a 44.2 percent recurrence rate over the same period. The advantage of prolonged maintenance medication was recently reported for the same cohort after

5 years (Kupfer, Frank, Perel, et al., 1992). However, caution is warranted, because the type of acute treatment to which patients initially respond may dictate the relative efficacy of different maintenance treatments (Greenhouse, Stangl, Kupfer, et al., 1991).

Several open-label continuation/maintenance phase studies of fluoxetine in major depressive disorder in adult or geriatric patients suggest long-term efficacy (Cohn and Wilcox, 1985; Feighner, 1984; Rickels, Smith, Glaudin, et al., 1985). One randomized, double-blind placebo-controlled maintenance phase trial was conducted over a 1-year period on 222 psychiatric outpatients with major depressive disorder and compared fluoxetine to placebo (Montgomery, Dufour, Brion, et al., 1988). All patients had initially responded to a 6-week open trial with fluoxetine during acute phase treatment, and all were symptom-free for 4 to 5 months (continuation phase) prior to randomization for this maintenance study. All patients had had at least two episodes of major depression in the 5 years preceding this study. One hundred eighty-two completed the 1-year maintenance trial or developed a recurrence. On fluoxetine, 26 percent had a recurrence, compared to 57 percent on placebo—a significant difference. In a recent placebo-controlled, randomized study of sertraline for 44 weeks following acute phase response, placebo was associated with a 45.7 percent relapse/recurrence rate, compared to 13.0 percent for sertraline (Doogan and Caillard, 1992). Similar results are suggested for paroxetine (Montgomery and Dunbar, 1991).

The only randomized, placebo-controlled maintenance study in adults of an MAOI (phenelzine) found that phenelzine (at 45 or 60 mg/day) was associated with a much lower recurrence rate (30 percent) than placebo (over 80 percent) in the first 12 months of maintenance (Robinson, Lerfald, Bennett, et al., 1991). A similarly robust maintenance effect with phenelzine was found in a randomized, double-blind placebo-controlled maintenance trial in geriatric patients (Georgotas, McCue, and Cooper, 1989).

Other extension studies of acute phase treatment without placebo controls reveal similar findings for maprotiline (Coppen, Montgomery, Gupta, et al., 1976), doxepin (Feighner and Cohn, 1985), bupropion (Mendels, Amin, Chouinard, et al., 1983; Othmer, Othmer, Preskorn, et al., 1988), and trazodone (Fabre and Feighner, 1983; Feighner, 1984; Mann, Georgotas, Newton, et al., 1981). No randomized continuation/maintenance phase studies for amoxapine, fluvoxamine, desipramine, doxepin, isocarboxazid, protriptyline, tranylcypromine, or trimipramine were found.

In summary, strong evidence supports the use of specific medications to prevent relapse/recurrence in most patients with recurrent forms of major depressive disorder. Whether this efficacy extends to unstudied antidepressants is an open question, though logic and basic pharmacologic principles suggest that it does. Whether some patients (and which ones) can forgo maintenance treatment after 2 to 3 years is unstudied. If the practitioner attempts to discontinue maintenance treatment, the patient should be monitored closely for the initial 6 to 12 months following discontinuation of the medication.

Frequency of Visits

Guideline: Patients who have responded fully in the acute phase of treatment need to be seen only once every 1 to 3 months during the continuation and maintenance phases to evaluate symptoms, efficacy, and side effects and to promote adherence. (Strength of Evidence = B.)

If there is significant symptom breakthrough, the patient should be seen more quickly and monitored more frequently so that timely action can be taken. Early treatment of new episodes reduces the overall time that the patient is ill (Kupfer, Frank, McEachran, et al., 1990).

Medication Dosage Adjustments and Antidepressant Blood Levels

Guideline: During both the continuation and maintenance phases of treatment, the medication dosage should be maintained at the full dosage initially required to attain symptom remission in the acute phase treatment. (Strength of Evidence = B.)

A maintenance therapy trial (Frank, Kupfer, Perel, et al., 1990) showed a comparatively lower recurrence rate for patients taking imipramine at the full acute phase dosage than for those taking the lower maintenance dosage used in previous studies (Prien, Balter, and Caffey, 1978).

There is no need to check blood levels routinely during continuation or maintenance treatment. However, blood level determinations for those antidepressants whose minimal and/or maximum therapeutic levels are known may be needed if patients develop a toxic reaction or if the depressive episode recurs. For patients who develop another nonpsychiatric medical disorder requiring medication(s) that modify antidepressant levels, blood level determinations may also be helpful.

Symptom Breakthrough

Ten to 20 percent of patients report that some depressive symptoms return during continuation or maintenance treatment. This symptom breakthrough is often brief, mild, and self-limited. Support and observation are indicated. If the breakthrough is severe or prolonged, action is indicated. In some cases, symptoms may result from a change in antidepressant blood level due to induction of metabolic enzymes. If this cause is suspected, a blood level determination may be informative for medications whose lower therapeutic and toxic levels are known. Alternatively, daily doses can be increased empirically until symptom remission is again achieved. Caution is necessary, however, because symptom breakthrough may be associated with blood levels in the toxic range and some patients do not show marked side effects at these levels. The adjusted dosage is then continued until drug treatment is discontinued. Increased side effects during symptom breakthrough may be a clinical clue to an excessive drug level.

In some patients, symptom breakthrough is the result of the inability of the current medication to suppress symptoms. If dosage adjustment fails, consultation, augmentation, or alternative medications should be considered.

Discontinuation of Medication

Guideline: Antidepressant medications are generally safe, even with long-term use. However, medications should be discontinued if they are not required. All patients with a single episode of major depressive disorder are advised to discontinue medication after 4 to 9 months of continuation treatment since only 50 percent will have another episode of major depressive disorder. Even then, the next episode may be years hence. Whenever possible, the decision to discontinue treatment is made collaboratively with the full participation and knowledge of the patient. If the full depressive episode recurs during or shortly after discontinuation, the episode has not "run its course," and the full therapeutic dosage is typically reinstated. (Strength of Evidence = A.)

If a patient is reluctant to discontinue medication, it may be continued for another 3 to 6 months. However, a discussion of the basis for this reluctance is indicated.

Guideline: It is advisable to taper all TCAs on discontinuation if the patient has had exposure at therapeutic dosages for 3 months or more. A tapering schedule over 2 to 4 weeks is usually well tolerated. (Strength of Evidence = A.)

Rapid discontinuation of medication can result in insomnia, aches and pains, and nausea. Patients should be warned to expect transient sleep disturbance during medication tapering. A recent report suggests that, for imipramine, a more abrupt discontinuation is associated with a higher recurrence rate than is a more gradual schedule (Greenhouse, Stangl, Kupfer, et al., 1991). Thus, tapering over 6 to 8 weeks is also an option. It is unclear whether it is necessary to taper maprotiline and amoxapine.

Guideline: There is no evidence that bupropion, MAOIs, fluoxetine, paroxetine, sertraline, or trazodone must be tapered. (Strength of Evidence = B.)

If anxiolytics or sedative hypnotics have been used, they should be tapered to avoid rebound anxiety/insomnia. (These medications should generally not be used for more than 12 weeks of treatment, because their efficacy has not been established beyond this time frame. Furthermore, anxiolytics and sedative hypnotics are usually not required as adjuncts to standard antidepressants.)

If the major depressive episode recurs during or shortly after discontinuation, the depressive episode has not "run its course," and the full therapeutic dosage should be reinstated. Clinician or self-report symptom severity measures may provide a rapid, objective evaluation that makes it possible to determine whether the syndrome is actually returning or the patient is only experiencing transient anxiety/worry. Some patients manifest a transient mild return of some symptoms during tapered discontinuation. If this occurs, the speed of tapering should be slowed, but it may be continued.

Once tapered off medication, patients should be encouraged to monitor their symptoms. (Some practitioners provide patients with self-report scales to be completed monthly and mailed back for followup.) Persons who develop a new episode are most likely to do so within 8 months following discontinuation (Prien and Kupfer, 1986). Early treatment, if the full syndrome returns, should include the same treatment to which the patient previously responded. Early intervention reduces the length of the episode (Kupfer, Frank, and Perel, 1989).

Continuation/Maintenance Phase Management with Psychotherapy

Guideline: Continuation psychotherapy to improve psychosocial functioning may be added to the treatment regimen for those who respond to acute phase medication. (Strength of Evidence = C.) Maintenance psychotherapy as the sole treatment to prevent recurrence is generally not recommended unless the patient, for some reason (e.g., pregnancy), needs to avoid medication. (Strength of Evidence = B.)

The objective of continuation psychotherapy is the same as that for medication—to maintain the patient in an asymptomatic state. The efficacy of continuation psychotherapy alone as a treatment is not well established.

Cognitive Therapy

There are no randomized controlled trials of continuation or maintenance phase cognitive therapy. Indirect evidence from a few studies suggests that some patients who respond to cognitive therapy in the acute phase of treatment may continue to reap a prophylactic benefit once acute phase cognitive therapy is stopped, compared to those treated with only antidepressant medication in the acute phase.

In a recent study of cognitive therapy as an adjunct to pharmacotherapy, Miller and colleagues (1989) determined that patients given standard treatment (i.e., hospital milieu and pharmacotherapy), or cognitive therapy plus standard treatment, or social skills training plus standard treatment did not differ in acute symptom reduction after 3 weeks of hospitalization. After an additional 20 weeks of outpatient continuation treatment, however, both cognitive therapy plus standard treatment and social skills training plus standard treatment reduced self-reported depressive symptoms more than did medication plus clinical management alone—effects that were maintained at 6- and 12-month followup. By the end of outpatient treatment, patients with higher levels of cognitive distortion had responded better to cognitive therapy plus standard treatment or to social skills training plus standard treatment than to standard treatment alone. Conversely, persons with lower levels of cognitive distortion showed no preferential response. These few findings provide a very tentative basis to consider continuation cognitive therapy or other psychotherapies for those with residual symptoms after acute phase treatment, especially if they are cognitive in nature.

Some evidence suggests that continuation cognitive therapy in responders is beneficial compared to no continuation cognitive therapy. The relapse/recurrence rate following acute phase cognitive therapy in responders is on the order of 40 to 60 percent, based on naturalistic followup studies (Beck, Hollon, Young, et al., 1985; Covi and Lipman, 1987; Gallagher and Thompson, 1982; Gallagher-Thompson, Hanley-Peterson, and Thompson, 1990; Kovacs, Rush, Beck, et al., 1981; O'Leary and Beach, 1990; Ross and Scott, 1985; Shea, Elkin, Imber, et al., 1992). In contrast, only a 23 percent relapse rate was detected at 1-year followup for cognitive therapy responders who received 8 months of continuation cognitive therapy (Blackburn, Eunson, and Bishop, 1986). Similarly, the relapse rate was 19 percent in cognitive therapy responders given biweekly to monthly continuation cognitive therapy over 8 months, compared to a 44 percent relapse rate for those (in a separate trial) who received only acute phase cognitive therapy (Jarrett, Ramanan, Eaves, et al., 1992). While both reports suggest that continuation cognitive therapy may help to sustain the response to acute phase cognitive therapy, both are open trials without randomized comparison groups. Only a true randomized continuation/maintenance trial following acute phase response to cognitive therapy versus a control condition can determine whether continuation/maintenance cognitive therapy is effective.

Behavioral Therapy

No randomized controlled or open trials have been performed for either continuation or maintenance phase behavioral therapy.

Interpersonal Psychotherapy

Two studies of continuation/maintenance phase interpersonal psychotherapy are available. The first revealed that interpersonal psychotherapy (acute/continuation phase) resulted in better social/occupational/marital adjustment 1 year later than did no interpersonal psychotherapy, but the followup was naturalistic (Klerman, DiMascio, Weissman, et al., 1974). The second showed that maintenance interpersonal psychotherapy alone delayed, but did not ultimately prevent, a new recurrence in outpatients with highly recurrent major depressive disorder, who responded during the acute phase of treatment to the combination of imipramine plus interpersonal psychotherapy and who sustained the well state for 16 weeks of combined continuation phase treatment (Frank, Kupfer, Perel, et al., 1990).

Marital Therapy

No randomized controlled or open trials have been undertaken for either continuation or maintenance phase marital therapy.

Brief Dynamic Psychotherapy

There are no randomized controlled or open trials of either continuation or maintenance phase brief dynamic psychotherapy.

Factors Affecting Decisions about Continuation/Maintenance Therapies

Maintenance psychotherapy as the sole treatment to prevent recurrence of major depressive disorder is generally not recommended for two reasons. First, for those who have one or two episodes, maintenance treatment is usually not indicated. Second, for those who have had three or more episodes, maintenance medication has established efficacy, but maintenance psychotherapy alone (without medication) is less effective at preventing the next episode (Frank, Kupfer, Perel, et al., 1990; Weissman, Prusoff, DiMascio, et al., 1979). In selected clinical situations, such as during pregnancy, efforts to become pregnant, or times during which occupational demands require patients to take no medication, maintenance psychotherapy may be used for a limited time in an attempt to maintain a medication- and symptom-free state.

Given the strong evidence for prophylaxis against a new episode in patients taking medication, the few studies of psychotherapy, and the relatively disappointing prophylactic effects of maintenance psychotherapy in these studies, medication is the essential, if not the only needed, treatment to maintain symptomatic remission in highly recurrent depressions. However, evidence from some studies suggests a broader domain of improvement if medication and psychotherapy are combined for acute phase treatment (Klerman, DiMascio, Weissman, et al., 1974; Weissman, Klerman, Prusoff, et al., 1981). By logical extension, similar findings may be expected for continuation phase combined treatment in some patients.

The optimal length of therapy used as an adjunct to medication to resolve associated psychosocial problems has not been established. In practice, it is typically determined individually, based on resolution of these associated problems. The only formal study of continuation interpersonal psychotherapy used up to 16 sessions, once patients had symptomatically responded to acute treatment with medication over 8 weeks (Weissman, Prusoff, DiMascio, et al., 1979).

Frequency of Visits

Research on the optimal frequency of continuation or maintenance phase psychotherapy visits is lacking. The patient in continuation phase psychotherapy alone usually contracts with the therapist for followup visits at a frequency indicated by the type of psychotherapy and the degree of need (usually one to three times each month). The practitioner should continue to be available to the patient after acute phase treatment, if the symptoms return. If the patient is in the continuation or maintenance phase of treatment and is receiving psychotherapy along with medication, psychotherapy visits may be needed weekly for up to 20 sessions. Once therapy is discontinued, the prescribing physician should still see the patient at least once every 2 to 3 months to evaluate symptoms, reinforce adherence, and check medication side effects until the medication is discontinued.

Symptom Breakthrough

Guideline: It is important to inform patients that symptoms may recur during continuation/maintenance treatment and that the practitioner should be informed of them. (Strength of Evidence = A.)

Some patients will feel that they have failed and drop out of treatment if symptoms return. The practitioner should anticipate this tendency and educate the patient before continuation or maintenance phase treatment is begun. In the event of symptom breakthrough during continuation phase psychotherapy alone, the practitioner must distinguish between transient mild symptoms and a full relapse. For mild transient symptoms, the number of therapy visits may be increased in an attempt to resolve these symptoms. It is essential that the patient be informed both at the onset (when selecting acute treatment) and at the time of any significant symptom breakthrough that medications are potentially effective options. If the symptoms are more severe, persistent, disabling, or if the patient requests it, acute phase treatment with medication should be strongly considered.

Continuation/Maintenance Phase Management with the Combination of Medication and Psychotherapy

Continuation phase combined treatment is not uncommon practice, especially for patients with the more chronic or complex forms of depression that are often seen in tertiary care settings. The rationale for combined continuation treatment is to maintain symptom remission and to improve psychosocial function. It is unclear which patients specifically benefit from this combination. The general principles outlined for continuation or maintenance management with either medication or psychotherapy hold for combined treatment.

Evidence for Efficacy

Guideline: Assuming a full response to combined treatment in acute or continuation phases, the evidence shows that medication alone may be all that is necessary to prevent a recurrence. A substantial number of clinicians believe that some patients will benefit from targeted psychotherapies in continuation or maintenance phases if only partial symptomatic response or psychosocial restoration was obtained with medication alone. (Strength of Evidence = B.)

In an open trial of interpersonal psychotherapy combined with imipramine, 8.5 to 15.3 percent of patients relapsed during continuation phase treatment (Frank and Kupfer, 1987). One study found that patients who responded to acute phase medication alone showed improved, longer term psychosocial adjustment when interpersonal psychotherapy was included in continuation treatment (Klerman, DiMascio, Weissman, et al., 1974). However, in a randomized controlled maintenance trial of combined treatment, the prevention of recurrences obtained could be accounted for by medication (Frank, Kupfer, Perel, et al., 1990). That is, combined treatment did not add to the prophylaxis attained by medication alone.

Since maintenance medication without formal psychotherapy leads to sustained symptom remission for many patients in the maintenance phase, both those responding in the acute phase to medication alone (Klerman, DiMascio, Weissman, et al., 1974; Weissman, Klerman, Prusoff, et al., 1981) and those responding in the acute phase to combined treatment (Frank, Kupfer, Perel, et al., 1990), continuation and maintenance medication is the mainstay of prophylaxis for recurrent forms of major depressive disorder. Whether psychotherapy meaningfully adds to the prophylaxis found with continuation medication is unknown. Many practitioners believe psychotherapy is helpful in symptomatically unstable patients and helps to prevent relapse, especially in those with associated personality disorders or those with a previously chronic or complex course.

It is also unknown whether combined maintenance treatment with medication and psychotherapy helps similar, particularly problematic patients. The one maintenance randomized controlled trial that tested combined treatment excluded patients who had partial or poor interepisode recoveries from the recurrently depressed sample (Frank, Kupfer, Perel, et al., 1990).

Discontinuation of Treatment

Principles for discontinuing medication are as described earlier.

A Second Opinion or Referral

Primary Care Practitioners

The primary care practitioner may wish to obtain a second opinion from a psychiatrist or other mental health care professional regarding one or more of the following:

- Recommended medication management.
- Need for psychotherapy.
- Need for maintenance medication.
- Diagnostic consultation.
- Severe, recurrent, or psychotic depression.
- Need for light therapy.
- Presence of complex general medical problems.
- Poor adherence.
- Partial response to initial treatment(s).
- Need for ECT.
- Need for hospitalization.
- Need for involuntary commitment.
- Patient request.
- Symptom breakthrough after a positive acute phase response.

In general, the more specific the question(s), the more useful the consultation will be. The major difficulties in obtaining the consultation are:

- Timely availability of consultants.
- Geographical availability of consultants.
- Patient reluctance to see the mental health care professional.

It is optimal to establish a working relationship with one or more such professionals, who should make themselves easily and readily available to the primary care provider. Several medical schools now offer consultation by telephone to primary care providers who may be in geographically remote locations.

Many cases of major depressive disorder can be effectively treated in primary care settings, especially if diligent attention is paid to symptom assessment, dosage adjustment, psychosocial disabilities, and adherence. As with the treatment of hypertension, diabetes, hypercholesterolemia, and most other medical conditions, treatment of depression aims at optimal regulation of the disorder—not simply improvement. Acceptance of a partial response when full symptomatic remission and restoration of psychosocial function are possible may lead to greater chronicity, difficulty in subsequent treatment, and disability from or difficulties in managing associated general medical disorders, as well as unneeded pain and suffering. The practitioner is strongly encouraged to aim for full remission and not to delay consultation inappropriately in those who are not remitting.

Patients and Families

Persuading a patient to see a consultant can be difficult. This goal can be facilitated by providing patients and families with information about depression and by reassuring them that most consultations require only one or two visits, that most do not require inpatient treatment, and that the more severe forms of depression are medical conditions for which a wide range of treatments are available.

The practitioner should inform patients and families that they may request a second opinion at any time and that the practitioner, while beginning treatment, may later ask for a second opinion as well. Bringing up the possibility of consultation early (though many patients will not require it) can often avoid the patient's later rejection of the consultation, as it is then seen as part of a larger treatment plan. This strategy also reduces the demand that these patients, should they fail to respond fully, can make on primary care providers. Since the treatment of depression is rapidly changing, special expertise for selected cases can save patients time, money, and suffering.

Consultations with Mental Health Care Professionals

It is important that mental health care professionals be readily available (same day or next day) to provide an optimal consultation or second opinion to busy primary care providers. Too often, mental health care professionals leave primary care providers to cope with depressed patients for weeks prior to consultation. This experience frustrates practitioners, unnecessarily delays treatment, and causes patients unneeded anxiety and suffering.

Mental health care professionals should outline specific options or steps for the primary care provider and should provide patients with the same information. The mental health care professional often wants to obtain a history from both the patient and a friend or family member. The primary care provider should alert the patient to that possibility. Patients may themselves have questions in addition to those already raised with the primary care provider. Patients and families should be encouraged to raise those questions with both primary care providers and consultants. Finally, mental health care professionals should provide a rapid oral response and a brief written response to the primary care provider and should be open to subsequent patient visits, if needed.

References

Abou-Saleh MT, Coppen A. Classification of depression and response to antidepressant therapies. Br J Psychiatry 1983;143:601-3.

Akiskal HS. A proposed clinical approach to chronic and "resistant" depressions: evaluation and treatment. J Clin Psychiatry 1985;46:32-6.

Altamura AC, Mauri M. Plasma concentrations, information and therapy adherence during long-term treatment with antidepressants. Br J Clin Pharmacol 1985;20(6):714-6.

American Medical Association. Drug evaluations. Chicago: AMA; 1990.

American Psychiatric Association. Diagnostic and statistical manual of mental disorders. 3rd ed. rev. Washington, DC: American Psychiatric Press; 1987.

Amsterdam J, Brunswick DJ, Mendels J. High dose desipramine, plasma drug levels and clinical response. J Clin Psychiatry 1979;40(3):141-3.

Amsterdam J, Brunswick DJ, Mendels J. The clinical application of tricyclic antidepressant pharmacokinetics and plasma levels. Am J Psychiatry 1980;137:653-62.

Anderson CM, Griffin S, Rossi A, Pagonis I, Holder DP, Treiber R. A comparative study of the impact of education vs. process groups for families of patients with affective disorders. Fam Process 1986;25(2):185-205.

Anton RF, Burch EA. Amoxapine versus amitriptyline combined with perphenazine in the treatment of psychotic depression. Am J Psychiatry 1990;147(9):1203-8.

Anton RF, Sexauer JD. Efficacy of amoxapine in psychotic depression. Am J Psychiatry 1983;140(10):1344-7.

Appelbaum PS, Russell GV, Orsulak PJ, Schildkraut JJ. Clinical utility of tricyclic antidepressant blood levels: a case report. Am J Psychiatry 1979;136:339-41.

Avery D, Lubrano A. Depression treated with imipramine and ECT: the DeCarolis study reconsidered. Am J Psychiatry 1979;136:559-62.

Avery D, Winokur G. The efficacy of electroconvulsive therapy and antidepressants in depression. Biol Psychiatry 1977;12(4):507-23.

Bandura A. Social learning theory. Englewood Cliffs, NJ: Prentice-Hall; 1977.

Baumann P. New aspects in research on blood levels and bioavailability of antidepressants. Psychopathology 1986;19 Suppl 2:79-84.

Beach SRH, Arias I, O'Leary KD. Risk for depression as a factor of social support. Paper presented at: Eastern Psychological Association; 1983; Philadelphia.

Beach SRH, Jouriles EN, O'Leary KD. Extramarital sex: impact on depression and commitment in couples seeking marital therapy. J Sex Marital Ther 1985;11:99-108.

Beasley CM, Sayler ME, Cunningham GE, Weiss AM, Masica DN. Fluoxetine in tricyclic refractory major depressive disorder. J Affect Disord 1990;20:193-200.

Beck AT, Hollon SD, Young JE, Bedrosian RC, Budenz D. Treatment of depression with cognitive therapy and amitriptyline. Arch Gen Psychiatry 1985;42:142-8.

Beck AT, Rush AJ, Shaw BF, Emery G. Cognitive therapy of depression. New York: Guilford Press; 1979.

Beck AT, Ward CH, Mendelson M, Mock J, Erbaugh J. An inventory for measuring depression. Arch Gen Psychiatry 1961;4:561-71.

Bellack AS, Hersen M, Himmelhoch JM. A comparison of social-skills training, pharmacotherapy and psychotherapy for depression. Behav Res Ther 1983;21(2):101-7.

Bialos D, Giller E, Jatlow P, Docherty J, Harkness L. Recurrence of depression after discontinuation of long-term amitriptyline treatment. Am J Psychiatry 1982;139(3):325-9.

Bielski RJ, Friedel RO. Prediction of tricyclic antidepressant response: a critical review. Arch Gen Psychiatry 1976;33:1479-89.

Blackburn IM, Bishop S. Changes in cognition with pharmacotherapy and cognitive therapy. Br J Psychiatry 1983;143:609-17.

Blackburn IM, Bishop S, Glen AIM, Whalley LJ, Christie JE. The efficacy of cognitive therapy in depression: a treatment trial using cognitive therapy and pharmacotherapy, each alone and in combination. Br J Psychiatry 1981;139:181-9.

Blackburn IM, Eunson KM, Bishop S. A two-year naturalistic follow-up of depressed patients treated with cognitive therapy, pharmacotherapy and a combination of both. J Affect Disord 1986;10:67-75.

Bothwell S, Weissman MM. Social impairments four years after an acute depressive episode. Am J Orthopsychiatry 1977;47:231-7.

Bourin MS, Kergueris MF, Lapierre YD. Therapeutic monitoring of treatment with antidepressants. Psychiat J Univ Ottawa 1989;14:460-2.

Bowers WA. Treatment of depressed in-patients: cognitive therapy plus medication, relaxation plus medication, and medication alone. Br J Psychiatry 1990;156:73-8.

Brandon S, Cowley P, McDonald C, Neville P, Palmer R, Wellstood-Eason S. Electroconvulsive therapy: results in depressive illness from the Leicestershire trial. Br Med J 1984;288(6410):22-5.

Brown GW, Harris T. Social origins of depressions: a study of psychiatric disorders in women. London: Tavistock Press; 1978.

Brown RA, Lewinsohn PM. A psychoeducational approach to the treatment of depression: comparison of group, individual, and minimal contact procedures. J Consult Clin Psychol 1984;52(5):774-83.

Brown RP, Frances A, Kocsis JH, Mann JJ. Psychotic vs non-psychotic depression: comparison of treatment response. J Nerv Ment Dis 1982; 170(10):635-7.

Brown RP, Sweeney J, Frances A, Kocsis JH, Loutsche E. Age as a predictor of treatment response in endogenous depression. J Clin Psychopharmacol 1983; 3:176-8.

Carney RM, Rich MW, Freedland KE, Saini J, teVelde A, Simeone C, Clark K. Major depressive disorder predicts cardiac events in patients with coronary artery disease. Psychosom Med 1988;50:627-33.

Carney RM, Rich MW, teVelde A, Saini J, Clark K, Freedland KE, editors. The incidence, significance and detection of depression in patients with suspected coronary artery disease. Proceedings of NIMH Conference on Mental Disorders in General Health Care Settings; 1985 Jun 26-27; Seattle. 1987a. p. 37-9.

Carney RM, Rich MW, teVelde A, Saini J, Clark K, Jaffe AS. Major depressive disorder in coronary artery disease. Am J Cardiol 1987b;60:1273-5.

Chan CH, Janicak PG, Davis JM, Altman E, Andriukaitis S, Hedeker D. Response of psychotic and nonpsychotic depressed patients to tricyclic antidepressants. J Clin Psychiatry 1987;48:197-200.

Charney DS, Nelson JC. Delusional and nondelusional unipolar depression: further evidence for distinct subtypes. Am J Psychiatry 1981;138:328-33.

Charney DS, Price LH, Heninger GR. Desipramine-yohimbine combination treatment of refractory depression: implications for the beta-adrenergic receptor hypothesis of antidepressant action. Arch Gen Psychiatry 1986;43(12):1155-61.

Cohn JB, Wilcox C. A comparison of fluoxetine, imipramine, and placebo in patients with major depressive disorder. J Clin Psychiatry 1985;46(3 Pt 2):26-31.

Cole JO, Schatzberg AF, Sniffin C, Zolner J, Cole JP. Trazodone in treatment-resistant depression: an open study. J Clin Psychopharmacol 1981;1 Suppl:49-54.

Coppen A, Ghose K, Montgomery S, Rama Rao VA, Bailey J, Christiansen J, Mikkleson PL, van Praag HM, van de Poel F, Minsker EJ, Kozulja VG, Matussek N, Kungkunz G, Jorgensen A. Amitriptyline plasma-concentration and clinical effect: a World Health Organisation Collaborative Study. Lancet 1978; 1(8055):63-6.

Coppen A, Mendelwicz J, Kielholz P. Pharmacotherapy of depressive disorders: a consensus statement. Geneva: World Health Organization; 1986.

Coppen A, Montgomery SA, Gupta RK, Bailey JE. A double-blind comparison of lithium carbonate and maprotiline in the prophylaxis of the affective disorders. Br J Psychiatry 1976;128:479-85.

Corne SJ, Hall JR. A double-blind comparative study of fluoxetine and dothiepin in the treatment of depression in general practice. Int Clin Psychopharmacol 1989;4(3):245-54.

Corney RH. Marital problems and treatment outcome in depressed women: a clinical trial of social work intervention. Br J Psychiatry 1987;151:652-9.

Covi L, Lipman RS. Cognitive behavioral group psychotherapy combined with imipramine in major depression. Psychopharmacol Bull 1987;23(1):173-6.

Cross design synthesis: a new strategy for medical effectiveness research. Washington, DC: US GAO; 1992. Report No. B244808.

Davidson JR, McLeod MN, Kurland AA, White HL. Antidepressant drug therapy in psychotic depression. Br J Psychiatry 1977;131:493-6.

Davidson J, McLeod M, Law-Yone B, Linnoila M. A comparison of electroconvulsive therapy and combined phenelzine-amitriptyline in refractory depression. Arch Gen Psychiatry 1978;35(5):639-42.

Davidson J, Pelton S. Forms of atypical depression and their response to antidepressant drugs. Psychiatry Res 1986;17:87-95.

de Jong R, Treiber R, Henrich G. Effectiveness of two psychological treatments for inpatients with severe and chronic depressions. Cognitive Ther Res 1986;10:645-63.

DeCarolis V, Gilberti F, Roccatagliata G, et al. Imipramine and electroshock in the treatment of depression: a clinical statistical analysis of 437 cases. Dis Nerv Syst 1964;25:29-42.

Depression Guideline Panel. Depression in primary care: detection, diagnosis, and treatment. Technical report. Number 5. Rockville, MD: US Department of Health and Human Services, Public Health Service; forthcoming.

DiMascio A, Klerman GL, Prusoff BA. Relative safety of amitriptyline in maintenance treatment of depression. Arch Gen Psychiatry 1975;160:34-41.

DiMascio A, Klerman GL, Weissman MM, Prusoff BA, Neu C, Moore P. A control group for psychotherapy research in acute depression: one solution to ethical and methodological issues. J Psychiatr Res 1979;15:189-97.

DiMascio A, Weissman MM, Prusoff BA, Neu C, Zwilling M, Klerman GL. Differential symptom reduction by drugs and psychotherapy in acute depression. Arch Gen Psychiatry 1979;36:1450-6.

Dinan TG, Barry S. A comparison of electroconvulsive therapy with a combined lithium and tricyclic combination among depressed tricyclic nonresponders. Acta Psychiatr Scand 1989;80:97-100.

Dobson KS. A meta-analysis of the efficacy of cognitive therapy for depression. J Consult Clin Psychol 1989;46(3):414-9.

Doogan DP, Caillard V. Sertraline in the prevention of depression. Br J Psychiatry 1992;160:217-22.

Dornseif BE, Dunlop SR, Potvin JH, Wernicke JF. Effect of dose escalation after low-dose fluoxetine therapy. Psychopharmacol Bull 1989;25(1):71-9.

Eddy DM, Hasselblad V, Schacter R. A Bayesian method for synthesizing evidence: the confidence profile method. Int J Technol Assess Health Care 1990;6:31-5.

Electroconvulsive therapy. Psychiatr Clin North Am 1991,14(4):793-1016.

Elkin I, Shea TM, Watkins JT, Imber SD, Sotsky SM, Collins JF, Glass DR, Pilkonis PA, Leber WR, Docherty JP, Fiester SJ, Parloff MB. National Institute of Mental Health Treatment of Depression Collaborative Research Program. General effectiveness of treatments. Arch Gen Psychiatry 1989;46:971-82.

Fabre LF Jr, Feighner JP. Long-term therapy for depression with trazodone. J Clin Psychiatry 1983;44(1):17-21.

Fairchild CJ, Rush AJ, Vasavada N, Giles DE, Khatami M. Which depressions respond to placebo? Psychiatry Res 1986;18(3):217-26.

Fawcett J, Scheftner W, Clark D, Hedeker D, Gibbons R, Coryell W. Clinical predictors of suicide in patients with major affective disorders: a controlled prospective study. Am J Psychiatry 1987;144:35-40.

Feet PO, Larsen S, Robak OH. A double blind study in out-patients with primary non-agitated depression treated with imipramine in combination with placebo, diazepam or dixyrazine. Acta Psychiatr Scand 1985;72(4):334-40.

Feighner JP. Trazodone in major affective disorders. Psychopathology 1984;17 Suppl 2:15-23.

Feighner JP, Brauzer B, Gelenberg AJ, Gomez E, Kiev A, Kurland ML, Weiss BL. A placebo-controlled multicenter trial of Limbitrol versus its components (amitriptyline and chlordiazepoxide) in the symptomatic treatment of depressive illness. Psychopharmacology 1979;61(2):217-25.

Feighner JP, Cohn JB. Double-blind comparative trials of fluoxetine and doxepin in geriatric patients with major depressive disorder. J Clin Psychiatry 1985;46(3):20-5.

Ferster CB. A functional analysis of depression. Am Psychol 1973;28(10):857-70.

Foley SH, Rounsaville BJ, Weissman MM, Sholomskas D, Chevron E. Individual vs. conjoint interpersonal psychotherapy for depressed patients with marital disputes. Paper presented at: Annual meeting of the American Psychiatric Association; 1987 May; Chicago.

Frances A, Brown RP, Kocsis JH, Mann JJ. Psychotic depression: a separate entity? Am J Psychiatry 1981;138:831-3.

Frank E, Kupfer DJ. Efficacy of combined imipramine and interpersonal psychotherapy. Psychopharmacol Bull 1987;23(1):4-7.

Frank E, Kupfer DJ. Axis II personality disorders and personality features in treatment-resistant and refractory depression. In: Roose SP, Glassman AH, editors. Treatment strategies for refractory depression. Washington, DC: American Psychiatric Press; 1990. p. 205-21.

Frank E, Kupfer DJ, Jacob M, Jarrett D. Personality features and response to acute treatment in recurrent depression. J Pers Disord 1987;1(1):14-26.

Frank E, Kupfer DJ, Perel JM, Cornes C, Jarrett DB, Mallinger AG, Thase ME, McEachran AB, Grochocinski VJ. Three-year outcomes for maintenance therapies in recurrent depression. Arch Gen Psychiatry 1990;47:1093-9.

Frank E, Prien RF, Jarrett JB, Keller MB, Kupfer DJ, Lavori P, Rush AJ, Weissman MM. Conceptualization and rationale for consensus definitions of terms in major depressive disorder: response, remission, recovery, relapse, and recurrence. Arch Gen Psychiatry 1991;48:851-5.

Freeman CPL, Basson JV, Creighton A. Double blind controlled trial of ECT and simulated ECT in depressive illness. Lancet 1978;1(8067):738-40.

Friedman AS. Interaction of drug therapy with marital therapy in depressed patients. Arch Gen Psychiatry 1975;32:619-37.

Gallagher DE, Thompson LW. Treatment of major depressive disorder in older adult outpatients with brief psychotherapies. Psychotherapy: theory, research, and practice 1982;19(4):482-90.

Gallagher DE, Thompson LW. Effectiveness of psychotherapy for both endogenous and nonendogenous depression in older adult outpatients. J Gerontol 1983;38(6):707-12.

Gallagher-Thompson D, Hanley-Peterson P, Thompson LW. Maintenance of gains versus relapse following brief psychotherapy for depression. J Consult Clin Psychol 1990;58(3):371-4.

Gangadhar BN, Kapur RL, Kalyanasundaram S. Comparison of electroconvulsive therapy with imipramine in endogenous depression: a double blind study. Br J Psychiatry 1982;141:367-71.

Georgotas A, McCue RE, Cooper TB. A placebo-controlled comparison of nortriptyline and phenelzine in maintenance therapy of elderly depressed patients. Arch Gen Psychiatry 1989;46:783-6.

Giles DE, Jarrett RB, Biggs MM, Guzick DS, Rush AJ. Clinical predictors of recurrence in depression. Am J Psychiatry 1989;146:764-7.

Giles DE, Jarrett RB, Roffwarg HP, Rush AJ. Reduced REM latency: a predictor of recurrence in depression. Neuropsychopharmacology 1987;1:33-9.

Giller E Jr, Bialos D, Harkness L, Jatlow P, Waldo M. Long-term amitriptyline in chronic depression. Hillside J Clin Psychiatry 1985;7(1):16-33.

Glassman AH, Kantor SJ, Shostak M. Depression, delusions, and drug response. Am J Psychiatry 1975;132(7):716-9.

Glassman AH, Schildkraut JJ, Orsulak PJ, et al. Tricyclic antidepressant blood level measurements and clinical outcome: an APA task force report. Am J Psychiatry 1985;142:155-62.

Glen AIM, Johnson AL, Shepherd M. Continuation therapy with lithium and amitriptyline in unipolar depressive illness: a randomized, double-blind, controlled trial. Psychol Med 1984;14(1):37-50.

Gonzales LR, Lewinsohn PM, Clarke GN. Longitudinal follow-up of unipolar depressives: an investigation of predictors of relapse. J Consult Clin Psychol 1985;53:461-9.

Goodwin FK, Jamison KR. Manic-depressive illness. New York: Oxford University Press; 1990.

Greenhouse JB, Stangl D, Kupfer DJ, Prien RF. Methodologic issues in maintenance therapy clinical trials. Arch Gen Psychiatry 1991;48(4):313-8.

Gregory S, Shawcross CR, Gill D. The Nottingham ECT study—a double blind comparison of bilateral, unilateral and simulated ECT in depression. Br J Psychiatry 1985;146:520-4.

Guy W. ECDEU assessment manual for psychopharmacology. Washington, DC: US Department of Health, Education, and Welfare; 1976.

Hall RCW, Popkin MK, Devaul RA, Faillace LA, Stickney SK. Physical illness presenting as psychiatric disease. Arch Gen Psychiatry 1978;35:1315-20.

Hamilton M. A rating scale for depression. J Neurol Neurosurg Psychiatry 1960;23:56-62.

Hamilton M. Development of a rating scale for primary depressive illness. Br J Soc Clin Psychol 1968;6:278-96.

Hamilton M. The effect of treatment on the melancholias (depressions). Br J Psychiatry 1982;140:223-30.

Hersen M, Bellack AS, Himmelhoch JM, Thase ME. Effects of social skills training, amitriptyline, and psychotherapy in unipolar depressed women. Behav Ther 1984;15:21-40.

Hinchliffe M, Hooper D, Roberts FJ. The melancholy marriage. New York: Wiley; 1978.

Hogg JA, Deffenbacher JL. A comparison of cognitive and interpersonal-process group therapies in the treatment of depression among college students. J Couns Psychol 1988;35(3):304-10.

Hollon SD, DeRubeis RJ, Seligman MEP. Cognitive therapy and the prevention of depression. Appl Prev Psychology 1992;1:89-95.

Hollon SD, Shelton RC, Loosen PT. Cognitive therapy in relation to pharmacotherapy for depression. J Consult Clin Psychol 1991;59:88-99.

Hooley JM, Orley J, Teasdale JD. Levels of expressed emotion and relapse in depressed outpatients. Br J Psychiatry 1986;148:642-7.

Hough RL, Landsverk JA, Karno M, Burnam MA, Timbers DM, Escobar JI, Regier DA. Utilization of health and mental health services by Los Angeles Mexican Americans and non-Hispanic whites. Arch Gen Psychiatry 1987;44:702-9.

Howarth BG, Grace MGA. Depression, drugs, and delusions. Arch Gen Psychiatry 1985;42:1145-7.

Jacobson NS, Holtzworth-Munroe A, Schmaling KB. Marital therapy and spouse involvement in the treatment of depression, agoraphobia, and alcoholism. J Consult Clin Psychol 1989;57(1):5-10.

Jacobson NS, Schmaling KB, Salusky S, Follette V, Dobson K. Marital therapy as an adjunct treatment for depression. Paper presented at: Annual meeting of the Association for the Advancement of Behavior Therapy; 1987 Nov; Boston.

Jarrett RB, Ramanan J, Eaves GG, Kobes R, Basco MR, Rush AJ. How prophylactic is cognitive therapy in treating depressed outpatients? Paper presented at: The World Congress of Cognitive Therapy; 1992 Jun; Toronto, Canada.

Johnson J, Weissman MM, Klerman GL. Service utilization and social morbidity associated with depressive symptoms in the community. JAMA 1992;267:1478-83.

Johnstone EC, Lawler P, Stevens M, Deakin JFW, Frith CD, McPherson K, Crow TJ. The Northwick Park Electroconvulsive Therapy Trial. Lancet 1980;2:1317-20.

Kane JM, Quitkin FM, Rifkin A, Ramos-Lorenzi JR, Nayak DD, Howard A. Lithium carbonate and imipramine in the prophylaxis of unipolar and bipolar II illness: a prospective, placebo-controlled comparison. Arch Gen Psychiatry 1982;39(9):1065-9.

Kaskey GB, Nasr S, Meltzer HY. Drug treatment in delusional depression. Psychiatry Res 1980;2(3):267-77.

Kathol RG, Wenzel RP. Natural history of symptoms of depression and anxiety during inpatient treatment on general medicine wards. J Gen Intern Med 1992;7:287-93.

Keitner GI, Ryan CE, Miller LW, Kohn R, Epstein NB. 12-month outcome of patients with major depression and comorbid psychiatric or medical illness (compound depression). Am J Psychiatry 1991;148:345-50.

Klerman GL, DiMascio A, Weissman MM, Prusoff B, Paykel ES. Treatment of depression by drugs and psychotherapy. Am J Psychiatry 1974;131(2):186-92.

Klerman GL, Weissman MM. Interpersonal psychotherapy (IPT) and drugs in the treatment of depression. Pharmacopsychiatry 1987;20:3-7.

Klerman GL, Weissman MM, Rounsaville BJ, Chevron RS. Interpersonal psychotherapy of depression. New York: Basic Books; 1984.

Kornblith SJ, Rehm LP, O'Hara MW, Lamparski DM. The contribution of self-reinforcement training and behavioral assignments to the efficacy of self-control therapy for depression. Cognitive Ther Res 1983;7(6):499-528.

Kovacs M, Rush AJ, Beck AT, Hollon SD. Depressed outpatients treated with cognitive therapy or pharmacotherapy: a one-year follow-up. Arch Gen Psychiatry 1981;38:33-41.

Kravitz HM, Fogg L, Fawcett J, Edwards J. Antidepressant or antianxiety? A study of the efficacy of antidepressant medication. Psychiatry Res 1990;32:141-9.

Kroessler D. Relative efficacy rates for therapies of delusional depression. Conv Ther 1985;1:173-82.

Kupfer DJ. Long-term treatment of depression. J Clin Psychiatry 1991;52(Suppl 5):28-34.

Kupfer DJ, Frank E, McEachran AB, Grochocinski VJ. Delta sleep ratio: a biological correlate of early recurrence in unipolar affective disorder. Arch Gen Psychiatry 1990;47(12):1100-5.

Kupfer DJ, Frank E, Perel JM. The advantage of early treatment intervention in recurrent depression. Arch Gen Psychiatry 1989;46:771-5.

Kupfer DJ, Frank E, Perel JM, Cornes C, Mallinger AG, Thase ME, McEachran AB, Grochocinski VJ. Five-year outcome for maintenance therapies in recurrent depression. Arch Gen Psychiatry 1992;49:769-73.

Kupfer DJ, Spiker DG. Refractory depression: prediction of non-response by clinical indicators. J Clin Psychiatry 1981;42:307-12.

Lambourn J, Gill D. A controlled comparison of simulated and real ECT. Br J Psychiatry 1978;133:514-9.

Last CG, Thase ME, Hersen M, Bellack AS, Himmelhoch JM. Patterns of attrition for psychosocial and pharmacologic treatments of depression. J Clin Psychiatry 1985;46(9):361-6.

Lewinsohn PM, Antonuccio DA, Steinmetz J, Teri L. The coping with depression course: a psychoeducational intervention for unipolar depression. Eugene, OR: Castalia Press; 1984.

Lewinsohn P, Clarke G. Group treatment of depressed individuals: the "coping with depression" course. Adv Behav Res Ther 1984;6:99-114.

Liebowitz MR, Quitkin FM, Stewart JW, McGrath PJ, Harrison W, Rabkin JG, Tricamo E, Markowitz JS, Klein DF. Psychopharmacologic validation of atypical depression. J Clin Psychiatry 1984;45(7 Pt 2):22-5.

Liebowitz MR, Quitkin FM, Stewart JW, McGrath PJ, Harrison WM, Markowitz JS, Rabkin JG, Tricamo E, Goetz DM, Klein DF. Antidepressant specificity in atypical depression. Arch Gen Psychiatry 1988;45(2):129-37.

Lipper S, Murphy DL, Slater S, Buchsbaum MS. Comparative behavioral effects of clorgyline and pargyline in man: a preliminary evaluation. Psychopharmacology 1979;62:123-8.

Luborsky L. Principles of psychoanalytic psychotherapy. New York: Basic Books; 1984.

Lustman PJ, Amado H, Wetzel RD. Depression in diabetics: a critical appraisal. Compr Psychiatry 1983;1:65-74.

Lustman PJ, Griffith LS, Clouse RE. Depression in adults with diabetes: results of 5-year follow-up study. Diabetes Care 1988;11:605-12.

Lustman PJ, Griffith LS, Clouse RE, Cryer PE. Psychiatric illness in diabetes: relationship to symptoms and glucose control. J Nerv Ment Dis 1986;174:736-42.

Lykouras E, Malliaras D, Christodoulou GN, Moussas G, Christodoulou D, Tzonou A. Delusional depression: phenomenology and response to treatment. Psychopathology 1986a;19(4):157-64.

Lykouras E, Malliaras D, Christodoulou GN, Papakostas Y, Voulgari A, Tzonou A, Stefanis C. Delusional depression: phenomenology and response to treatment: a prospective study. Acta Psychiatr Scand 1986b;73(3):324-9.

Magni G, Fisman M, Helmes E. Clinical correlates of ECT-resistant depression in the elderly. J Clin Psychiatry 1988;49:405-7.

Maj M, Veltro F, Pirozzi R, Lobrace S, Magliano L. Pattern of recurrence of illness after recovery from an episode of major depression: a prospective study. Am J Psychiatry 1992;149:795-800.

Malan DH. The frontier of brief psychotherapy. New York: Plenum Press; 1976.

Malan DH. Individual psychotherapy and the science of psychodynamics. London: Butterworths; 1979.

Mandel MR, Welch CA, Mieskie M, McCormick M. Prediction of response to ECT in tricyclic-intolerant or tricyclic-resistant depressed patients. McLean Hosp J 1977;2:203-9.

Mann, J. Time-limited psychotherapy. Cambridge, MA: Harvard University Press; 1973.

Mann JJ, Georgotas A, Newton R, Gershon S. A controlled study of trazodone, imipramine, and placebo in outpatients with endogenous depression. J Clin Psychopharmacol 1981;1(2):75-80.

McDonnell-Douglas Employee Assistance Program Study, 1989, 1990 study.

McGrath PJ, Stewart JW, Harrison W, Quitkin FM. Treatment of tricyclic refractory depression with a monoamine oxidase inhibitor. Psychopharmacol Bull 1987;23:169-72.

McLean PD, Hakstian AR. Clinical depression: comparative efficacy of outpatient treatments. J Consult Clin Psychol 1979;47(5):818-36.

McLean PD, Hakstian AR. Relative endurance of unipolar depression treatment effects: longitudinal follow-up. J Consult Clin Psychol 1990;58(4):482-8.

McLean PD, Ogston K, Grauer L. A behavioral approach to the treatment of depression. J Behav Ther Exper Psychiatry 1973;4:323-30.

Medical Research Council. Clinical trial of the treatment of depressive illness. Br Med J 1965;5439:881-6.

Mendels J, Amin MM, Chouinard G, Cooper AJ, Miles JE, Remick RA, Saxena B, Secunda SK, Singh AN. A comparative study of bupropion and amitriptyline in depressed outpatients. J Clin Psychiatry 1983;44(5 Pt 2):118-20.

Miller IW, Norman WH, Bishop SB, Keitner GI, Dow MG. Cognitive-behavioral treatment of depressed inpatients. Behav Ther 1989;20:25-47.

Mindham BA. A comparison of maprotiline (Ludiomil) and amitriptyline (2). J Int Med Res 1977;5 Suppl 4:25-33.

Mindham RHS, Howland C, Shepherd M. An evaluation of continuation therapy with tricyclic antidepressants in depressive illness. Psychol Med 1973;3:5-17.

Minter RE, Mandel MR. A prospective study of the treatment of psychotic depression. Am J Psychiatry 1979a;136(11):1470-2.

Minter RE, Mandel M. The treatment of psychotic major depressive disorder with drugs and electroconvulsive therapy. J Nerv Ment Dis 1979b;167(12):726-33.

Mintz J, Mintz LI, Arruda MJ, Hwang SS. Treatments of depression and the functional capacity to work. Arch Gen Psychiatry 1992;49(10):761-8.

Montgomery SA, Dufour H, Brion S, Gailledreau J, Laqueille X, Ferrey G, Moron P, Parant-Lucena N, Singer L, Danion JM, et al. The prophylactic efficacy of fluoxetine in unipolar depression. Br J Psychiatry 1988;153(Suppl 3):69-76.

Montgomery SA, Dunbar GC. Paroxetine and placebo in the long-term maintenance of depressed patients. Paper presented at: American College of Neuropsychopharmacology; 1991 Dec; San Juan, Puerto Rico.

Moon CA, Davey A. The efficacy and residual effects of trazodone (150 mg nocte) and mianserin in the treatment of depressed general practice patients. Psychopharmacology (Berlin) 1988;95 Suppl:S7-13.

Moradi SR, Muniz CE, Belar CD. Male delusional depressed patients: response to treatment. Br J Psychiatry 1979;135:136-8.

Murphy GE, Simons AD, Wetzel RD, Lustman PJ. Cognitive therapy and nortriptyline, singly and together, in the treatment of depression. Arch Gen Psychiatry 1984;41:33-41.

Myers ED, Calvert EJ. Information, compliance and side-effects: a study of patients on antidepressant medication. Br J Clin Pharmacol 1984;17:21-5.

Neimeyer RA, Feixas G. The role of homework and skill acquisition in the outcome of group cognitive therapy for depression. Behav Ther 1990;21:281-92.

Neimeyer RA, Heath A, Strauss J. Personal reconstruction during group cognitive therapy for depression. In: Epting F, Landfield AW, editors. Anticipating personal construct psychology. Lincoln, NE: University of Nebraska Press; 1985. p. 180-95.

Neimeyer RA, Weiss ME. Cognitive and symptomatic predictors of outcome of group therapies for depression. J Cognitive Psychother: Int Q 1990;4(1):23-32.

Nelson JC, Bowers MB Jr. Delusional unipolar depression: description and drug response. Arch Gen Psychiatry 1978;35:1321-8.

Nezu AM. Efficacy of a social problem-solving therapy for unipolar depression. J Consult Clin Psychol 1986;54:196-202.

Nezu AM, Perri MG. Social problem-solving therapy for unipolar depression: an initial dismantling investigation. J Consult Clin Psychol 1989;57(3):408-13.

NIMH Consensus Development Conference Statement. Mood disorders: pharmacologic prevention of recurrences. Am J Psychiatry 1985;142:469-76.

NIMH Consensus Development Conference: The diagnosis and treatment of depression in late life. Bethesda, MD: 1991 Nov 4-6.

Nolen WA, Van De Putte JJ, Dijken WA, Kamp JS. L-5HTP in depression resistant to reuptake inhibitors: an open comparative study with tranylcypromine. Br J Psychiatry 1985;147:16-22.

Nolen WA, Van De Putte JJ, Dijken WA, Kamp JS, Blansjaar BA, Kramer HJ, Haffmans J. Treatment strategy in depression: II. MAO inhibitors in depression resistant to cyclic antidepressants: two controlled crossover studies with tranylcypromine versus L-5-hydroxytryptophan and nomifensine. Acta Psychiatr Scand 1988;78:676-83.

O'Leary KD, Beach SRH. Marital therapy: a viable treatment for depression and marital discord. Am J Psychiatry 1990;147(2):183-6.

Oren DA, Rosenthal NE. Seasonal affective disorders. In: Paykel ES, editor. Handbook of affective disorders. 2nd ed. London: Churchill Livingstone; 1992. p. 551-67.

Othmer E, Othmer SC, Stern WC, Van Wyck Fleet J. Long-term efficacy and safety of bupropion. J Clin Psychiatry 1983;44(5):153-6.

Othmer SC, Othmer E, Preskorn SH, Mac D. Differential effect of amitriptyline and bupropion on primary and secondary depression: a pilot study. J Clin Psychiatry 1988;49(8):310-2.

Overall JE, Biggs J, Jacobs M, Holden K. Comparison of alprazolam and imipramine for treatment of outpatient depression. J Clin Psychiatry 1987;48(1):15-9.

Parloff MB. Psychotherapy research evidence and reimbursement decisions: Bambi meets Godzilla. Am J Psychiatry 1982;139(6):718-27.

Paul SM, Extein I, Calil HM, et al. Use of ECT with treatment resistant depressed patients at the National Institute of Mental Health. Am J Psychiatry 1981; 138:486-9.

Paykel ES, DiMascio A, Haskell D, Prusoff BA. Effects of maintenance amitriptyline and psychotherapy on symptoms of depression. Psychol Med 1975;5:67-77.

Paykel ES, DiMascio A, Klerman GL, Prusoff BA, Weissman MM. Maintenance therapy of depression. Pharmakopsychiatr Neuropsychopharmakol 1976; 9(3):127-39.

Paykel ES, Myers JK, Dienelt MN, Klerman GL, Lindenthal JJ, Pepper MP. Life events and depression: a controlled study. Arch Gen Psychiatry 1969;21:753-60.

Pecheur DR, Edwards KJ. A comparison of secular and religious versions of cognitive therapy with depressed Christian college students. J Psychol Theol 1984;12(1):45-54.

Peet M, Harvey NS. Lithium maintenance: 1. A standard education programme for patients. Br J Psychiatry 1991;158:197-200.

Perry PJ, Morgan DE, Smith RE, Tsuang MT. Treatment of unipolar depression accompanied by delusions. J Affect Disord 1982;4:195-200.

Persons JB. Psychotherapy outcome studies do not accurately represent current models of psychotherapy. Am Psychol 1991;46:99-106.

Persons JB. Outcome of psychotherapy for unipolar depression. In: Giles T, editor. Effective psychotherapy: a handbook of comparative research. New York: Plenum Press; in press.

Persons JB, Burns DD, Perloff JM. Predictors of dropout and outcome in cognitive therapy for depression in a private practice setting. Cognitive Ther Res 1988;12(6):557-75.

Peselow ED, Filippi AM, Goodnick P, Barouche F, Fieve RR. The short- and long-term efficacy of paroxetine HCl: A. Data from a 6-week double-blind parallel design trial vs. imipramine and placebo. Psychopharmacol Bull 1989a; 25(2):267-71.

Peselow ED, Filippi AM, Goodnick P, Barouche F, Fieve RR. The short- and long-term efficacy of paroxetine HCl: B. Data from a double-blind crossover study and from a year-long term trial vs. imipramine and placebo. Psychopharmacol Bull 1989b;25(2):272-6.

Physician's desk reference. Oradell, NJ: Medical Economics Co.; 1992.

Pilkonis PA, Frank E. Personality pathology in recurrent depression: nature, prevalence, and relationship to treatment response. Am J Psychiatry 1988;145(4):435-41.

Post RM. Transduction of psychosocial stress into the neurobiology of recurrent affective disorder. Am J Psychiatry 1992;149(8):999-1010.

Potter WZ, Murphy DL, Wehr TA, Linnoila M, Goodwin FK. Clorgyline: a new treatment for patients with refractory rapid-cycling disorder. Arch Gen Psychiatry 1982;39:505-10.

Preskorn SH, Dorey RC, Jerkovich GS. Therapeutic drug monitoring of tricyclic antidepressants. Clin Chem 1988;34:822-8.

Preskorn SH, Kent TA. Mechanisms and interventions in tricyclic antidepressant overdoses. In: Stancer HC, Garfinkel PE, Rakoff VM, editors. Guidelines for the use of psychotropic drugs. New York: Spectrum Publications; 1984. p. 63-75.

Preskorn SH, Simpson S. Tricyclic-antidepressant-induced delirium and plasma drug concentration. Am J Psychiatry 1982;139:822-3.

Preskorn SH, Weller E, Jerkovich G, Hughes CW, Weller R. Depression in children: concentration-dependent CNS toxicity of tricyclic antidepressants. Psychopharmacol Bull 1988;24:140-2.

Prien RF, Balter MB, Caffey EM Jr. Hospital surveys of prescribing practices with psychotherapeutic drugs. A critical examination. Arch Gen Psychiatry 1978;35(10):1271-5.

Prien RF, Klett CJ, Caffey EM. Lithium carbonate and imipramine in prevention of affective episodes. Arch Gen Psychiatry 1973;29:420-25.

Prien RF, Kupfer DJ. Continuation drug therapy for major depressive episodes: how long should it be maintained? Am J Psychiatry 1986;143:18-23.

Prien RF, Kupfer DJ, Mansky PA, Small JG, Tuason VB, Voss CB, Johnson WE. Drug therapy in the prevention of recurrences in unipolar and bipolar affective disorders. Report of the NIMH Collaborative Study Group comparing lithium carbonate, imipramine, and a lithium carbonate-imipramine combination. Arch Gen Psychiatry 1984;41(11):1096-1104.

Prudic J, Sackeim HA, Devanand DP. Medication resistance and clinical response to electroconvulsive therapy. Psychiatry Res 1990;31:287-96.

Prusoff BA, Weissman MM, Klerman GL, Rounsaville BJ. Research diagnostic criteria subtypes of depression: their role as predictors of differential response to psychotherapy and drug treatment. Arch Gen Psychiatry 1980;37:796-801.

Quitkin FM, Harrison W, Stewart JW, McGrath PJ, Tricamo E, Ocepek-Welikson K, Rabkin JG, Wager SG, Nunes E, Klein D. Response to phenelzine and imipramine in placebo nonresponders with atypical depression. Arch Gen Psychiatry 1991;48:319-23.

Quitkin FM, McGrath PJ, Stewart JW, Harrison WM, Tricamo E, Wager SG, Ocepek-Welikson K, Nunes E, Rabkin JG, Klein DF. Atypical depression, panic attacks, and response to imipramine and phenelzine: a replication. Arch Gen Psychiatry 1990;47:935-41.

Quitkin FM, Stewart JW, McGrath PJ, Liebowitz MR, Harrison WM, Tricamo E, Klein DF, Rabkin JG, Markowitz JS, Wager SG. Phenelzine versus imipramine in the treatment of probable atypical depression: defining syndrome boundaries of selective MAOI responders. Am J Psychiatry 1988;145(3):306-11.

Rehm LP. Behavior therapy for depression. New York: Academic Press; 1979.

Rehm LP. Psychotherapies for depression. In: Bloom BL, Schlesinger K, editors. Boulder symposium on clinical psychology: depression. Hillsdale, NJ: Erlbaum; in press.

Rehm LP, Kaslow NJ, Rabin AS. Cognitive and behavioral targets in a self-control therapy program for depression. J Consult Clin Psychol 1987;55(1):60-7.

Rehm LP, Kornblith SJ, O'Hara MW, Lamparsky DM, Romano JM, Volkin JI. An evaluation of major components in a self-control behavior therapy program for depression. Behav Modif 1981;5:459-89.

Reimherr FW, Wood DR, Byerley B, Brainard J, Grosser BI. Characteristics of responders to fluoxetine. Psychopharmacol Bull 1984;20(1):70-2.

Reynolds CF, Frank E, Perel JM, Imber SD, Cornes C, Morycz RK, Mazumdar S, Miller MD, Pollock BG, Rifai AH, et al. Combined pharmacotherapy and psychotherapy in the acute and continuation treatment of elderly patients with recurrent major depression: a preliminary report. Am J Psychiatry 1992;149(12):1687-92.

Richards HH, Midha RN, Miller S. A double-blind study of trazodone and mianserin in the treatment of depression in general practice. J Int Med Res 1982;10(3):147-56.

Rickels K, Case WG. Trazodone in depressed outpatients. Am J Psychiatry 1982;139(6):803-6.

Rickels K, Chung HR, Csanalosi IB, Hurowitz AM, London J, Wiseman K, Kaplan M, Amsterdam JD. Alprazolam, diazepam, imipramine, and placebo in outpatients with major depression. Arch Gen Psychiatry 1987;44(10):862-6.

Rickels K, Gordon PE, Jenkins BW, Perloff M, Sachs T, Stepansky W. Drug treatment in depressive illness. Dis Nerv Syst 1970;31(1):30-42.

Rickels K, Smith WT, Glaudin V, Amsterdam JB, Weise C, Settle GP. Comparison of two dosage regimens of fluoxetine in major depression. J Clin Psychiatry 1985;46(3 Pt 2):38-41.

Robin A, De Tissera S. A double-blind controlled comparison of the therapeutic effects of low and high energy electroconvulsive therapies. Br J Psychiatry 1982;141:357-66.

Robinson DS, Lerfald SC, Bennett B, Laux D, Devereaux E, Kayser A, Corcella J, Albright D. Continuation and maintenance treatment of major depression with the monoamine oxidase inhibitor phenelzine: a double-blind placebo-controlled discontinuation study. Psychopharmacol Bull 1991;27:31-9.

Roper Reports. Report to Medicaid: what people do for minor health problems. New York: Roper Organization; 1986. p. 86-8.

Ross M, Scott M. An evaluation of the effectiveness of individual and group cognitive therapy in the treatment of depressed patients in an inner city health centre. J Royal Gen Pract 1985;35:239-42.

Rost KM, Smith GR. The deliberate miscoding of major depression in the primary care setting. Paper presented at: the Society for General Internal Medicine; 1992 Apr; Washington, DC.

Roth D, Bielski R, Jones M, Parker W, Osborn G. A comparison of self-control therapy and combined self-control therapy and antidepressant medication in the treatment of depression. Behav Ther 1982;13:133-44.

Rounsaville BJ, Weissman MM, Prusoff BA. Psychotherapy with depressed outpatients: patient and process variables as predictors of outcome. Br J Psychiatry 1981;138:67-74.

Rounsaville BJ, Weissman MM, Prusoff BA, Herceg-Baron RL. Marital disputes and treatment outcome in depressed women. Compr Psychiatry 1979;20(5):483-90.

Rude SS. Relative benefits of assertion or cognitive self-control treatment for depression as a function of proficiency in each domain. J Consult Clin Psychol 1986;54(3):390-4.

Rush AJ. Pharmacotherapy and psychotherapy. In: Derogatis LR, editor. Clinical psychopharmacology. Menlo Park, CA: Addison-Wesley Publishing Co.; 1986. p. 46-67.

Rush AJ. Cognitive approaches to adherence. In: Frances AJ, Hales RJ, editors. Annual review of psychiatry. Vol. 7. Washington, DC: American Psychiatric Press; 1988. p. 625-40.

Rush AJ, Beck AT, Kovacs M, Hollon SD. Comparative efficacy of cognitive therapy and pharmacotherapy in the treatment of depressed outpatients. Cognitive Ther Res 1977;1:17-37.

Rush AJ, Cain JW, Raese J, Stewart RS, Waller DA, Debus JD. Neurological bases for psychiatric disorders. In: Rosenberg RN, editor. Comprehensive neurology. New York: Raven Press; 1991. p. 555-603.

Rush AJ, Erman MK, Schlesser MA, Roffwarg HP, Vasavada N, Khatami M, Fairchild C, Giles DE. Alprazolam versus amitriptyline in depressions with reduced REM latencies. Arch Gen Psychiatry 1985;42(12):1154-9.

Rush AJ, Hollon S, Beck AT, Kovacs M. Depression: must pharmacotherapy fail for cognitive therapy to succeed? Cognitive Ther Res 1978;2:199-206.

Rush AJ, Watkins JT. Group versus individual cognitive therapy: a pilot study. Cognitive Ther Res 1981;5(1):95-103.

Rush AJ, Weissenburger J. Melancholic symptom features: a review and options for DSM-IV. In: Frances AJ, Widiger T, editors. DSM-IV sourcebook. Washington, DC: American Psychiatric Press; in press.

Sackeim HA, Prudic J, Devanand DP. Treatment of medication resistant depression with electroconvulsive therapy. In: Tasman A, Goldfinger SM, Kaufman CA, editors. Annual review of psychiatry. Vol. 9. Washington, DC: American Psychiatric Press; 1990. p. 91-115.

Sackeim HA, Prudic J, Devanand DP, Decina P, Kerr B, Malitz S. The impact of medication resistance and continuation pharmacotherapy on relapse following response to electroconvulsive therapy in major depression. J Clin Psychopharmacol 1990;10:96-104.

Schatzberg AF, Rothschild AJ. Psychotic (delusional) major depression: issues for DSM-IV. In: Frances AJ, Widiger T, editors. DSM-IV sourcebook. Washington, DC: American Psychiatric Press; in press.

Schuckit MA, Feighner JP. Safety of high-dose tricyclic antidepressant therapy. Am J Psychiatry 1972;128(11):1456-9.

Schweizer E, Rickels K, Amsterdam JD, Fox I, Puzzuoli G, Weise C. What constitutes an adequate antidepressant trial for fluoxetine? J Clin Psychiatry 1990;51(1):8-11.

Scogin F, Jamison C, Davis N. Two-year follow-up of bibliotherapy for depression in older adults. J Consult Clin Psychol 1989;58(5):665-7.

Scogin F, Jamison C, Gochneaur K. Comparative efficacy of cognitive and behavioral bibliotherapy for mildly and moderately depressed older adults. J Consult Clin Psychol 1989;57:403-7.

Scott AIF. Which depressed patients will respond to electroconvulsive therapy? The search for biological predictors of recovery. Br J Psychiatry 1989;154:8-17.

Scott MJ, Stradling SG. Group cognitive therapy for depression produces clinically significant reliable change in community-based settings. Behav Psychother 1990;18:1-19.

Secunda SK, Katz MM, Friedman R, Schuyler D. Special report: the depressive disorders. Washington, DC: National Institute of Mental Health, US Government Printing Office; 1973.

Selmi PM, Klein MH, Greist JH, Sorrell SP, Erdman HP. Computer-administered cognitive-behavioral therapy for depression. Am J Psychiatry 1990;147(1):51-6.

Seltzer A, Roncari I, Garfinkel P. Effect of patient education on medication compliance. Can J Psychiatry 1980;25:638-45.

Shapiro DR, Quitkin FM, Fleiss JL. Response to maintenance therapy in bipolar illness: effect of index episode. Arch Gen Psychiatry 1989;46(5):401-5.

Shapiro S, Skinner EA, Kessler LG, von Korff M, German PS, Tischler GL, Leaf PJ, Benham L, Cottler L, Regier DA. Utilization of health and mental health services: three epidemiologic catchment sites. Arch Gen Psychiatry 1984;41:971-8.

Shaw BF. Cognitive-behavior therapies for major depression: current status with an emphasis on prophylaxis. Psychiatr J Univ Ottawa 1989;14(2):403-8.

Shaw BF, Elkin I, Vallis TM, Dobson SD, Olmsted M. Therapist competency and adherence ratings with prediction of outcome in the cognitive therapy for depression. Unpublished manuscript, 1993.

Shaw BF, Olmsted M. Competency ratings in relation to protocol adherence and clinical outcome. Paper presented at: The Society for Psychotherapy Research; 1989 Jun: Toronto, Canada.

Shea MT, Elkin I, Imber SD, Sotsky SM, Watkins JT, Collins JF, Pilkonis PA, Beckham E, Glass DR, Dolan RT, et al. Course of depressive symptoms over follow-up: findings from the NIMH Treatment of Depression Collaborative Research Program. Arch Gen Psychiatry 1992;49(10):782-7.

Shea MT, Pilkonis PA, Beckham E, Collins JF, Elkin I, Sotsky SM, Docherty JP. Personality disorders and treatment outcome in the NIMH Treatment of Depression Collaborative Research Program. Am J Psychiatry 1990;147(6):711-8.

Sher TG, Baucom DH, Larus JM. Communication patterns and response to treatment among depressed and nondepressed maritally distressed couples. J Fam Psychol 1990;4(1):63-79.

Simons AD, Murphy GE, Levine JL, Wetzel RD. Cognitive therapy and pharmacotherapy for depression: sustained improvement over one year. Arch Gen Psychiatry 1986;43:43-8.

Simpson GM, Lee JH, Cucuilc Z, Kellner R. Two doses of imipramine in hospitalized depressives. Arch Gen Psychiatry 1976;33(9):1093-1102.

Soloff PH, George A, Nathan RS, Schulz PM. Characterizing depression in borderline patients. J Clin Psychiatry 1987;48:155-7.

Sotsky SM, Glass DR, Shea MT, Pilkonis PA, Collins JF, Elkin I, Watkins JT, Imber SD, Leber WR, Moyer J, et al. Patient predictors of response to psychotherapy and pharmacotherapy: findings in the NIMH Treatment of Depression Collaborative Research Program. Am J Psychiatry 1991;148(8):997-1008.

Spiker DG, Weiss JC, Dealy RS, Griffin SJ, Hanin I, Neil JF, Perel JM, Rossi AJ, Soloff PH. The pharmacological treatment of delusional depression. Am J Psychiatry 1985;142(4):430-6.

Stein MK, Rickels K, Weise CC. Maintenance therapy with amitriptyline: a controlled trial. Am J Psychiatry 1980;137(3):370-1.

Steinmetz JL, Lewinsohn PM, Antonuccio DO. Prediction of individual outcome in a group intervention for depression. J Consult Clin Psychol 1983;51(3):331-7.

Stern SL, Rush AJ, Mendels J. Toward a rational pharmacotherapy of depression. Am J Psychiatry 1980;187:545-52.

Stern WC, Harto-Truax N, Bauer N. Efficacy of bupropion in tricyclic-resistant or intolerant patients. J Clin Psychiatry 1983;44(5 Pt 2):148-52.

Steuer JL, Mintz J, Hammen CL, Hill MA, Jarvik LF, McCarley T, Motoike P, Rosen R. Cognitive-behavioral and psychodynamic group psychotherapy in treatment of geriatric depression. J Consult Clin Psychol 1984;52(2):180-9.

Stoudemire A, Frank R, Hedemark N, Kamlet M, Blazer D. The economic burden of depression. Gen Hosp Psychiatry 1986;8:387-94.

Strober M. Familial aspects of depressive disorder in early adolescence. In: Weller EB, Weller RA, editors. Current perspectives on major depressive disorders in children. Washington, DC: American Psychiatric Press; 1984. p. 38-48.

Strober M, Carlson G. Bipolar illness in adolescents with major depression: clinical, genetic, and psychopharmacologic predictors in a three- to four-year prospective followup investigation. Arch Gen Psychiatry 1982;39:549-55.

Strupp HH, Binder JL. Psychotherapy in a new key. New York: Basic Books; 1984.

Tamayo M, Fernandez de Gatta MM, Gutierrez JR, Carcia MJ, Dominguez-Fil A. High levels of tricyclic antidepressants in conventional therapy: determinant factors. Int J Clin Pharmacol Ther Toxicol 1988;26:495-9.

Teri L, Lewinsohn PM. Individual and group treatment of unipolar depression: comparison of treatment outcome and identification of predictors of successful treatment outcome. Behav Ther 1986;17:215-28.

Terman M, Williams JBW, Terman JS. Light therapy for winter depression: a clinician's guide. In: Keller P, editor. Innovations in clinical practice: a source book. Sarasota, FL: Pro Resource; 1991. p. 179-221.

Thase ME, Carpenter L, Kupfer DJ, Frank E. Clinical significance of reversed vegetative subtypes of recurrent major depression. Psychopharmacol Bull 1991;27:17-22.

Thase ME, Frank E, Mallinger A, Hamer T, Kupfer DJ. Treatment of imipramine-resistant recurrent depression: III. Efficacy of monoamine oxidase inhibitor. J Clin Psychiatry 1992;53(1):5-11.

Thase ME, Hersen M, Bellack AS, Himmelhoch JM, Kupfer DJ. Validation of a Hamilton subscale for endogenomorphic depression. J Affect Disord 1983;5:267-78.

Thase ME, Mallinger AG, McKnight D, Himmelhoch JM. Treatment of imipramine-resistant recurrent depression: IV. A double-blind, cross-over study of tranylcypromine in anergic bipolar depression. Am J Psychiatry 1992; 149(2):195-8.

Thompson LW, Gallagher DE. Efficacy of psychotherapy in the treatment of late-life depression. Psychological treatment of unipolar depression: special issue. Adv Behav Res Ther 1984;6(2):127-39.

Thompson LW, Gallagher DE, Breckenridge JS. Comparative effectiveness of psychotherapies for depressed elders. J Consult Clin Psychol 1987;55(3):385-90.

Thompson LW, Gallagher D, Czirr R. Personality disorder and outcome in the treatment of late-life depression. J Geriatr Psychiatry 1988;21(2):133-46.

Turner RW, Wehl CK. Treatment of unipolar depression in problem drinkers. Adv Behav Res Ther 1984;6:115-25.

Usaf SO, Kavanagh DJ. Mechanisms of improvement in treatment for depression: test of a self-efficacy and performance model. J Cognitive Psychother: Int Q 1990;4(1):51-70.

USP. Drug information for the health care professional. Volumes 1A, 1B. 12th ed. Rockville, MD: US Pharmacopeial Convention; 1992.

van Gent EM, Zwart FM. Psychoeducation of partners of bipolar-manic patients. J Affect Disord 1991;21(1):15-8.

von Korff M, Ormel J, Katon W, Lin E. Disability and depression among high utilizers of health care: a longitudinal analysis. Arch Gen Psychiatry 1992;49:91-100.

Voris JC, Morin C, Kiel JS. Monitoring outpatients' plasma antidepressant-drug concentrations as a measure of compliance. Am J Hosp Pharm 1983;40:119-29.

Watson M. Psychosocial intervention with cancer patients: a review. Psychol Med 1983;13:839-46.

Weisman A, Worden J. The existential plight in cancer: significance of the first 100 days. Psychiatry Med 1976-1977;7:1-15.

Weissman MM. The psychological treatment of depression: evidence for the efficacy of psychotherapy alone, and in comparison with, and in combination with pharmacotherapy. Arch Gen Psychiatry 1979;36:1261-9.

Weissman MM, Jarrett RB, Rush AJ. Psychotherapy and its relevance to the pharmacotherapy of major depression: a decade later (1976-1985). In: Meltzer H, editor. Psychopharmacology: the third generation of progress. New York: Raven Press; 1987.

Weissman MM, Kasl SV, Klerman GL. Follow-up of depressed women after maintenance treatment. Am J Psychiatry 1976;133:757-60.

Weissman MM, Klerman GL, Prusoff BA, Sholomskas D, Padian N. Depressed outpatients: results one year after treatment with drugs and/or interpersonal psychotherapy. Arch Gen Psychiatry 1981;38:51-5.

Weissman MM, Prusoff BA, DiMascio A, Neu C, Goklaney M, Klerman GL. The efficacy of drugs and psychotherapy in the treatment of acute depressive episodes. Am J Psychiatry 1979;136(4B):555-8.

Wells KB. Depression as a tracer condition for the national study of medical care outcomes—background review. Santa Monica: RAND; 1985.

Wells KB, Golding JM, Burnam MA. Psychiatric disorder and limitations in physical functioning in a sample of the Los Angeles general population. Am J Psychiatry 1988a;145:712-7.

Wells KB, Golding JM, Burnam MA. Psychiatric disorder in a sample of the general population with and without chronic medical conditions. Am J Psychiatry 1988b;145:976-81.

West ED. Electric convulsion therapy in depression: a double-blind controlled trial. Br Med J 1981;282(6261):355-7.

Wilson PH. Cognitive-behavior therapy for depression: empirical findings and methodological issues in the evaluation of outcome. Behav Change 1989; 6(2):85-95.

Winokur G. Familial (genetic) subtypes of pure depressive disease. Am J Psychiatry 1979;136:911-3.

Winokur G. Mania and depression, a classification of syndrome and disease. Baltimore: Johns Hopkins University Press; 1991.

Winokur G, Kadrmas A. A polyepisodic course in bipolar illness: possible clinical relationships. Compr Psychiatry 1989;30:121-7.

Winokur G, Wesner R. From unipolar depression to bipolar illness: 29 who changed. Acta Psychiatr Scand 1987;76:59-63.

Winsauer HJ, O'Hair DE. Rapid onset of action of amoxapine in depressive illness. Curr Ther Res 1984;35(5):815-25.

Wolberg LR. Short-term psychotherapy. New York: Grune & Stratton; 1967.

Woody GE, Luborsky L, McLellan AT, O'Brien CP, Beck AT, Blaine J, Herman I, Hole A. Psychotherapy for opiate addicts. Does it help? Arch Gen Psychiatry 1983;40(6)[JC:72c]:639-45.

Youssel FA. Compliance with therapeutic regimens: a follow-up study for patients with affective disorders. J Adv Nurs 1983;8:513-7.

Yudofsky SC. Electroconvulsive therapy in general hospital psychiatry: a focus on new indications and technologies. Gen Hosp Psychiatry 1981;3(4):292-6.

Zuckerman DM, Prusoff BA, Weissman MM, Padian NS. Personality as a predictor of psychotherapy and pharmacotherapy outcome for depressed outpatients. J Consult Clin Psychol 1980;48(6):730-5.

Acronyms

AHCPR	Agency for Health Care Policy and Research
BDI	Beck Depression Inventory
BMT	Behavioral marital therapy
CGI	Clinical Global Impression
CPM	Confidence profile method
ECT	Electroconvulsive therapy
FDA	Food and Drug Administration
GAD	Generalized anxiety disorder
HAM-D	Hamilton Rating Scale for Depression
MAOI	Monoamine oxidase inhibitor
NIMH	National Institute of Mental Health
SSRI	Selective serotonin reuptake inhibitor
TCA	Tricyclic antidepressant

Glossary

Acute Treatment. Formally defined procedures used to reduce and remove the signs and symptoms of depression and to restore psychosocial function.

Adequate Treatment Analysis. Analysis of data in terms of the relationship between the number of patients who received a predetermined minimum amount of treatment and the number who responded.

Agoraphobia. A disorder characterized by a fear of open, public places or of situations where crowds are found.

Anhedonia. An absence of or the inability to experience a sense of pleasure from any activity.

Behavioral Therapy. A form of psychotherapy that focuses on modifying observable problematic behaviors by systematic manipulation of the environment.

Bipolar Disorder. A major mood disorder characterized by episodes of major depression and mania or hypomania, formerly called manic-depressive psychosis, circular type. The diagnosis of bipolar I disorder requires one or more episodes of mania. The diagnosis of bipolar II disorder requires one or more episodes of hypomania and is excluded by the history or presence of a manic episode. Current episode may be manic, depressed, hypomanic, or mixed manic type.

Clinical Management. Education of and discussion with patients and, when appropriate, their families about the nature of depression, its course, and the relative costs and benefits of treatment options. It also includes assessment and management of the patient while in treatment, along with resolution of obstacles to treatment adherence, monitoring and management of treatment side effects, and assessment of outcome.

Cognitive Therapy. A treatment method that focuses on revising a person's maladaptive processes of thinking, perceptions, attitudes and beliefs. Cognitive therapy has been developed for different specific disorders, including depression.

Completer Analysis. Analysis of data in terms of the relationship between the number of patients whose condition improved and the number who completed the treatment protocol.

Continuation Treatment. Treatment designed to prevent the return of the most recent mood episode.

Cyclothymic Disorder. A mood disorder of at least 2 years' duration characterized by numerous periods of mild depressive symptoms not sufficient in duration or severity to meet criteria for major depressive episodes interspersed with periods of hypomania. Some view this condition as a mild variant of bipolar disorder.

Dementia. A group of mental disorders involving a general loss of intellectual abilities, including memory, judgment, and abstract thinking. There may be associated poor impulse control and/or personality change. Dementias may be progressive, reversible, or static and have a variety of causes.

Dysthymia. A mood disorder characterized by depressed mood and loss of interest or pleasure in customary activities, with some additional signs and symptoms of depression, that is present most of the time for at least 2 years. Many patients with dysthymia go on to develop major depressive episodes.

Electroconvulsive Therapy. A treatment method usually reserved for very severe or psychotic depressions or manic states that often are not responsive to medication treatment. A low-voltage alternating current is sent to the brain to induce a convulsion or seizure, which accounts for the therapeutic effect.

Hypomania. An episode of illness that resembles mania, but is less intense and less disabling. The state is characterized by a euphoric mood, unrealistic optimism, increased speech and activity, and a decreased need for sleep. For some, there is increased creativity, while others evidence poor judgment and impaired function.

Intent-to-Treat Analysis. Analysis of data in terms of the relationship between the number of patients randomized to treatment and the number whose condition improved.

Interpersonal Psychotherapy. A time-limited psychotherapeutic approach that aims at clarification and resolution of one or more of the following interpersonal difficulties: role disputes, social isolation, prolonged grief reaction, or role transition. The patient and therapist define the nature of the difficulty and work to its resolution.

Maintenance Treatment. Treatment designed to prevent a new mood episode (e.g., depression, mania, hypomania).

Major Depressive Disorder. A major mood disorder characterized by one (single) or more (recurrent) episodes of major depression, with or without full recovery between episodes.

Mania. An episode of illness usually seen in the course of bipolar I disorder and characterized by hyperexcitability, euphoria, and hyperactivity. Rapid thinking and speaking, agitation, a decreased need for sleep, and a marked increase in energy are nearly always present. During manic episodes, some patients also experience hallucinations or delusions. Manic episodes can also be caused by selected general medical disorders.

Melancholic Features. Symptoms usually found in severe major depressive episodes, including marked loss of pleasure, psychomotor retardation or agitation, weight loss, and insomnia.

Mood Disorders. A grouping of psychiatric conditions that have as a central feature a disturbance in mood (usually profound sadness or apathy, euphoria, or irritability). These disorders may be episodic or chronic.

Obsessive-Compulsive Disorder. A condition that is characterized by the presence of obsessions and/or compulsions. Obsessions are recurrent, intrusive thoughts—usually irrational worries—that often necessitate behaviors to prevent untoward consequences (e.g., fears of contamination from dirt requiring the individual to wear gloves at all times). Compulsions are recurrent behaviors beyond the normal range that the individual feels compelled to undertake, usually to preserve personal safety, to avoid embarassment, or to perform adequately (e.g., checking multiple times to see that the gas is turned off before leaving home). The disorder affects 1 to 2 percent of the population.

Open Trial. A trial of a treatment in which both patient and practitioner are aware of the treatment being used.

Panic Disorder. An anxiety disorder characterized by discrete intense periods of fear and associated symptoms. Panic disorder may be accompanied by agoraphobia.

Remission. A return to the asymptomatic state, usually accompanied by a return to the usual level of psychosocial functioning.

Somatization Disorder. A disorder characterized by multiple, often long-standing somatic complaints of bodily dysfunction (e.g., pain complaints, gastrointestinal disturbances). The disorder usually begins before the age of 30 and has a chronic, albeit fluctuating, course.

Supportive Therapy. Psychotherapy that focuses on the management and resolution of current difficulties and life decisions using the patient's strengths and available resources.

Symptom Breakthrough. The return of symptoms in the course of either continuation or maintenance phase treatment.

Vegetative Symptoms. A group of symptoms that refer to sleep, appetite, and/or weight regulation.

Contributors

These guidelines could not have been developed without the expertise and assistance of many types of contributors who, together, made the effort feasible. All of those listed here willingly assisted in the intense effort required to develop guidelines on an issue as complex as the appropriate treatment of major depressive disorder. The resulting document reflects the many important interactions that occurred during the guideline development process.

Depression Guideline Panel Members: Biosketches

A. John Rush, MD, *Chair*
Betty Jo Hay Distinguished Chair in Mental Health
Professor and Vice Chairman for Research, Department of Psychiatry
University of Texas Southwestern Medical Center
Dallas, Texas

Dr. Rush received his BA from Princeton University and his MD from the College of Physicians and Surgeons of Columbia University.

He is currently the Director of the Mental Health Clinical Research Center, an NIMH-funded center studying the biology, psychology, pharmacology, and psychotherapy of mood disorders. Dr. Rush has published extensively on both the psychology and biology of depression. He has received several NIMH grants to study depression and has helped develop and study the efficacy of cognitive therapy in treatment of depressed outpatients. His research has sought to identify biologic and psychological predictors of specific treatment responses, as well as relapse and recurrence. He serves as the Chair of the DSM-IV Work Group on Mood Disorders for the American Psychiatric Association.

Dr. Rush is a Fellow of the American College of Psychiatry, the American Psychiatric Association, and the American College of Neuropsychopharmacology. He is Past President of the Society for Psychotherapy Research.

William E. Golden, MD
Director, General Internal Medicine
Associate Professor, Department of Medicine
University of Arkansas for Medical Sciences
Little Rock, Arkansas

Dr. Golden received his AB from Brown University (1975) and his MD from Baylor College of Medicine (1978). He completed his internal medicine residency and chief residency at Rush-Presbyterian St. Luke's

Medical Center in Chicago (1983). Dr. Golden is Director of the Quality Assurance Research and Education Center, Director of the Division of General Internal Medicine, and Associate Professor of Medicine at the University of Arkansas for Medical Sciences. He is currently Chairman of the Quality Assurance Committee of University Hospital. He has had several funded projects in quality assurance and has expertise in perioperative care and medical informatics. He has authored more than 40 journal articles and book chapters on perioperative care, medical education, and quality improvement.

Dr. Golden is a trustee of the American Society of Internal Medicine and a member of the board of directors of the American Medical Review Research Center. He serves on the American Medical Association Council on Medical Education and has recently been appointed to the Liaison Committee on Medical Education. He is a member of many internal medicine societies and has served numerous roles in educational activities and policy-making matters for these organizations.

Gladys Walton Hall, PhD, MSW
Associate Professor, School of Social Work
Howard University
Washington, District of Columbia

Dr. Hall received her BS from Morgan State University (1966), MSW from the University of Connecticut (1971), and PhD from the University of Maryland (1982). She recently completed a post-doctoral fellowship at the National Institute of Mental Health (1990).

Dr. Hall teaches clinical social work methods courses and is a licensed clinical social worker with experience in the private and public sectors. Her private practice is in a comprehensive medical setting and includes the treatment of depressed women. She has authored several publications in the area of depression (childhood depression) and served on various professional boards, both national and local (including the D.C. Mental Health Association). Her research focus is on the psychosocial factors related to the co-morbidity of depression and conduct disorder among children.

Col. Moses Herrera, MD
Chief, Primary Care Clinic
Robins Air Force Base Hospital
Robins Air Force Base, Georgia

Dr. Herrera is a Fellow of the American Academy of Family Practice. He has many years of experience in the practice of family medicine, including obstetrics, geriatrics, pediatrics, and adolescent medicine, as well as in short-term psychotherapy and in the diagnosis and treatment of depression. He has served on the Mental Health Committee of the American Academy of Family Practice. With his experience, Dr. Herrera can speak with particular regard to the utility of guidelines as they may be applied to family practice in military medicine.

Artie Houston
Consumer Representative
Fort Worth, Texas

Mrs. Houston represents patients (consumers). She has lived successfully with manic-depressive illness, which was diagnosed in 1968. She played a prominent role in the establishment of the National Depressive and Manic-Depressive Association (NDMDA) and served as its executive vice president and president in 1988-89. Mrs. Houston founded the first NDMDA chapter in Tarrant County, Texas, and served as its president for 2 years. She has a background in business and public relations. She served for 15 years as the business director of a large blood center in Fort Worth, Texas. Mrs. Houston has an extensive history of volunteer work in the areas of depression, manic-depressive illness, and hemophilia.

Roger G. Kathol, MD
Professor of Psychiatry and Internal Medicine
University of Iowa Hospitals and Clinics
Iowa City, Iowa

Dr. Kathol received his BA from the University of Kansas (1970) and his MD from the University of Kansas School of Medicine (1974). He completed his residency in internal medicine at the University of Iowa (1978) and his residency in psychiatry at the University of Iowa (1980). He completed a 1-year fellowship in endocrinology at the University of Otago in Wellington, New Zealand (1981).

Dr. Kathol is the director of the combined Internal Medicine/Psychiatry Unit and the General Hospital Psychiatry Services at the University of Iowa Hospitals and Clinics. He currently teaches both psychiatrists and internists about the diagnosis and treatment of medical and psychiatric disorders in patients with complex and combined medical/psychiatric difficulties. He has received NIMH and private foundation grants for clinical research on depressive disorders in the medically ill, on endocrine changes in patients with primary depression, and on pharmacokinetic drug interactions. His research has contributed to the understanding of depression in the medically ill, as well as the potential relationship of hypothalamic-pituitary-adrenal axis dysfunction in patients with primary affective disorder.

Dr. Kathol has lectured widely, is on the editorial board of several journals, holds membership on the boards of national organizations, and is published widely in the area of psychiatric pathology as seen in medically ill patients. He is board-certified in both internal medicine and psychiatry, and is a Fellow of the American College of Physicians, the American

Psychiatric Association, and the American Academy of Psychosomatic Medicine. He is the current president of the Academy of Clinical Psychiatry and is a founding officer of the Association of Medicine and Psychiatry.

Wayne Katon, MD
Professor of Psychiatry
Chief of Consultation-Liaison Psychiatry
University of Washington Medical School
Seattle, Washington

Dr. Katon received his BA from the University of Vermont (1971) and his MD from the University of Oregon (1976). He completed his residency in psychiatry at the University of Washington (1979).

Dr. Katon is Chief of the Division of Consultation-Liaison at the University of Washington and head of the Psychiatry Liaison Service to Family Medicine at University and Providence Medical Centers. Dr. Katon received the American Academy of Family Practice Award for Excellence in Teaching. He has taught medical students, psychiatric residents, and family medicine practitioners in the area of psychiatric disorders in family practice and primary care. He has received independent NIMH funding for the study of depression and chronic tinnitus, a randomized trial of psychiatric consultation for patients who are high medical service utilizers, and a randomized trial of psychiatric consultation in treatment of major depression in primary care.

Dr. Katon has published widely in the area of psychopathology (depression, panic disorders, and somatization) in the primary care setting. He has authored more than 100 journal articles and chapters and a book commissioned by NIMH entitled *Panic Disorder in the Medical Setting*. His research has sought to identify the psychological and social factors associated with medically unexplained somatic symptoms (chest pain, back pain, irritable bowel syndrome, tinnitus, pelvic pain, and dizziness). He is a recognized national and international authority on psychiatric disorders in family practice and general internal medicine.

Catherine L. Matchett, MD
Matchett Medical Center, President
Grapevine, Texas

Dr. Matchett is a Fellow of the American Academy of Family Practice in private practice, who serves approximately 3,500 families in the North Texas area. She completed a rotating internship and 2 years in a psychiatry residency, passing the written boards in psychiatry before completing a family practice residency.

Dr. Matchett is Vice President of the Dallas Chapter of the American Academy of Family Practice. She has a strong interest in preventive medicine and patient education. She has developed and lectured on the utilization of patient education materials and educational methods to facilitate detection and recognition of a wide variety of common health problems, including several disorders that are commonly missed or misdiagnosed by primary care physicians, including depression, anxiety disorders, premenstrual syndrome, and headache disorders. These materials are used to engage patient participation in the process of identification and translation of symptoms into a proper diagnosis so that recognized treatment strategies may be employed. There is an assumption that patient compliance with treatment increases when the patient is educated and actively involved in the treatment process.

Frederick Petty, PhD, MD
Associate Professor, Department of Psychiatry
Veterans Administration Medical Center
University of Texas Southwestern Medical Center
Dallas, Texas

Dr. Petty received his PhD from the Georgia Institute of Technology (1971) and his MD from the University of Tennessee (1976). He completed his residency in psychiatry at the University of Iowa (1980).

Dr. Petty is the recipient of a Research Career Development Award from the Department of Veterans Affairs. He was the Director of the Consultation/Liaison Service at both the Iowa City and Dallas Department of Veterans Affairs Medical Centers. He conducts both basic and clinical research on the biology of stress and depression, as well as on biologic markers for alcoholism. Dr. Petty has received independent, peer-reviewed funding to conduct his research from the Veterans Administration Merit Review Board, NIMH, and NIAAA. He has lectured widely to family practice and general internal medicine physicians regarding the differential diagnosis and management of mood disorders. Dr. Petty is Director of the Depression Clinic at the Department of Veterans Affairs Medical Center in Dallas.

Herbert C. Schulberg, PhD
Professor of Psychiatry, Psychology and Medicine
University of Pittsburgh School of Medicine
Pittsburgh, Pennsylvania

Dr. Schulberg received his BA from Yeshiva College (1955), his PhD from Columbia University, and his MS Hygiene from the Harvard School of Public Health (1963). He completed 2 years of pre-doctoral internships in clinical psychology at several Veterans Administration facilities.

Dr. Schulberg is Director of the Primary Care Consultation Program at the Western Psychiatric Institute and Clinic. He is a Fellow of the American Psychological Association, and was previously president of the American College of Mental Health Administration and a Visiting Scientist at the NIMH. He has published more than 125 peer-reviewed articles, chapters, and books that focus on the delivery and evaluation of psychiatric services, as well as the recognition, differential diagnosis, and treatment of depression and other psychiatric disorders in the primary care setting. Dr. Schulberg is a recognized national authority in this area. He has received several NIMH grants that support his research efforts. Presently, Dr. Schulberg is directing an NIMH-funded 4-year study of the clinical efficacy and cost efficiency of various treatments for major depression in primary care practice.

G. Richard Smith, Jr., MD
Professor and Director
Centers for Mental Healthcare Research
VA HSR&D Field Program for Mental Health
University of Arkansas for Medical Sciences
Little Rock, Arkansas

Dr. Smith received his MD from the University of Arkansas (1977), where he completed his residency in psychiatry. He was a Fellow in Psychiatry and Medicine at the University of Rochester (1980-81). He has served as residency director in the Department of Psychiatry at the University of Arkansas. He has published in the areas of alexithymia, somatization disorder, consultation-liaison, and immunology. He has received NIMH and Robert Wood Johnson Foundation research support for studies of somatization disorder and psychosocial disabilities associated with myocardial infarction. He has been developing disease-specific outcome modules for psychiatric conditions.

Dr. Smith currently serves as Chair of the NIMH Initial Review Group on Mental Health Services Research. He is Director of the Centers for Mental Healthcare Research, which include the NIMH Center for Rural Mental Healthcare Research and the Veterans Affairs Field Program for Mental Health.

Gail Wiscarz Stuart, PhD, RN, CS
Associate Professor and Chief, Division of Psychiatric Nursing
Department of Psychiatry and Behavioral Sciences
Professor, College of Nursing
Medical University of South Carolina
Charleston, South Carolina

Dr. Stuart received her MS in psychiatric nursing from the University of Maryland (1973) and her PhD in behavioral sciences from Johns Hopkins University (1985). She is a certified specialist in adult psychiatric and mental health nursing from the American Nurses Association and maintains a private practice of psychotherapy.

Dr. Stuart's clinical and research interests involve the study of depression, anxiety disorders, and mental health care delivery systems. As Chief of the Division of Psychiatric Nursing, in the Department of

Psychiatry, Dr. Stuart is responsible for overseeing the clinical inpatient units at the Institute of Psychiatry. She is also the coordinator of the graduate program in psychiatric nursing at the Medical University of South Carolina in Charleston.

Dr. Stuart has received multiple honors and awards for her work from a large number of organizations and is a Fellow of the American Academy of Nursing. She serves on the NIMH Task Force on Psychiatric Nursing and the NIMH Research Resource Panel for the Severely Mentally Ill, among other national appointments. Dr. Stuart has been the principal investigator or coinvestigator on several independent research grants, including studies of the pharmacotherapy and childhood environments of patients with panic disorder, bulimia, and depression. She has written several nationally recognized textbooks on psychiatric nursing and has a substantial list of peer-reviewed journal publications in both the areas of psychiatric disorders and the role of nursing in health care delivery.

Reviewing Consultants for Treatment Issues[1]

Patient Compliance in Affective Illness
Monica Ramirez Basco, PhD
University of Texas
Southwestern Medical Center
Dallas, Texas

The Role of Social Support in Depression: A Selected Review of the Evidence
Linda S. Beeber, PhD, RN
Syracuse University
College of Nursing
Syracuse, New York

The Role of Occupational Therapy in the Management of Depression
Elizabeth B. Devereaux,
MSW, ACSW/L, OTR/L, FAOTA
Associate Professor,
Department of Psychiatry
Marshall University
School of Medicine
Huntington, West Virginia

The Efficacy of Long-Term Psychotherapy in the Treatment of Depression
Gretchen L. Haas, PhD
Department of Psychiatry
University of Pittsburgh
School of Medicine
Western Psychiatric Institute
and Clinic
Pittsburgh, Pennsylvania

The Efficacy of Combined Drugs and Psychotherapy for Depression
Steven D. Hollon, PhD
Kirsten Haman, BS
Department of Psychology
Vanderbilt University
Nashville, Tennessee

Short-Term Psychotherapy and Depression
Robin B. Jarrett, PhD
Melinda Down, BS
University of Texas
Southwestern Medical Center
Dallas, Texas

Treatment of Depression with Electroconvulsive Therapy (ECT)
Charles H. Kellner, MD
Carol M. S. Burns, RNC
Hilary J. Bernstein, LMSW
Medical University of
South Carolina
Charleston, South Carolina

Diagnosis and Treatments for Patients with Comorbid Anxiety and Mood Disorders
Karla Moras, PhD
Richard E. Zinbarg, PhD
David H. Barlow, PhD
Department of Psychiatry
State University of New York
at Albany
Albany, New York

Therapeutic Monitoring of Antidepressant Drugs
Paul J. Orsulak, PhD, MBA
Pei Ke Liu, MD
Departments of Psychiatry
and Pathology
University of Texas
Southwestern Medical Center
Dallas, Texas

---

[1]Being listed in this section does not necessarily imply endorsement of the guideline.

Treatment of Depression with Anxiolytic Medications

Frederick Petty, PhD, MD
Madhukar Trivedi, MD
Department of Psychiatry
Dallas Veterans Affairs
Medical Center
University of Texas
Southwestern Medical Center
Dallas, Texas

Light Therapy for Winter Depression

Michael Terman, PhD
New York State Psychiatric Institute
New York, New York
Jiuan Su Terman, PhD
Department of Psychiatry
Columbia College of Physicians
and Surgeons
New York, New York

Strategies for Treatment Resistant Depression

Michael E. Thase, MD
Department of Psychiatry
University of Pittsburgh
School of Medicine
Western Psychiatric Institute
and Clinic
Pittsburgh, Pennsylvania

The Efficacy of Heterocyclic and SSRI Antidepressant Medications

Madhukar Trivedi, MD
A. John Rush, MD
Department of Psychiatry
University of Texas
Southwestern Medical Center
Dallas, Texas

The Efficacy of Tricyclic Antidepressant Medications

Madhukar Trivedi, MD
William A. Hendrickse,
MD, MRCP
A. John Rush, MD
Department of Psychiatry
University of Texas
Southwestern Medical Center
Dallas, Texas

Scientific Reviewers[2]

Hagop S. Akiskal, MD
Senior Science Advisor,
Office of the Director
National Institute of Mental Health
Rockville, Maryland

Deborah Allen, MD
Professor and Chairman,
Department of Family Medicine
Indiana University
School of Medicine
Indianapolis, Indiana

Kenneth Z. Altshuler, MD*
Professor and Chairman,
Department of Psychiatry
University of Texas
Southwestern Medical Center
Dallas, Texas

Aaron T. Beck, MD*
Professor, Department of Psychiatry
University of Pennsylvania
Philadelphia, Pennsylvania

W. Eugene Broadhead,
MD, PhD, FAAFP
Associate Professor, Department of
Community and Family Medicine
Duke University Medical Center
Durham, North Carolina

C. Robert Cloninger, MD*
Washington University
Medical School
St. Louis, Missouri

Allen J. Frances, MD*
Professor and Chairman,
Department of Psychiatry
Duke University Medical Center
Durham, North Carolina

Ellen Frank, PhD*
University of Pittsburgh
School of Medicine
Western Psychiatric Institute
and Clinic
Pittsburgh, Pennsylvania

Jack Froom, MD
Professor, State University of
New York at Stony Brook
Stony Brook, New York

Junius J. Gonzales, MD
Chief, Primary Care
Research Program
Services Research Branch
National Institute of Mental Health
Rockville, Maryland

Frederick K. Goodwin, MD
Director, National Institute
of Mental Health
Bethesda, Maryland

Philip S. Holtzman, PhD*
Harvard University
Cambridge, Massachusetts

Neil Jacobson, PhD
Professor, Department of
Psychology
Center for Clinical Research
University of Washington
Seattle, Washington

Lewis L. Judd, MD
Mary Gilman Marston Professor
and Chair, Department of
Psychiatry
UCSD School of Medicine
La Jolla, California

---

[2]Being listed in this section does not necessarily imply endorsement of the guideline.
*Scientific Reviewer, Group II.

T. Byram Karasu, MD
Professor of Psychiatry
Albert Einstein College of Medicine
Bronx Municipal Hospital Center
Jacobi Hospital
Bronx, New York

Donald F. Klein, MD
Columbia University, College of Physicians & Surgeons
New York, New York

Gerald Klerman, MD (deceased)
Professor, Department of Psychiatry
Director of Research
New York Hospital/
Cornell Medical Center
Payne Whitney Clinic
New York, New York

Rodger Kobes, MD, PhD*
Timberlawn Psychiatric Hospital
University of Texas
Southwestern Medical Center
Dallas, Texas

Helena Chmura Kraemer, PhD
Stanford University
Stanford, California

David J. Kupfer, MD
Western Psychiatric Institute and Clinic
University of Pittsburgh
Pittsburgh, Pennsylvania

Jerome Levine, MD*
Department of Psychiatry (MPRC)
University of Maryland
School of Medicine
Baltimore, Maryland

William T. McKinney, MD*
University of Wisconsin
School of Medicine
Madison, Wisconsin

Kathleen Merikangas, PhD*
Yale University School of Medicine
New Haven, Connecticut

Deborah M. Nadzam, PhD, RN*
Associate Director of Outcomes Research and Development
Joint Commission on Accreditation of Healthcare Organizations
Oak Brook Terrace, Illinois

Robert M. Post, MD*
National Institute of Mental Health
Bethesda, Maryland

Lon S. Schneider, MD*
University of Southern California
School of Medicine
Los Angeles, California

Myrna M. Weissman, PhD*
Columbia University
New York, New York

Thomas N. Wise, MD
Professor of Psychiatry
Georgetown University
Washington, District of Columbia

*Scientific Reviewer, Group II.

Organizations and Individuals Providing Peer and Pilot Review[3]

American Nurses Association
Washington, District of Columbia
Contact: Karen O'Connor, MA, RN

Sandra E. Benter, DNSC, RN, CS
Psychotherapy and Consultation Practice
Owings Mills, Maryland

John M. Davis, MD
Illinois State Psychiatric Institute
Chicago, Illinois

David L. Dunner, MD
Professor, Department of Psychiatry
University of Washington
Seattle, Washington

William H.M. Finney, MD, MPH
Shepherd's Clinic
Baltimore, Maryland

Terry E. Fitzgerald
National Council,
Community Mental Health Centers
Rockville, Maryland

Frederick K. Goodwin, MD
Director, National Institute of Mental Health
Bethesda, Maryland

Edgar Heim, MD
Professor and Co-chair
Psychiatrische Univ. Poliklinik
Bern, Switzerland

Shirley Hibbeln
Education Consultant
National Depressive and Manic-Depressive Association
Chicago, Illinois

Robert M.A. Hirschfeld, MD
Professor and Chairman,
Department of Psychiatry
University of Texas Medical Branch
Galveston, Texas

IMCARE Practice Guidelines Network
IMCARE (Internal Medicine Center to Advance Research and Education)
American Society of Internal Medicine
Washington, District of Columbia
Contact: Bernard M. Rosof, MD, President
Betty F. King, Executive Director

Harold A. Kaminetzky, MD, FACOG
Director, Practice Activities
American College of Obstetricians and Gynecologists
Washington, District of Columbia

Gerald Klerman, MD (deceased)
President
Association for Clinical Psychosocial Research

Don R. Lipsitt, MD
President, American Association of General Hospital Psychiatrists
Cambridge, Massachusetts

Russ Newman, PhD, JD
Deputy Executive Director for Professional Practice
American Psychological Association
Washington, District of Columbia

---

[3]Being listed in this section does not necessarily imply endorsement of the guideline.

Pharmaceutical Manufacturers Association
Health Outcomes Work Group
Washington, District of Columbia
Contact: Hugh H. Tilson, MD, DrPH

Harold Alan Pincus, MD
American Psychiatric Association
Washington, District of Columbia

John B. Reichman, MD
American Academy of Clinical Psychiatry
Pocatello, Idaho

Lorraine Richter, BS
Education Chairman
National Depressive and Manic-Depressive Association
Chicago, Illinois

Joseph A. Rogers
Mental Health Association of Southeastern Pennsylvania
Philadelphia, Pennsylvania

Peter M. Silberfarb, MD
Dartmouth Medical School
Dartmouth Hitchcock Medical Center
Lebanon, New Hampshire

Jeff Susman, MD
Department of Family Medicine
University of Nebraska Medical Center
Omaha, Nebraska

Robert L. Thomas
National Association of Private Psychiatric Hospitals
Washington, District of Columbia

Joyce E. Thompson, CNM, DrPH, FAAN
University of Pennsylvania School of Nursing
Philadelphia, Pennsylvania

Organizations and Individuals Providing Additional Scientific, Technical, and Administrative Support

University of Texas Southwestern Medical Center, Dallas, Texas
M. Trivedi, MD, Scientific Assistant to the Chair
M. White, MM, Project Manager
L. Arnold
W. Hendrickse, MD, MRCP
G. Kramer
D. Savage

Agency for Health Care Policy and Research, Rockville, Maryland
J.J. Clinton, MD, Administrator
K. McCormick, PhD, RN, Director, Office of the Forum
E. Corrigan
C. Crofton, PhD
G. Hernandez, RN
S. King, MD
V. Montgomery
K. Pearson, RPh, MPH
R. Siegel
L. Williams

Editorial Associates, Washington, District of Columbia
G. Martin

Fast Word, Dallas, Texas

Health Systems Research, Washington, District of Columbia

MedStat Systems, Inc., Ann Arbor, Michigan

Mikalix & Company, Waltham, Massachusetts
M. Madison, MPA, and staff

Moshman and Associates, Bethesda, Maryland

National Institute of Mental Health, Bethesda, Maryland
F. Goodwin, MD, Director
J. Burke, MD, MPH
J. Gonzales, MD
A. Leshner, PhD
G. Norquist, MD, MSPH

National Library of Medicine, Bethesda, Maryland
I. Auston, MLS, and staff

University of California at Los Angeles, California
D. Schriger, MD, MPH

University of California at Berkeley, California
T.W. Hu, PhD

University of Pittsburgh Medical Center, Pittsburgh, Pennsylvania
M. McDonald, MFA

Washington Consulting Group, Inc., Washington, District of Columbia
C.L. Smith

Index

R

☆ U. S. GOVERNMENT PRINTING OFFICE : 1993 - 352-320 QL 3